HERB TRADER

HERB TRADER

A TALE OF TREACHERY AND ESPIONAGE IN THE GLOBAL MARIJUANA TRADE

by

A.R. Torsone

CONTENTS

South East Asia

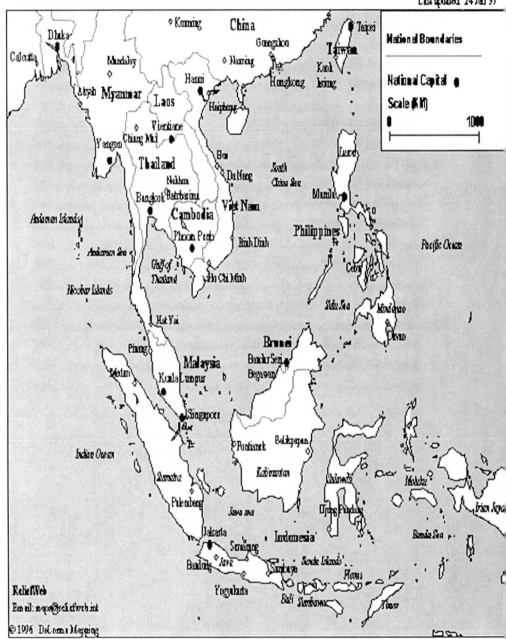

National Boundaries

National Capital ●

Scale (KM)

0   1000

China · Kunming · Nanning · Guangzhou · Taipei · Taiwan · Kaoh Isiung · Hongkong

Dhaka · Calcutta · Mandalay · Atyub · Myanmar · Hanoi · Haiphong · Laos · Vientiane · Chiang Mai · Yangon · Thailand · Bua · Da Nang · South China Sea · Luzon · Manila

Andaman Islands · Nakhon Ratchasima · Bangkok · Cambodia · Viet Nam · Philippines · Pacific Ocean

Andaman Sea · Phnom Penh · Binh Dinh · Cebu

Nicobar Islands · Gulf of Thailand · Ho Chi Minh · Sulu Sea · Mindanao · Davao

Hat Yai

Penang · Melan · Malaysia · Brunei · Bandar Seri Begawan · Kuala Lumpur · Singapore

Indian Ocean · Sumatra · Pontianak · Balikpapan · Sulawesi · Molukas · Irian Jaya · Kalimantan · Banda Sea

Palembang · Java sea · Ujung Pandang · Jakarta · Semarang · Indonesia · Bandung · Java · Surabaya · Sunda Islands · Flores · Yogyakarta · Bali · Sumbawa · Timor

DEDICATION

To Barbara Jean

Without her love and guidance I surely would have ended up where I had started.

AUTHOR'S NOTE

THE Thai-Cambodian mission rocked my life and soul to their core. It became desperately important for me to write my story in its entirety. This book was born from that compulsion.

Prologue

December 3, 1998

A Cambodian soldier peered into the American's confined, solitary cell, just as he had done every morning. This time, however, something was wrong. The American looked unusually still. The soldier was already sweating in the stifling Southeast Asian heat as he searched for his key to the old, rusty padlock that secured the dungeon's door.

The dark-skinned man squatted down beside the pale, wasted body lying face up on the floor before him. He shook the American's shoulder and loudly commanded him to rise. There was no response. Even though the Cambodian spoke Khmer, the American should have sat up at the outburst.

The soldier began to feel panicked. With his thumb, he opened the man's eyelid and saw the lifeless stare that he had seen many times before. The soldier turned and ran down the empty hallway. His footsteps echoed off the stone walls as he made his way to his commander's office.

Suddenly, Colonel Hing Peo's interrogation center exploded in confusion and excitement – as did the U.S. Embassy in Phnom Penh, the capital city of Cambodia. Word had gone out that the American was dead.

U.S. agents and U.S. Embassy personnel raced to Colonel Hing Peo's base. In the commotion, an Embassy staffer closely checked the American.

"He's alive! Get him to a hospital in Bangkok!"

A months-long effort to track this American (on the part of U.S. and foreign agents) had gone terribly awry. Now, even identification seemed impossible as they struggled to measure up the identity of the bone-thin, comatose body before them. They searched, but found no passport or identification.

Through U.S. diplomatic channels, Prime Minister Hun Sen of Cambodia agreed to release the American's two good friends, Captain Chin and Michael "the Bird," from Asia's notorious T.3 prison, also located in Phnom Penh. They were rushed directly to Hing Peo's base.

"Do you know this man?" the agent asked.

The Bird, disheveled and weak, stepped forward. He squinted as he looked into the face of the American. "Hmm . . . " he said. "No. I don't know him."

"You don't recognize this man? He's your buddy, Max!"

"That ain't Max," the Bird said.

"The hell it isn't. That's your friend Max!" the agent wailed.

The Bird moved in closer. He looked down and surveyed the gaunt, somber body. Then he glanced down at his feet. "Yeah," he said. "Yeah, that's Max. I can tell by his shoes."

U.S. agents and Cambodian soldiers carried Max to the Phnom Penh Airport, only to be turned away by the commercial airliner captain.

"We don't fly dead bodies!" the pilot protested.

So, under the direction of U.S. Ambassador Quinn, Max's comatose body was raced to the better of the two hospitals in Phnom Penh.

Two days later, at Max's bedside, a woman from the U.S. Embassy leaned down close to him and called out loudly, "Can you hear me? When did you eat last? Can you speak?"

Max's eyes flickered as he regained consciousness. The woman, now relieved, left with her male aide to notify the U.S. Ambassador.

In a blur, Max could make out the images of two Khmer soldiers sitting at the foot of his bed. Slowly, he forced out the words, "Do . . . you . . . have gun?"

One soldier nodded affirmatively.

Max inched up his shaking arm and pointed to his chest. "Shoot me," he said. "Shoot me . . . shoot . . . me."

A Khmer doctor quickly stepped up to Max as two American government agents entered the room and dismissed the soldiers. A long moment of silence hung in the air as the doctor examined Max.

Finally, almost impatiently, one of the agents stepped forward. "We ordered some food," he said. "And here's a cell phone. You want to call your family?"

Max gazed straight ahead.

"Don't you want to get back to America and see your children?"

Max nodded.

"Here," the agent said. "Your daughter's on the line."

Instead of talking, Max listened and silently cried.

Later that day, the U.S. government agents removed Max from Phnom Penh during Cambodia's most turbulent political era since the Pol Pot killing fields.

The unexpected discovery of his comatose condition had changed the U.S. government's plan to use a military aircraft to airlift Max from Southeast Asia. After an emotional exchange between Cambodian and U.S. authorities at the Phnom Penh Airport in the blazing Southeast Asian sun, Max was flown to Bangkok, the capital of neighboring Thailand. In Bangkok, the U.S. agents made sure he ate well. They apparently didn't want him to return to civilization looking like he had when they found him in Colonel Hing Peo's dungeon.

Six days later, Max and his entourage flew from Thailand to Singapore. There, after several hours of political negotiations, the go-ahead was given to fly on to Bali, Indonesia. The U.S. government had to be careful through which countries they traveled because they feared any situation that might provide Max with the possibility of political asylum.

In the Bali countryside, Max was placed in a quiet outdoor holding cell that was used by the Indonesian Military Police. The U.S. agents left him there while they went out to contact their headquarters.

A tropical rain blew in as the Bali twilight slowly turned into night. Max sat alone. He was still weak – still shaky from his long, drawn-out ordeal.

Max was lucky, though. Three other foreigners abducted in Cambodia – one from England, one from France, and another from Australia – were not. General Nuon Paet's Khmer Rouge soldiers killed them all because ransom money had not been paid quickly enough.

In Max's situation, he was surrounded by treachery. His involvement in a covert U.S. government-orchestrated, multi-ton marijuana operation had gone awry.

From Bali, they flew on to Guam – a historic island that Max remembered well. Only a year before, he had nearly perished in a furious tropical storm while on an almost impossible rescue mission in the Philippine Sea off the coast of Saipan.

In Guam, Max found his lost friends Captain Chin and the Bird at the

Federal Detention Center. Max spotted the Bird on the opposite side of the wire fence. His body was bone-thin.

"Michael! Michael!" Max yelled as he gripped the fence.

The Bird ran over, shouting, "When did you get here?"

"This is a mind-killing farm!" Max said in a manic frenzy. "Can't you see they're feeding us so much food and giving us beds to sleep on? We must resist. They're brainwashing us!"

Max was delusional, still recovering from dysentery and malaria.

The Bird, wide-eyed, cried, "Just leave me alone!"

Max fired back, "We must . . . we must call our lawyers immediately!"

"Calm down! Calm down!" the Bird wailed in a panic. "Wait till we return to the States!"

From the Guam Federal Detention Center, the two friends were transported separately to Seattle. After the long flight, U.S. Marshals brought Max into King County Jail in Seattle.

The admission guard behind the desk glanced up as the marshal stared straight into the guard's eyes and said, with purpose in his voice, "This is the guy from Cambodia."

The guard nodded. The marshal handed over Max's paperwork and retreated into the Seattle rain.

Max stood, waiting to be brought to his cell.

"Hey, you hungry?" the guard asked.

"Sure," Max replied.

"Have a seat in the lounge and watch the Jets game. I'll get you something to eat."

It all seemed surreal to the prisoner. The sights and sounds of this football game and the soft, cushiony armchairs all made him feel as if he had just arrived in another dimension of time and space.

Max spent the night in King County Jail. It was there, after feeling overcome by the desire to write down what had happened to him, where he wrote in painful detail an eleven-page letter to his daughter recounting moments of his experience in Southeast Asia.

If I die, he thought, *at least someone will know the truth.*

~ ~ ~

DECEMBER 21, 1998

Max was transferred to the Federal Detention Center near Seattle's SeaTac Airport.

This was a new, clean facility designed for short-term visits. In his single room, Max continued to write. Soon after his arrival, he was called out of his room to see Dr. Lo, the FDC psychologist. Apparently, this was a routine step for new arrivals.

Dr. Lo turned out to be an attractive Asian woman, smartly dressed and friendly. In her office, she sat to Max's left in a slightly higher chair with a notepad resting on her knee.

"So, Mr. Torsone," she began, a slight Asian accent rippling just beneath the surface of her clinical voice. "How are you today?"

"Fine," Max replied. The prisoner noticed her beautiful, long, dark hair. It reminded him of someone close to him – someone he loved very much.

Ahm . . . Ahm, he thought.

"I understand from the report I have that you came in from Southeast Asia," Dr. Lo said.

"Yes," Max replied.

"It also states here that you were in a Cambodian prison. Must've been terrible. Can you tell me about the experience?"

Max started to speak, but suddenly, his throat closed. He couldn't voice a word. His throat felt like it was filled with all the pain that he'd been carrying with him since his capture in Koh Kong. His eyes began to burn.

Sensing the prisoner's sudden discomfort and loss of composure, Dr. Lo rose from her chair and moved closer to Max. "It's okay," she said. "Just breathe slowly."

After the pain had subsided, Max stood to leave. As he opened the door, Dr. Lo spoke again.

"Are you going to be all right?"

Max nodded slightly and left.

The American didn't sleep that night. He just couldn't stop writing. The words poured out of him like the Mekong River pours into the South China Sea during the rainy season.

~~~

APRIL 1, 2000

By now, Max's battle with the U.S. State Department had drained his faith in the existence of truth and justice. Max sat and conversed with his new lawyer in the attorney-client visitation room at SeaTac. Before them lay a stack of legal papers that included a detailed information package that Max had printed. He hoped to bring his latest lawyer up to speed as quickly as possible.

The lawyer looked at the top document and seemed confused. "What does Prime Minister Hun Sen, the Cambodian leader, have to do with you and your situation?" he finally asked.

Max looked at him blankly, feeling overwhelmed. He didn't know where to begin. The document outlined the kind of sordid global chess game about the politics of contraband that this young lawyer hadn't even read about in books.

The American leaned back in his chair and gazed steadily at the man across the table. "Are you ready?" he asked.

His attorney pulled a legal pad out of his briefcase. "Ready," he said.

"It's not a matter of reason or justice. We all get involved
in a moment of emotion and then we cannot get out."
                              – Graham Greene, *The Quiet American*

BOOK ONE

Chapter 1

1:00 PM : October 25, 1978 : Poughkeepsie, New York

I received the call from my partners. They were strategically occupying a table at the Windows on the World restaurant on top of the World Trade Center. From this vantage, they could scan the shipping lanes that led to the Hudson River. To the patrons and restaurant workers, the four well-dressed men surely appeared to be Wall Street businessmen.

Their true purpose there, however, was to get a visual of a ship that had traveled from Columbia carrying 23,000 pounds of gold-bud marijuana.

"She's in!" my New York City-based partner announced over the phone.

Now the task of offloading this precious cargo was mine, so I immediately called my men. They knew that, when the call came in, they were to meet me at my younger brother's Sunoco Station, where we had two eighteen-foot, straight-body trucks ready to go. It would take all 25 of us to offload this marijuana-heavy ship in the four hours that we had to finish the job.

By 8:00 PM, everyone was piling into the back of the two trucks. It took 45 minutes to reach the offload site 70 miles north of NYC. The industrial pier was part of a giant construction material manufacturing complex. Big Al, my contact man, met us at the entrance. Tonight, the giant pier would be clear for my use.

I dropped off one man with a walkie-talkie in a wooded area opposite the main entrance.

"If you see anything out of place," I told him, "radio me."

The trucks moved in past the checkpoint to the weigh station, where they parked. They would wait for my signal to move to the pier.

Big Al and I rode together in his pickup truck to the bridge that spanned the railroad tracks running parallel to the Hudson River. On the bridge was parked a mammoth D-8 bulldozer, which prevented anyone from passing through.

I was delirious and my adrenaline was pumping. We would soon be trucking to the safe houses $9 million worth of herb that would take us no longer than 90 days to sell.

Big Al signaled the dozer operator and we drove over the bridge to the pier.

It was time.

I radioed the two truck operators. Moments later, the trucks backed into place. I ran up to the upper level and stood behind one of them, pulling the lever over and raising the steel door. The men inside all froze, their eyes dark and intense. They clearly had no idea where they were.

"Come on out," I barked.

They all jumped down and stood in a cluster. They were scared and confused – but alert.

I turned toward the river. There was a new moon, and the darkness made the lights along the water more intense.

I noticed a green, blinking light coming up the river. I flashed my white flashlight three times in response. Suddenly, the vessel turned and headed toward me.

It's happening, I thought. *It's really fucking happening.*

Next thing I knew, I was tying off the vessel's ropes to the pier. The captain came on deck and climbed down to where I was standing. We hugged each other. He looked good considering the long voyage he had just completed. I couldn't say the same for his crew.

I directed the men to open the forward and rear hatches. The captain instructed them on how to move the bales out of the hull of the ship in the most efficient manner. We established a bucket brigade, and suddenly, 80-pound bales of Columbian Gold started moving up the incline and into the trucks. For three and a half hours, we worked like ancient Egyptian slaves, almost collapsing from exhaustion.

Every now and then, Big Al would sound the alarm. The signal reminded me of a WWII submarine klaxon preparing to dive. In our case, Big Al alerted us whenever a ship was passing by. We would all stop working and take a low profile on the pier. It was our only respite.

When we'd finished, I stared back out into the darkness lining the pier. The dampness in the air made me shiver as I stood alone – the trucks had left without my realizing.

I was gathering my senses when Big Al came down from the lookout point. He stood on the upper tier, looking down at me. The large man smiled and held his meaty hands on his hips. "Max, you're something else!" he bellowed.

We had just moved eleven and a half tons of Columbian Gold marijuana – priced at $400 per pound.

The prospect of such large sums of money seemed to change everyone. As I paid the men in giant wads of cash the next morning, I could see that a new dimension had been introduced into their lives. They had had a taste of adventure. Now they wanted more.

CHAPTER 2

OCTOBER 1975

I sat with Daniel, my herb contact in New York, in his weathered barn next to a large, antique paned-glass window. We smoked a joint as a beam of warm sunlight poured down onto the single pound of Columbian herb cradled on Daniel's lap. We had been sitting face to face on wooden crates as the pungent fragrance of hay bales and baskets of fresh-picked corn, tomatoes, squash, and melons filled our lungs with sweet, organic scents. Outside our sanctuary, autumn's awesome beauty flowed on into the horizon.

Daniel's huge, bountiful vegetable garden rested beside our cozy spot in the barn. I remember seeing his wife in her flowered country dress picking honeydew melons for lunch, her long, golden hair flowing over her shoulders. She carried her six-month-old son under her left arm. Their three-year-old daughter, wearing a little blue jumpsuit, walked in tow, holding a freshly-picked honeydew.

Since his arrival on this old farm in the spring of 1975, Daniel had been working for me. He had responded to an ad that I had placed in the classifieds for a position working for my company called Abbey Lane Landscape Designers and Contractors.

All summer long, Daniel and I had worked together in the hot sun, breathing in the fresh country air and sweating as we built retaining walls, planted nursery stock, and constructed blue-stone patios. We had many things in common, one being our proximity in age. He was 25; I was 23. But overall, what bonded us together more than anything was our love for marijuana.

After work, we'd often kick back under a shade tree, smoke a freshly-rolled joint of Mother Nature and dream of what could be.

On this crisp fall day, Daniel had called and asked if I could come over to his place. He had something important to speak to me about.

We now sat facing each other in the rustic barn. Daniel's long, blonde hair was tied in a ponytail and glowed in the strong autumn sunbeam. He spoke slowly and deliberately, explaining how his people in New York City were beginning to trust him again. As a result, they had supplied him with herb for distribution.

Daniel held the golden herb in his upturned hands as he slowly raised them up. The intense sunbeam magnified the colors of the buds. They were gold-laced with threads of green, red, and purple – just like the mountains surrounding us.

In a sermon-like voice, Daniel spoke. "This is our energy. This is our life."

He slowly handed me the pound of gold bud. The moment was magical.

Through our many conversations, I had learned that Daniel didn't consider herb to be a drug. He explained that he would never work with anyone who was involved with drugs. He said in his Brooklyn accent, "If I hear you're dealing with con artists or drug dealers, I'll have to discontinue our relationship. People who deal drugs have weak people around them. When they get into trouble, they're capable of hurting you. Yet herb people have good karma and tend not to be strung out or desperate. You'll have fewer hassles."

Daniel was street smart, so I took his advice seriously.

In the early seventies, I had sold small amounts of herb to pay my way through college. Now I had a substantial connection. Daniel and his people were capable of supplying me with hundreds, if not thousands, of pounds of Columbian herb. Seemingly overnight, my herb distribution business grew. It stretched from New York City to the mountains of Lake Placid and to many points in between.

As the herb business expanded, I recruited my childhood friends, John and Eric. As children, we had lived next to each other in our parents' ranch-style homes in the suburbs of Poughkeepsie. Since the age of four, John and Eric had been like brothers to me. Now we were all in our twenties.

John was 5'10" with a solid build. He had black, thinning hair, a mustache, and intense eyes like his grandfather – a man who, ironically, had made big money bootlegging booze during prohibition.

Eric was an all-star football player in high school. His height and weight were similar to John's, but Eric was athletically gifted. He had wavy, brown hair and an easy smile. His Mark Twain sense of humor had come from his father.

In those days, we would drive down to the city to meet Daniel and his people in order to receive our loads and drop off cash from the previous week's load. We would also meet our customers to pick up cash and drop off herb. This naturally created a scene that was more social than professional. Nearly every week, we and our new business associates would dine at New York's finest restaurants. We would hit every hot spot in the city. Sometimes, Daniel would meet us for a Japanese massage, where shiatsu and a steam room would make a safe place to discuss new loads coming in.

Occasionally, John would disagree with me regarding our profit margin. "So what?" he'd say. "We have a strong network. We also don't have any real money because you're practically giving the product away."

"Don't worry," I'd say. "You'll see. We keep our profits low and our network will expand. Simple economics, man. We'll muscle out the competition with low prices. Plus, we're still making good money – and you know it."

We were moving hundreds of pounds per month. The only element that ever caused problems was the occasional drought. Having no control over the supply side, we were always at the mercy of others – a problem I set out to rectify.

I recall the summer of 1978, when Daniel asked me to come alone to dine with him at the Tavern on the Green. This New York City landmark had giant chandeliers, each a different color: red, yellow, green, and blue crystal. Sparkling over our heads like celestial bodies, each one must have weighed hundreds of pounds. The high glass ceiling and walls carried an antique greenhouse design. Outside, stately oak trees covered with millions of twinkling white lights dazzled the patrons inside the restaurant. The interior was a combination of Victorian and French décor, ornately painted in pastels with flowers everywhere.

The food and champagne were exquisite. We would often see famous people sitting next to us, like Richard Nixon, John Travolta, and Carly Simon.

It was within this ambiance that Daniel proposed the next big thing. "My friends and I need a place to dock a ship for an offload," he said. "We're bringing in an ocean-going vessel with herb from Columbia. If you know a place to offload, you could make some real money."

The carnival atmosphere surrounding me, the champagne, and this request to become involved in an herb trip all seemed like a pre-written script. While hiding my excitement, I told Daniel that I'd check into it and get back to him in a week.

The next day, I met with John and Eric, and told them the big news. Our excitement was contagious.

We checked every place that we could think of on the Hudson River, looking for an offload site. This was our stomping ground. My years of rowing on the Poughkeepsie High School crew team finally paid off. I knew every cove, dock, and inlet on the Hudson.

John suddenly lit up. "Hey! What about your buddy Big Al? He runs that huge stone-crushing plant on the Hudson River. They have big docks . . . and ships and barges go there all the time. Maybe he'd be interested."

"You think I should broach the subject with him?" I asked. "I mean, I hardly know him. If he turns me down, we're exposed."

"He's our only shot. We won't be able to do this offload if he says no!"

That day, I went to the immense stone-crushing plant to see Big Al. The man was in his late fifties, had a full head of gray hair, and was built like a Mack truck. He was an old-fashioned guy and I liked his no-bullshit personality. I located him at the crusher-towers.

"Hey, Max!" Big Al said jovially. "How you doing? What can I do for you?"

His wide smile and robust face gave me the confidence I needed to pop the big question. Practically yelling to overcome the noise, I told Al that a good friend of mine was coming from the Caribbean in a ship carrying untaxed rum, and explained that we were willing to pay good money to use his dock to offload it.

Big Al stood there as the ominous crusher-towers behind him made a sound like rolling thunder. He rubbed his chin with his powerful right hand. The expression on his face was that of a calculating giant. "You know these guys well?" he asked in a deep voice, now shouting at me because of the noise coming from the crushers.

I yelled back at him, "I know one guy pretty good. The rest of them I've known through him for about two years. I've been working closely with them. I trust them!" I paused a moment before belting out, "You can meet them if you want to!"

The sounds of heavy equipment, train engines, and the mammoth stone crushers all made the earth under my feet rumble. In these surroundings, Big Al appeared bigger and stronger. His huge body seemed to be trying to break out of his white shirt. I felt intimidated, and thought, *If I fuck this up, this guy's going to kill me.*

Eventually, the giant smiled and became Big Al again. He said with a friendly roar, "Max, for you, I'll do it!"

"Great!" I said.

I stopped myself from jumping up and giving him a bear hug. Instead, we shook hands.

~ ~ ~

When the Hudson project was complete, we were all basking in the glow of success. I moved into a contemporary new home on the Hudson with my wife Virginia and our two-month-old daughter Ari. The river views were spectacular. The sun reflected off the water, shimmering on the walls of the interior living space. At night, ships would anchor near the house to take on water from an underground spring. The lights of the ship would reflect off the river and create a very romantic setting. The rolling hills lining the river valley made me feel as if I was in one of the most beautiful places on Earth.

The men I had brought into this adventurous life would come to visit, one by one. "When's the next ship coming in?" they would ask. "What do you want me to do?"

I could see how fast the money was being spent. Everyone had bought new cars: Volvos, Mercedes', and BMWs. Some started businesses. Outsiders began noticing. You don't go from a pickup truck to a Benz and designer clothes and not get noticed.

I had to educate everyone. I told them, "If you don't have a business or a means to support your lifestyle, stay low-key. We don't need the attention."

~ ~ ~

A meeting I had with Daniel exposed the politics of the herb business.

"They fucked me out of my share," Daniel said. "They manipulated me while my mother was dying so they could get control of the project. Now I have to split with them and you have to decide who you're going with. And you better say me, because I brought you into this business."

"I'm with you," I said without hesitation.

"I'm glad to hear that. Skip is coming with me, too. I've got my own things happening. We don't need those other guys."

Skip was an Al Pacino look-alike. He had grown up with Daniel and was part of the NYC group.

Later, Daniel came up to my house. "I've got people interested in your offload site," he said. "I can have them come up to see it, if you want."

I reminded him that security was extremely important and that only very qualified and trustworthy people should be brought there. I told Daniel that a $20,000 deposit was necessary for anybody who wanted to take a look at our site. The deposit money would then be credited if they actually used the place.

The following day, I met with Eric and John. They expressed their thoughts to me about Daniel.

"He's a flake, Max," Eric said with a chuckle. They both thought that I should align myself with the NYC group instead.

I explained to them that I couldn't, so the three of us worked out a compromise. John and Eric would go with the NYC group and I would go with Daniel. We also split up our distribution networks. It was a loose arrangement, but one that we could live with.

I ran the set-up by Daniel and he said, "They're your friends – you can do what you want with them."

It was spring of 1979. I sold my horticulture business to John and began my life working full-time in the herb business. This gave me more free time to spend with my family.

Exciting as things were getting, I tried to maintain a sensible head in those days. The stakes had changed now that I had a wife and children.

"It's only herb," I would tell myself. "Soon, it'll be legalized. In any event, the cops are after drugs, not weed."

Chapter 3

MY brother Junior, who is four years younger than me, was now working full-time with my operation. Early on, he struck up a relationship with a gun shop owner named Idema. Junior explained to me that this guy was in the U.S. Army Special Forces and that he had a couple of buddies I might be interested in meeting.

Idema didn't know exactly what I was doing; he only knew that it was something covert.

One night, Junior called me. "Hey, I'm here at Adventure World," he said. "Idema has his Army buddies visiting him and they'd like to meet you. I think you should come. They look like guys you might be able to utilize."

I drove over to Adventure World. The store was closed, but the door was open. I found them in the back. There, I was introduced to a set of identical twins – Sam and Bob Übel. They were almost my height at six feet tall. They both had short blonde hair cut in a conservative style and icy blue eyes. The twins were built like they were in training. They wore new gray suits and polished shoes. Their moves were calculated, smooth, and serious. I could sense their dangerous personas.

We talked for an hour, all the while not touching on what my business was. I asked them what they had been doing since they had left the Army Special Forces and what their plans were now. Bob handed me a business card. The plain white card with black letters read *Special Services*, and had his name in the bottom right-hand corner.

He spoke to me in a military style. "We're experts in underwater demolition, covert insurgencies, protection, and abductions. Basically, we can handle anything that seems close to impossible. *Anything.*"

I felt uneasy around these two, but I broke up the meeting on a positive note and made plans to get together with them again. Sam seemed friendlier than his twin and soon became my brother's almost constant companion. Sometimes, Junior would take Sam over to our mother's house for home-cooked Italian dinners, and on occasion, Sam would stay the night there instead of driving back to his home in Springfield, Pennsylvania. Sam also sometimes lived in Deland, Florida with his girlfriend.

My brother and I discussed the possibility that these special forces, do-or-die, 007 types could develop with us. I was concerned about security.

"Forget about it," Junior said. "These guys are perfect for you. I know Sam. He's going to become your most valuable man."

Later, Junior invited Sam to a meeting with me at my home on the Hudson. Together, Sam, my brother and I shot our new arsenal of guns and talked about our various interests. Sam brought his own .45 caliber automatic.

My suspicions were starting to fade when I realized that, by having Sam observe my home and its contents, I was essentially and tacitly introducing him to what our secret life was all about. The nautical and aviation charts, the globe of the world, and the navigation dividers on my large map desk were all in plain view for Sam to interpret.

He took a closer look and I let the exposure happen. I enjoyed studying his reactions as he began to realize what was unfolding. I judged his responses as a positive sign.

Sam then informed me that he was a licensed pilot and sea captain. My brother was right: these twins would become great assets to us.

Chapter 4

I knew that if I didn't develop something soon, I'd lose my momentum, so I stopped at Eric's safe house to touch base with him. Lately, Eric had been pushing hard to do a Jamaican trip with me. He explained that he had a supply of high-quality herb in Jamaica worth three to four times as much as the Columbian stuff we'd just run. Our new value to weight ratio would enhance our chance of success because we could use a small aircraft this time and still earn a very good profit.

I told him that, within a week, I would find out if I could put this project together.

After our meeting, I focused on finding a suitable plane, settling on a Cessna 310 capable of carrying a payload of approximately 800 pounds for about 1,500 miles without refueling. The only thing left, then, was finding an airport that was within that range from Jamaica to the U.S mainland.

The airport in Deland, Florida, of all places, was brought to my attention by a colleague named Gene, who was a pilot and a bit of an aviation expert. He claimed that the landing strip was large enough for my plane to land legitimately and then taxi to the rear end of the airfield, where it would be secluded enough to discharge its cargo. The plane could then continue to clear customs and fulfill its flight plan. The gear, of course, would have to be trucked up the coast.

With a plane in my possession and a landing strip arranged, all that was left was hiring a pilot and co-pilot. Gene and his friend Jim volunteered for the positions.

Back at Eric's safe house, I explained that I had a plane, a pilot, and a co-pilot.

I added that I was soon going to verify an offload site in Florida. Eric agreed to book a flight to Jamaica so he could start procuring the load.

The only trouble with this new plan was that the expense for the operation would completely deplete my cash reserves. So in other words, if we succeeded, I would be in a position to continue working and earning toward my early retirement. If we failed, I was in big trouble.

I flew down to Deland for a meeting with Sam, who was living with his girlfriend at the time. I told him what I was doing and offered him the chance to join us. Sam was elated. This was the perfect opportunity for him to engage in the kind of lifestyle that he had been trained for.

Together, we looked at the Deland Airport. Gene had been right. It was perfect.

So I formulated a plan. Sam, Eric, and I would procure and load the herb onto the aircraft in Jamaica. Jim and Gene would fly the cargo back to Deland. John and Nile, a solid friend and Vietnam vet, would oversee the task of retrieving the duffel bags from the drop point. John would organize drivers and load cars to move the cargo from Florida to our safe house in Upstate New York where my brother Junior would be standing by.

Before leaving for Jamaica, I took the time to be with my family. Virginia knew that I had to go. She said she'd be fine, and I left her enough money so she didn't have to worry. I hugged and kissed my little daughter Ari, looking forward with joy to when she would speak her first words. I was close to her and knew that I had to return in one piece. I wouldn't let her grow up without a father as I had.

~~~

OCTOBER 1979

I departed for Jamaica to meet with Eric. In a few weeks, Sam would fly down with Jim and Gene in the Cessna 310. This was the peak time for the Sensi herb harvest in Jamaica.

"Shit, it's hot down here!" I groaned as Eric helped me carry my luggage out of the Montego Bay International Airport.

We got into his car and immediately headed for the small town of Negril on the west coast of Jamaica. Eric had rented a teak-style bungalow with a thatched roof and an outdoor shower. This tropical shelter was called Citronella – and was perched upon a rocky ledge overseeing the turquoise Caribbean Sea.

Nearby was Rick's Café, and across the dirt path was the Banana Shout Bungalows, an enterprise managed by Eric's local contact Monzi. The whole scene was a haven for hedonistic tourists looking to escape their jobs in America, Europe, and Canada. This laid-back village also featured Rastafarian touts hoping to sell you anything from shells to ganja.

The boom of reggae music filled the smoky air within Rick's Café. At any time of the day or night, cold Red Stripe beer and Jamaican delicacies could be found here. Had I been a tourist, I would have enjoyed this colorful scene. But I was there for a very different reason. In addition, I was a stressed-out wreck.

It wasn't long after I had arrived that we faced a new dilemma. Eric informed me that Monzi couldn't fulfill the order of 800 pounds of ganja for the agreed price of $100 per pound.

Eric had brought his backpack filled with Red Stripe beer, spicy beef jerky, and Sensi. The sun was setting and the sound of the sea crashing against the rocky cliffs below mesmerized me.

As we slowly ate and drank, Eric said confidently, "We can solve this problem. We can bypass Monzi and go into the mountains ourselves. Buy the herb from independent farmers for cash, store it, package it, and pay the police to move it to an airstrip."

I chewed on the spicy jerky and cooled my burning mouth with cold Red Stripe. "Your buddy Monzi is a piece of shit," I hissed between swigs of beer.

"Let's just dig in here and do this job and leave," Eric said defensively. "We might need Monzi's help in locating an airstrip – I know that he has police connections that can be trusted. So don't create a bad scene, all right?"

"I won't. I just don't like the situation," I said. "Seems like a three-man job. One of us has to be with the cargo to manicure and package it while two of us have to travel the countryside to purchase the ganja. I'll fly Sam down here soon."

"It's your call, man." Eric passed a big spliff of Sensi to me and then dozed off in his hammock. It wasn't long before I was out, too.

~ ~ ~

The next day, Eric and I headed out to start accumulating our load. We drove on the dangerous mountain roads of Cockpit Country in the Westmoreland region. The Jamaicans drove like crazy people in huge Leyland trucks that raced around hairpin turns, cutting off oncoming cars. The roads cut through the mountains above 100-foot-tall canyons. The heat, coupled with Eric's erratic and defensive driving, made me dizzy.

Eric explained that he and Monzi had traveled this whole Sensi growing area before I arrived and that he knew where to go to locate the small farmers we'd now need to deal with.

After each stop with a farmer, we would drop a crocus bag stuffed with sweet, fresh Sensi into the trunk of our Toyota. By the time we'd finished, the trunk was filled to the brim with high-grade ganja that we would have no problem selling in the States for $2,000 per pound.

We returned to our bungalows late that night, having decided to speak to Monzi about a deal to store our cargo, supply the airstrip, and provide police protection.

Monzi, a light-skinned Jamaican, sat in our bungalow while he smoked and drank Red Stripe.

"Come on, Monzi," Eric pressed, "you fucked us up by giving us the wrong information. Now you have to compromise."

Monzi smiled and exhaled a huge plume of smoke. In his Jamaican twang, he said, "But you are Americans. You can get more money from back home. Then we can do this business right."

"Fuck you, Monzi," Eric responded. "We've already got the ganja. Make yourself ten grand by doing this easy shit or we'll find someone else!"

Monzi smiled and slowly replied, "I don't care about money. I only care to make you happy, mon."

Eric and I rolled our eyes and laughed at this jungle hustler. Monzi laughed with us and finally agreed.

We started storing our herb at Monzi's inland family home. Monzi's wife and children got a kick out of seeing "da white people" working the countryside instead of playing the tourist role and lounging around the holiday hotels that lined the sandy beaches.

We paid his wife to cook for us while we manicured the buds and packaged them at Monzi's place.

Caring for the weed was a slow process. October had come and gone. It was now late November, and only half of the load had been gathered and properly packaged.

I notified my brother and asked him to send Sam down with the plane. I would send Jim and Gene back to the States on a commercial flight and Sam would stay to help speed things up. Our aircraft would remain at the Montego Bay Airport in Jamaica, fueled and ready to fly.

Several times, Eric and I faced close calls with thieves. By then, people knew that we were carrying cash for ganja, so we were constantly on guard for a rip-off. In this volatile area, it would be easy to kill us and take our money, clothes, and car. We would never be heard from again. Sam's presence and military background, in that regard, would certainly come in handy.

After a trip home for the winter holidays, I returned with more cash. We had procured approximately 700 pounds at that point. I sat with Eric and Sam on Monzi's veranda.

"Let's get the fuck out of here, man," Eric pleaded. "It's getting dangerous to wait any longer."

Sam agreed. The risk-to-value ratio, as he explained it, was way off the charts. The load, manicured and packaged, was worth more to a Jamaican gang than we were worth alive.

We had accumulated enough cargo to fly our load into Deland by that point, anyway. After a last-minute ganja deal with a local farmer, we packed the 750 pounds of product into U.S. Army surplus olive-drab duffel bags with straps that made them easy to carry during the offload procedure.

The airstrip in Jamaica was located inside a vast sugarcane plantation in Westmoreland. With the plan finally coming to fruition, I flew Jim and Gene down to Montego Bay and checked them into a hotel near the airport. I then drove them out to inspect the airstrip. They agreed that it was rough, but as long as the landing gear held up, the strip would be long enough for landing and takeoff.

John and my brother coordinated everyone in the States. It was time for our move.

Gene and Jim stayed with the plane, making sure that it was ready. They knew that if they saw a burning flare, they were to abort the landing, proceed to Kingston Airport, and wait at the Pegasus Hotel for further instructions. After reviewing every phase of the operation, I turned and gave a thumbs-up to Jim and Gene.

"See you on the other side!" I said as I departed the tarmac.

In the oppressive Jamaican heat, Monzi delivered the cargo with a police escort. Eric, Sam, and I waited with nervous anticipation at the plantation airstrip.

Right on time, the white and red twin-engine Cessna 310 with the identification number N77769 circled and landed in a plume of dust. Sam gave the pilot, Jim, hand signals as the aircraft spun around to face the airstrip for takeoff. Dust blew out in billows as the powerful engines roared. Our load-truck pulled up to the plane's fuselage.

Ten minutes later, the door was shut and the aircraft exploded down the runway like rolling thunder. I could feel the loud vibrations against my face as she roared over my head.

With the first phase completed, Eric and I could breathe again.

Eric, Sam, and I set up base at the Carlyle Hotel in Montego Bay and established communication with the ground crew in Florida. It would take six hours to fly to Deland from Jamaica. I notified my brother of the ETA. Eric stayed near the front desk in the hotel lobby so he could see if the switchboard operator was listening in on us as Sam and I waited for the call upstairs.

In the morning, we received word that the mission, up to that point, was a success. The plane had landed at the Deland Airport and the cargo was in the load cars on their way to New York.

Kevin Charter, a deputy sheriff who had worked for me at the offload site on the Hudson project, cancelled at the last minute so my brother hired a friend of his to drive in his place. I thought to myself how crazy it was that Kevin, who was always bugging me to work again, cancelled when work had finally arrived. I didn't like it at all.

Eric, Sam, and I flew back the next day and were home in New York before the load cars were scheduled to arrive. The following day, when I was catching up on some much-needed sleep, the phone rang. It was one of the drivers.

"Hey, Max! Listen, I just crossed the Newburgh Beacon Bridge and all the load cars except mine got stopped by New York State Troopers. They didn't see me, so I just kept on going. What should I do?"

I could tell by the sound of his voice that he was upset. I told him to hide the car in John's barn and disappear.

Soon, it was confirmed that all the drivers had been arrested except one, who was now in hiding. I communicated with everybody and hired lawyers immediately. The arrests didn't stop.

One by one, everyone was arrested except Sam, Gene, Jim, and myself. I felt sick. My friends were busted and the source of the heat was still unknown. I had to move quickly to salvage the remaining load-car. Then I could pay for everyone's legal expenses with the profits its cargo generated.

Sam and I watched the barn and the surrounding area carefully before entering the building and unloading the duffel bags from the trunk of the one successful load-car. I then drove to New York City to meet Daniel. He was extremely impressed with the quality of the herb and with what we had just accomplished, but he was upset over the bust and asked if there was anything he could do to help. I explained that the cash from the sale of the remaining cargo would pay for all the lawyers and the bail.

All seven of the men who had been arrested as part of the sting, including Eric, John, and my brother, were released on bail.

Shortly thereafter, Peter McMann, one of the lawyers and an old friend of mine, called me into his office. He asked me if I knew Kevin Charter.

"Yes," I said.

"Well," Pete said, "he's your informant."

Charter had been busted for a small amount of coke and had turned in his friends to avoid jail time. I was angry – I'd told Kevin never to get involved with coke. "It'll bring you problems," I had said.

Days later, Peter McMann walked out of court smiling. This was the finest day of his legal career. The judge had written the wrong date on the warrant to seize the cars, so all charges had been dropped. Everyone was ecstatic except me.

The reason was simple. One of the other well-known criminal lawyers on our case, Don Michaels, had told me in his office that the district attorney and the state police had another informant working for them. I was the target to be arrested for conspiracy to import marijuana from Jamaica. Don didn't know who the informant was, but he said he was close to me.

It didn't take me long to guess who the bastard was.

When Gene came to my house to talk about what he wanted to do with the plane, I said, "Hey, nice tie . . . is that silk?" I ran my hand along his shirt, feeling for a wire. I sensed that he was nervous and saw something in his face that I had never seen before.

I had several meetings with Gene after that, and each time, he gave me more reason to feel like he was the informant.

One morning, he called and asked me to have breakfast with him at a local diner. When we'd sat down, he ordered a bagel with cream cheese. I had an omelet. Gene, meanwhile, was acting and looking strange.

"Gene," I said, "I've always been good to you. I gave you money when you needed it. I paid you for this job even though I lost money. I've been honorable to you. In the future, we'll make more money together. But what means the most to me is loyalty. Do right by me and I'll always do right by you."

Gene looked at me through his glazed, sleepless eyes and said, "Don't you worry about me. You'll never have any problems in your life because of me." He then went on to explain that the plane needed repairs and that he was going to fly to Jim's place to have the work done.

Gene never touched the bagel.

We walked outside to our cars. He shook my hand as he said goodbye, which I thought was odd. After we had entered our vehicles and started our engines, Gene rolled down his window.

"Listen!" he yelled to me. "Jim had a stroke and is in the hospital! He's lost much of his recent memory." With that, he drove away.

I didn't even get a chance to question him further. I sat in my car in shock. *Jim had a stroke? Lost his memory?*

That afternoon, I received a page from my lawyer. I called him right back. Don answered the phone in a huff.

"Hi, it's me," I said.

In a nervous voice, he strained out his words. "Max, get out of town, now!" he said.

"Why?" I responded, my heart pounding.

"Gene's dead. He was killed in a plane crash this morning. The DA thinks you're behind it. Gene was their informant. They think you were onto him and that you sabotaged the plane. The Federal Aviation Administration and Federal Bureau of Investigation are examining the plane right now. If they find anything suspicious, they're going to pick you up and accuse you of murder!"

"I'm not going anywhere!" I snapped. "I didn't hurt anyone."

Don interrupted. "You're their number one suspect!"

"I don't care. I'm not leaving," I said. "I'll come see you."

My head was spinning.

Soon, the newspapers, radio, and everyone knew. The story made front-page news, with photos of the plane all smashed up.

The FAA completed their investigation. Their report said "pilot error" was the cause. Eyewitnesses said they saw the plane fly straight into a wooded hillside.

Regardless, I decided to stay out of the air and on the ground for the time being. As for Kevin Charter, he was killed in a car accident several months later.

Bad karma. Bad, bad karma.

Chapter 5

DANIEL'S partner Skip and his girlfriend lived in Woodstock, New York. I often visited this colorful area that was filled with art, music, and theater. Woodstock was the last bastion of the hippy generation, and I always had a good feeling when I was there. When Skip decided to move back to Brooklyn, I took over his lease on a beautiful post-and-beam contemporary home nestled in a hemlock grove just outside of town.

I felt that things were getting a little too hot where I was living in Duchess County. Several weeks after the plane crash, Virginia, Ari, and I moved into this artistic house that had a rustic scent of cedar. We immediately felt at home there. The change was good and it had a relaxing effect on me. Before, our home on the Hudson River was constantly bombarded by visitors at all hours of the day and night. Now we could enjoy the peace and serenity that our new life provided.

Although I was living off my distribution network, the inner and exterior pressure to do another operation gnawed at me. So, through Don Michaels, I managed to purchase a 42-foot Columbia sloop named *Cool Breeze*. The sloop sat comfortably in Fort Lauderdale, Florida.

Our agreement would keep Don Michaels' pockets lined and me on the water. It wasn't long before I transferred the deposit money on the initial charter and went into gear to organize a sailboat trip from Jamaica to the U.S.

Chapter 6

AS hard-up as I was for a new job, it was nice to have so much time at home. I loved waking up in my own bed knowing that Ari was safe in her room only a few feet away from me. Our new cedar home had a wonderful feeling about it.

It was late August of 1980. Virginia, Ari, and I ate out almost every night, and during the day we did whatever we pleased. On hot days, we would go to a small lake in Wilson State Park. Sometimes we would meet a friend of Virginia's there who had a daughter about Ari's age.

Virginia's friend was a perceptive woman. Maybe her Columbian background made her more aware. Whatever it was, she took it upon herself to bring a friend of hers named Chandler to meet me at the lake. She thought we would get along. She was right.

Virginia's friend introduced us while we stood in knee-high lake water near the children. It was an instant friendship that would turn out to be a long and enduring one.

Chandler had a mustache and a thin face. He was 42 years old, 5'11" and slender. He had an easy-going personality, was divorced, and had raised his only son, Tony – who was a good looking eighteen-year-old.

Everybody liked Chandler. He had been an actor and had worked on TV shows like *Dark Shadows* and the *Hallmark Theater* series. He had also worked on Broadway. He even got to choke Joan Crawford once in a scene.

A movie producer friend of Chandler's had a close friend who was a world-class sailor – a guy Chandler thought I should meet. The guy was from New

Zealand, but just happened to be in town visiting the producer. At my request, Chandler set up the meeting.

Not long after, I met the movie producer's friend. His name was Damian. Captain Damian was a model-handsome, intelligent 30-year-old who spoke with a British accent. His global experience made me feel confident that we would get along well. His son Hopi was slightly older than my daughter Ari. His wife Deli, who was from Nice, was Virginia's age. We all got along great.

Captain Damian was eager to devote his life to our ongoing Caribbean operation – which entailed shipping Jamaican herb to our customers in America.

Autumn was the best season to work in Jamaica, so there was no time to waste. John, Nile, my brother, and I, met and organized the new project, settling on a southern offload site off the intra-coastal waterway in southern Georgia. Through some more of Chandler's contacts, I would have an end in Jamaica that seemed a little more reliable this time.

It was the second week of September of 1980, and I had little time to organize the operation. Don paged me to let me know that I should come to his law office. He had someone there who wanted to meet me.

"Who?" I asked.

"Just come over," he replied. "It's a surprise."

"I'll be over," I said and hung up.

I arrived at Don's office and walked into his reception area, where he greeted me warmly.

"Well, who's this mysterious person you want me to meet?" I asked.

Don wore his crazy smile, so I knew that it was going to be good. "Remember the judge who was involved in the case that your friends were arrested for?" he asked.

"Yeah."

"Well, he's here in my office and wants to see you."

"What about?"

"Relax, Max, he's a very close friend of mine. We own a marina and restaurant on the Hudson together. Just listen to what he has to say."

I reluctantly walked into Don's office. The judge was sitting behind the lawyer's desk.

"Hello, your honor," I said as I extended my hand.

The judge stood up and we shook hands. "It's a pleasure to finally meet you, Max," he said.

"I'll step out while you two talk," Don said, retreating out the door.

The judge was in his mid-forties and had a medium build with a full head of dark brown hair. He was almost nerdy-looking with his crooked glasses. "You know, Max," he said, "I'd like to say that I was very impressed with the way you handled the problem you had. You took real good care of your friends when everyone clammed up. It turned out pretty good for you all, I see."

"Yes, it did," I replied.

"You know, everyone got off because I placed the wrong date on the search warrant. I'll be frank with you. I don't believe in putting people in jail on marijuana charges. I think that marijuana should be legal."

"Yes, I agree with you on that," I said, wondering where all this was going.

The judge just smiled at me and gave me a slight nod. I listened and watched him very carefully, not really detecting any deceit or danger.

"You know, Max, my wife and I love to sail. We don't own a sailboat, but we do have a little houseboat that we keep on the Rondout River."

"Yes," I said, "I'm familiar with that area off the Hudson."

"Listen, Max," he said. "Next time you're looking for a crew to sail your boat from Jamaica, just let me know. I think a husband and wife crew – and the fact that I'm a judge – would be a perfect front."

Smelling a set-up, I replied that I would definitely consider this option.

"Good!" the judge said. "When you're ready, let me know. You can meet my wife and me on our houseboat."

"Very good," I said. "I'll get back to you very soon. We're actually in the process of developing a new project as we speak."

"Well, count us in," he said and stood up to shake my hand.

I met Don in the front office on my way out. He was sitting on the edge of a desk with the lit, excited face that I'd become accustomed to seeing.

I looked at him and said, "Is this for real?"

"One hundred percent," he replied.

"Listen, Don, I've got a professional captain from New Zealand ready to go. I'll bring him over so you can fill out the charter. Throw an ad in *The New York Times* and Captain Damian will respond and call for an appointment. He can meet the judge then."

Don laughed and headed for his rear office to talk to our new crewmember.

On my way back to the car, I wondered whether I had done the right thing by speaking to this guy.

~~~

Nile and John returned to New York from their reconnaissance work in Georgia. Their report was favorable. They had located the campground on the intra-coastal waterway. We needed to park our 40-foot camper there a few weeks in advance so rapport could be established with the other campers who apparently had stayed there all season long.

Nile and his wife, Louise, would stay there as newlyweds for several weeks before our ETA. Everyone would become comfortable seeing Nile go fishing every evening and having barbecues with his pretty young wife.

Captain Damian needed a car, so I gave him my 450 SEL 4.5 Mercedes Benz to use. I didn't hear any complaints. Can't say as I blame him – a beautiful car, expense money with the possibility of a windfall, and a sleek sailboat to tool around in – all were at his disposal. During the day, he kept busy by outfitting the *Cool Breeze* for the voyage at Don's Marina.

Meanwhile, I needed to develop my in-country team for Jamaica, so I contacted Eric. He would work with me on loading the *Cool Breeze*.

During our conversation, Eric explained how he and a mutual friend named Joel had recently tried to make an herb trip. When Joel and the pilot had come in for a landing in Jamaica, they had come in too hot and crashed the plane on the runway. No one had been seriously hurt, but Eric was pissed at Joel.

Eric was hoping to place the herb from the crashed plane trip on the *Cool Breeze*. I felt a little funny about this, but because of my close relationship with him, I agreed.

My next meeting did not turn out well. Sam Übel was in my living room with tears in his eyes.

"I can't go on this mission, Max. My brother in Thailand has taken your advice and nurtured a relationship with an Australian marijuana exporter."

"Let your brother know that I'm one hundred percent behind this move and to keep me in mind when he's ready to move herb," I said. "No hard feelings."

Now Sam was leaving to join his brother in Bangkok. We were both sorry to be parting.

"I'll stay in close contact with you," Sam said.

"Great!" I replied. I also warned him that the most beautiful girls in the world lived there and to be extra careful.

Sam smiled and said, "Don't worry. I'll keep my guard up."

Chapter 7

THE rain was pouring down heavily as I followed the column of Jamaican Bushmen and Rastafarians through the untamed, humid jungle. The men in front hacked away with their machetes and made a narrow path for the dozen Jamaicans who were carrying large bales of ganja and supplies on their heads.

The procession was led by our chief ganja supplier, Old Man Charlie. We all moved into a clandestine area of the jungle near Old Man Charlie's farm where we could do our manicuring and packaging. We set up our camp next to a shallow cave in the thick, tropical forest. The farm was on top of one of two mountains that looked very similar. They were shaped like dolphins, hence the name "Dolphin Hill."

For two weeks, it rained every day. In the tropical heat, we built tents with plastic tarps and sat in circles around small campfires as we packaged our cargo of fresh, sweet Sensi. Eric, Chandler, and I took turns working shifts around the clock. We removed the dense buds from the stems and hand-packed them in plastic bags. The bags were then placed in duffel bags for easy handling.

In the light of a kerosene lantern, I told the workers, "All meat, no bones." My shadow flickered against the rock ledge behind me.

This gathering could have taken place centuries ago and still looked the same. Our hands were covered in sticky, brownish-green resin from the manicuring process. We rubbed the resin off our fingers and made little hash balls. The smoke this hash would create was exquisite – a rare delicacy.

So far, the herb was fresh and of a high quality.

Old Man Charlie and his partner Lloyd were the contacts that Chandler had spoken about back in the States. Lloyd's Sydney Poitier looks and educated British accent were a switch from the Jamaican personas we had used before.

Old Man Charlie's farm almost appeared to be under siege considering all the workers. For security reasons, Old Man Charlie didn't want people coming and going from his farm, so cooking for and feeding everyone was a daily problem. At one point, I told Charlie to kill one of his goats for our dinner because no one had eaten for 24 hours and there wasn't a place to purchase food nearby.

Old Man Charlie did as he was told. That night, everyone ate curried goat. Later, an irate Old Man Charlie said to me, "No more killing goats," which was fine as far as I was concerned. I had not liked watching this poor goat gyrate, wiggle, and make gurgling sounds as its owner hung it upside down and slit its throat.

The Jamaican rain seemed as if it would never stop. Walking from the campsite to Old Man Charlie's farmhouse was a journey that always left us soaked and covered in mud.

We were close to finishing the load that had been delivered, but I could see that we were still 50 percent short of the 1,000 pounds that Lloyd had promised us.

In response, Lloyd told Old Man Charlie to go out and speak to the other farmers in the Dolphin Hill area in order to accumulate the other half of the load. Old Man Charlie wasn't looking forward to doing this. Asking for favors in the ganja business was risky.

Late the next day, we heard Old Man Charlie coming up the mountain before we could see him. His crying and cursing was not a good sign. When he came into view, he could be seen beating his chest and wailing in Jamaican slang.

"Ras clot. Bumbaclot! Ras-clot-bumbaclot!"

His shirt was wrinkled, and his sleeves rolled up. He looked haggard and beaten, with his hat disheveled on his head. By the time he made it to his farmhouse porch, he was acting as if he was dying. His wife brought him something to drink while he lay on his porch chair, mumbling deliriously – something about how he couldn't reason with anyone, how he couldn't get any more ganja.

Lloyd sat there, looking distracted. In his deep, well-spoken voice, he said, "I'll take care of it myself. I'll be back in a few days, and then we can finish up our work."

Eric suggested that, while Lloyd was away, the rest of us go to Negril to see our old friends and maybe collect some cargo from there. Also, we needed a break from weeks of jungle living.

I paid Old Man Charlie to watch our cargo. We had become friendly with most of the Rastas there and I promised to bring food and beer upon my return. I knew that this would make them happy.

In preparation for our journey, Eric, Chandler, and I picked up John, who was staying in a Montego Bay Hotel. John's job was to stay by the phone to communicate with the States and the crew of the *Cool Breeze*. In an emergency, he would come to our location to pass on any news.

When we met him at the hotel, he informed us that he had received a telegram message from Captain Damian. It read, "The *Cool Breeze* was boarded by the Jamaican Coast Guard on her approach to the island. The soldiers' boots scuffed the deck and the judge gave them hell. He showed the lieutenant his justice I.D. and the Coast Guard officer apologized and left them alone, calling off their planned search."

The *Cool Breeze* was now docked at the Montego Bay Yacht Club. The captain and crew were comfortable and ready to sail. While Lloyd was off doing his thing, Eric, Chandler, John, and I stayed next to Rick's Café in the same old bungalow that we had used before. We had good food and cold beer delivered to us – just what we needed to clear our heads. The salt water repaired our mosquito-bitten skin as we spear-fished and explored the caves along the rocky ledge below the bungalow.

Meanwhile, Eric and I spoke to Monzi in an attempt to recover Eric's crashed plane cargo.

"Storage fees gobbled up the remaining cargo, mon!" Monzi explained in his Jamaican twang. "You should have returned sooner!"

Angry with Monzi, I thought about going to see the supplier from an earlier trip, but decided to wait and see what Lloyd developed first. We picked up provisions for the farm and headed back to Old Man Charlie's to meet Lloyd.

~~~

The long drive up the mountain was treacherous. The hairpin turns next to the sheer, hundred-foot drop-offs reminded me that one wrong move would be enough to ensure that our bodies would never be found in these jungle canyons.

We finally made it to the farm, and Lloyd was waiting for us on the veranda.

We all sat together and listened to what Lloyd had to say. He announced that he had located an old friend, Dylan Hayes, a Jamaican who had a home in England. Hayes owned property in St. James and St. Elizabeth, and he had a sawmill on the coast in Westmoreland.

"He has the connections to fulfill our order," Lloyd said.

The next day, Eric, Chandler, Lloyd, and I drove down the mountain to see Hayes at his sawmill. He had arrived in his brown Mercedes Benz. This balding 40-year-old Jamaican with big round eyes and a perpetual smile moved quickly and impatiently, ordering his workers around faster than they could react to him. His heavy English accent, coupled with a hint of Jamaican, was pleasant to listen to. A full-fledged character, I felt that we would have to be careful with this guy.

Hayes said that he could deliver the load that we needed, so we all squeezed into his car and drove around St. James, St. Elizabeth, and Negril. As we traveled through these towns and villages, he would stop and roll down his window so the locals could run to his car and talk to him. All day, this went on.

Eric and I looked at each other, wondering whether or not we should work with this guy. Later, since we both agreed that he might not be trustworthy, we decided to split up. Eric and Chandler would go back to the farm and watch over the cargo. Lloyd and I would stay with Hayes to organize our new task of accumulating the rest of the load.

Before leaving, Eric pulled me aside. "If Old Man Charlie catches on that he's losing control and that we're leaving him," he said, "he might take it the wrong way and steal our load."

I agreed and told him to keep everyone calm. "We'll talk to Old Man Charlie and make him understand," I said. "He's still earning and doesn't need to worry."

Eric rolled his eyes and left with Chandler for Dolphin Hill.

It was getting late. Hayes had summoned his men to help him. I pulled Lloyd aside and questioned him again. "Are you sure Hayes can come up with the rest of the load on credit?"

Lloyd had already spent the cash we had available for the load that was now sitting on Dolphin Hill. "I'm telling you, mon, if dis mon can't do it, nobody can. First, we must move da load off da mountains tonight and secure it wit him."

Hayes had made arrangements to get a big diesel flatbed truck. He also brought on three men who worked for him on projects such as this. Their names were Ringo, Jolly, and the Fat Man.

Ringo was thin and wiry. He carried a gun and had a reputation for using it. He hardly ever spoke. I found out later that he was wanted for murder in Kingston.

Jolly was a hefty young man with a large Rasta hat that he never took off. He was talkative and likeable.

The Fat Man, of course, was fat. He also wore a Rasta hat and was normally in a good mood. He was a lousy driver and couldn't stop eating.

Hayes assembled his small gang at the sawmill as darkness fell and the rain returned. Hayes, Lloyd, and I followed the men in the flatbed truck. Several times, the truck came so close to the edge of the canyon that I was amazed they hadn't gone over already.

The huge truck went up the steep, muddy hill, slowly and in low gear. Halfway up this final hill, a set of headlights could be seen coming down from the farm. The road was not wide enough for the two trucks to pass. The two huge diesel trucks stopped only six feet apart. Their headlights were on each other like two prizefighters standing face to face before a fight. No blinking, no reversing. They just stared each other down in an attempt to intimidate.

I jumped out of the car and ran up to the front of the two trucks. A large group of men surrounding Old Man Charlie were heading toward me. In the pouring rain, Eric appeared from the darkness. He joined me between the loud, vibrating diesel trucks. In the bright light from the headlights, Eric spoke while trying to catch his breath.

"I couldn't contact you to warn you that that guy Hayes is a thief and a killer! He's got plans to steal our load and then take us to his sawmill to kill us!"

"Well, it's too late now," I said, "because here he comes right now."

Hayes stepped into the headlights as Old Man Charlie appeared from the other side. The two stood nose to nose.

Hayes spoke first in a confident voice with his gunmen behind him. "Charlie," he said, "you going to let me pass and let me get on with my business here?"

Old Man Charlie, knowing that he was in a weaker position to fight, lowered his head and backed away. Hayes turned and waved his arm at his truck in a forward motion. Old Man Charlie's truck had to back up slowly to the top of the hill.

I grabbed Lloyd and said, "Why didn't you tell me that Hayes was a thief and a killer?"

Lloyd, with stress and pain in his voice, said, "Don't worry. He can get our load, mon. He got da muscle to do dis job!"

That night was the night from hell. Jamaican Rastas, farmers, and workers on Dolphin Hill went on a rampage. The Dolphin Hill project was coming to an abrupt end and everyone was looting the place!

Eric, Chandler, Lloyd, and I protected the load from the thieves. Kerosene lanterns, tarps, leftover duffel bags, flashlights and provisions were all disappearing. Old Man Charlie barricaded himself in the house and swore to shoot the first man trying to set foot on his porch. Eric fought a worker trying to steal a bale. He later said how amazed he was at how strong the man was for his old age. I had fought a man in the dark, but lost him when he ran into the dense jungle.

Eric and I had to walk to the truck in the dark while anticipating that someone might ambush or shoot us from the thick jungle on either side of the path. The pouring rain made it difficult to hear anyone's movements.

After moving the load past Old Man Charlie's open window – where we could see the barrel of his shotgun pointing at us – we were ready to leave Dolphin Hill.

Hayes' men were inside the truck. Lloyd stayed in the back of the truck with the load. It was still raining heavily. Eric, Chandler, and I rode with Hayes in his car. We started our descent down the hill as if it were a race.

The rain was still pouring down. There was lightning and loud thunder all around us. The red clay surface of the road was slick as ice as the big truck barreled down the mountain, sometimes sliding sideways around turns.

I turned to Hayes. "What the hell is wrong with your fucking driver?" I asked. "He's going to kill himself and everyone with him!"

Hayes just gave a "what can I do about it" gesture. The truck took another hairpin turn at a high speed, and this time, it nearly went tumbling down the cliff. It was halfway over the edge and rocking up and down. The front wheels were extended over the canyon.

Ringo, Jolly, and the Fat Man slowly crawled out of the cab. They carefully stepped onto the running boards. One wrong step and they would have fallen to certain death in the canyon. The three of them climbed onto the back of the truck to add more weight as Hayes sent Jolly back to get a tractor and chains.

Forty-five minutes later, a big farm tractor arrived. Soon, the truck was pulled back to safety and everyone went back to their previous positions. I yelled to the driver, "Take it easy this time! We're in no rush!"

They took off again like a bunch of assholes.

"You have mentally ill men working for you," I said to Hayes.

Just like a recurring nightmare, the truck slid right into a ditch next to the road. It took two hours before the same tractor managed to pull the truck out. This time, Hayes actually made a point to speak to the Fat Man.

Finally, the truck made it to the paved road on the coast. We followed it to a place that looked familiar, but with the rain and darkness, I couldn't tell exactly where we were. Someone opened a gate and both our vehicles pulled in and parked next to a large building. Hayes said that we could store the ganja there and that it would be safe.

We all got out of the car. Behind us was a large sign that read, *Hayes Sawmill.*

Eric gave me a look as if to say, "They are going to steal our ganja and then kill us."

Chandler, Eric, and I stood near each other while Lloyd, Hayes, and his men finished stowing away the cargo. In the humid Jamaican night, I saw Hayes and his men walking toward us.

When he was standing before us, Hayes said, "There is just one more thing we need to take care of."

We were prepared to fight at the first sign of a gun.

"We need a cook," he said. "Someone to feed everybody at the farm where we are going tomorrow."

"Oh shit yeah!" I said, relieved. "A cook."

Chandler raised his hand. "I'll cook!" he said, even though he was the world's worst cook.

"Meet here tomorrow afternoon," Hayes said. "Then we'll head to my place to begin the work."

We were exhausted, hungry, and drenched, so we drove to the bungalow near Rick's Café and crashed. At sunrise, we all jumped into the sea to wash off the fear, filth, and sweat from the night of hell on Dolphin Hill.

The next day, after a much-needed sleep, we moved the cargo to Hayes' secret hilltop farm. It was deserted and desolate except for several old wooden structures that would protect the cargo and us from the rain and sun. This would be where the packaging would take place.

I needed to communicate with Captain Damian while Hayes was getting more herb for us, but I didn't want to meet him at the Yacht Club. I instructed him to meet me at the Intercontinental Hotel in Rose Hall.

As chance would have it, we were doing this operation in the middle of Jamaica's most turbulent election. Many people had died as a result of the power struggle during the election campaign between Prime Minister Michael Manly's People's National Party and Edward Seaga's Jamaica Labor Party.

En route to the hotel to meet Damian, we were stopped by a log that had been placed across the road. On both sides of us were high cliffs. Suddenly, men on both sides of the road started throwing rocks down at our car, demanding to know what party we were with. The sign of the fist was that of the JLP and the victory sign was that of the PNP. If we gave the wrong sign, we knew that the mob would kill us. We told them the truth – that we were on ganja business and didn't care about elections – so they let us go.

Despite the delay, Eric and I arrived at the Intercontinental Hotel on time. Something was happening there – the parking lot was packed and hundreds of Jamaicans were gathered at the entrance. We were standing on the lawn area when a huge Army helicopter hovered over us, preparing to land. We moved toward the hotel as the chopper landed. A big, sweaty Army general stepped out with his entourage.

Everyone went into the hotel. Eric and I were swept along into the lobby, surrounded by confusion. The fact that all the tourists had left because of the election meant that we were the only white men in the entire hotel – which made us stand out.

We searched for Captain Damian, but had no luck. At one point, we walked into a large ballroom packed with people. They were chanting something and shaking their fists to the chant. I looked at Eric and rolled my eyes.

We quickly turned around and entered an elevator to check the upper mezzanine level. Before the doors could close, two soldiers holding automatic weapons stepped inside. They never turned around. We faced each other, nose to nose, while the mellow elevator music played on the PA system.

The door opened and the two soldiers stepped out backwards. Eric and I walked straight for the steps and left the hotel for fear of being arrested or worse.

We later decided that the whole scene looked like a Michael Manly rally. His supporters had been trying to figure out how they could maintain control.

Edward Seaga's supporters, on the other hand, were trying to get back into power. We learned that, over a twenty-year period, Seaga and Manly had taken turns being Prime Minister several times.

Eric and I drove to the Yacht Club in Montego Bay, arriving in the late afternoon. Eric waited in the car while I walked over to the *Cool Breeze* which was docked in front of the marina. The aircraft carrier, the *USS Forrestal,* was also using this marina to shuttle the 5,000 sailors to and from the ship. All day and night, they shuttled sailors back and forth near the *Cool Breeze.*

Captain Damian spotted me walking toward him. He ran up before I could come any closer.

"What happened?" I asked.

"Shit!" Captain Damian said. "I couldn't get a taxi to take me to Rose Hall. They said it was too dangerous. Too many rallies. Plus, they're making a killing off these sailors, bringing them girls, ganja, tours of Montego Bay's nightlife. You name it. I figured you'd come here, so I looked out for you."

"You're right, it's dangerous. That's why I was so worried about you! Speaking of which, how're the judge and his wife?"

"They're having a great time. They're at a swingers resort in Negril called Hedonism II."

"Great," I said. "We might not be able to pull them out of there."

"Don't worry about that. They really enjoyed the trip over here. They're really getting into it."

"Let's hope they stay out of trouble."

"They will. You worry too much."

"Ha! That'll be the day. Looks like we'll depart in about two weeks. You all set over here?"

"Yes, sir!" Captain Damian replied. "I've gone over my checklist and we're ready."

"I can't believe the cover crew we're using," I said.

"Considering the area of the world that we're working in, it's perfect."

"I know. It's all in the art of deception. Meantime, I'll stay in close touch with you. Probably every other day, I'll call you here at the Yacht Club."

"Very good," Captain Damian said.

Eric drove as we smoked a spliff.

"This ganja tastes spicy," I said. "I like it."

"As long as everybody else likes it, that's what counts," Eric said.

~~~

After ten days, Dylan Hayes and his three gunmen had come up with absolutely nothing.

I was fired up. "I've got four days left and you haven't done a fucking thing. You drove me from one end of this fucking island to the other, all over the mountains, and still nothing," I yelled at Lloyd, Hayes, and everybody near him.

Hayes kept making excuses, but it was clear that I needed new suppliers. The next day, Lloyd introduced me to two more Jamaican Rastafarians – Raymond and Builder. They knew herb and said they could only get two or three hundred pounds on short notice.

Better than nothing, I thought, and made plans to organize the loading procedure.

Hayes came up with a small amount of product at the eleventh hour. We had three quarters of a load that weighed about seven hundred pounds, and I couldn't wait any longer. I had to keep my ETA in Georgia. Raymond and Builder hadn't brought their share yet, but they assured me that it was coming. I kept moving the load so thieves couldn't locate it.

The night before our departure, I had a meeting with Captain Damian and showed him the loading point on the chart. The Harbor Police would bring the cargo out to him at 24:00 hours.

Captain Damian and I hugged.

"See you on the other side!" I said as I left to prepare for our departure.

The departure point had a dock and a deep water frontage. It was raw land with trees and a concrete seawall.

At 23:00 hours, the Harbor Police showed up at the dock. All the ganja was there except for Raymond and Builder's share. We loaded the stuff onto the Harbor Police boat and waited for Raymond, Builder, and Chandler to return with their three hundred pounds.

Three hours went by and the Harbor Police said they couldn't wait any longer – they had to leave. I was furious. The amount that we had loaded onto the police boat barely made the trip worthwhile, and that was after pay cuts. I tried to reason with them to wait, but soon it would be sunrise and the *Cool Breeze* needed to depart from its station.

I was sick. We had spent all this time here, and now, in the last hours, the project was becoming a disaster. At that moment, I hated Jamaica. I hated these thieves I had to work with. I hated being lied to, robbed, and conned.

The Harbor Police were ready to pack it in when the pickup truck arrived. Chandler had gone with Raymond and Builder as insurance that they'd return.

"What the fuck happened?" I yelled.

"Don't ask," Chandler snapped, clearly frustrated, as he started to unload the bales.

The three hundred pounds of cargo was moved onto the police boat. Chandler went with the Harbor Police with our load while Eric and I stayed on shore.

It was going to take the men only an hour to load the *Cool Breeze*. Morning came and the temperature rose when the sun appeared over the sea. The police boat returned to our dock. Chandler looked haggard, but gave the thumbs up as he jumped off the boat onto the dock. The loading procedure was completed, and we all needed sleep desperately. It was a relief to get the job off our hands but I was concerned about whether we were going to make any money with this load. I was hoping that the market conditions were going to be favorable.

The next day, our team departed for New York. I was homesick and mentally fatigued. I was tired of sleeping in the hot and humid jungle . . . tired of fears, tired of the pressure to overcome obstacles.

Captain Damian's ETA was two weeks away. He would contact us on his Single Side Band radio when he neared the Florida coast.

Back home, I felt as if I had been born again. I had felt so good and everything seemed clean and safe.

I spent as much time as possible with my daughter, although there was a feeling of distance and coldness between Virginia and me. I couldn't figure my wife out. The sex was always hot, but there was no tenderness. We never even kissed.

I didn't want to go to Georgia and leave Virginia and Ari behind again. I felt that if we could spend more time together, maybe that would help. I figured that I would take them with me and have them stay in a nice hotel in Savannah while I finished my work in Brunswick. Nile and I would complete the operation while Virginia, Ari, and his wife Louise stayed at the hotel, removed from the operation.

A week went by in a flash. It was a drag to have slept in a soft bed, eaten familiar food, and then have to leave again.

Nile picked us up at the airport in Georgia. In Savannah, we checked into a beautiful and elegant hotel with brick and wrought iron décor. Louise stayed with Virginia and Ari while Nile and I departed for the campground next to the Crooked River.

At the campground, there was a six-foot slope to the water's edge from the top of the parking area. There were other campers parked along the water as well. Whenever the neighbors were around, Nile would go fishing so everyone knew that he liked being by the water.

The campers were only eight to ten feet apart. The door that led into our camper was on the rear side closest to the water. From there, it was a 30-foot walk to the river. From the neighbors' unit, only ten feet away, Nile and I could easily be seen coming from our RV if they should happen to look. This meant that, the night that we worked, we needed to carry fishing poles to and from the water's edge – so that if we were seen with a duffel bag, it could be explained as fishing gear and camping equipment. The large but low-profile Zodiac raft would not be seen because of the steep drop-off, unless someone came right down to look. Our possible exposure time for the raft was only a few minutes – and that was a calculated risk.

The duffel bags would be dropped off in the dark shadows on the shoreline. Nile and I would carry them, one by one, up the slope and into the camper until we had completed the load.

Junior verified that Captain Damian had made contact. He was on time. At 11:30 PM, everyone was in for the night. Most everyone at this hour, including the people at the RV right next to us, had the TV on. I could hear the Johnny Carson show.

My heart was pounding. Any minute, they would arrive.

Nile and I laid low by the water's edge. My mind was reeling. *What if we're hot and being watched,* I thought. *What if someone sees us?* My palms were sweating and my chest beat like a bass drum. A mist hovered over the calm water. It looked like a horror film. The sounds of crickets and water life seemed louder than usual.

Suddenly, I could faintly hear paddles in the water. The sound drew nearer and then the Zodiac approached on schedule with two dark figures inside.

Using sign language to communicate with one another, we offloaded the raft with duffel bags. Captain Damian and the judge seemed to know what to do. After we offloaded the Zodiac of its precious cargo, they silently disappeared into the thick layer of fog and darkness.

One by one, Nile and I carried the heavy bags up the slope and into the RV. Covered in sweat from the hard, physical work, Nile and I brought the last two duffel bags into the bedroom of the RV and shut the exit door. I collapsed on the dining area seat and looked at the familiar bags piled on the bed and floor. They reminded me of Jamaica. These were the same bags – the ones that I had protected at Old Charlie's farm, the ones that I had carried through the Jamaican rain, mud, and thick jungle, and the ones that nearly went off a cliff to nowhere.

I was cooled down now and was dying to take a whiff of this delicious herb that we had sacrificed so much for. I wanted to smoke a joint right there to celebrate our success, so I pulled out a duffel bag and opened the top. I remembered the sweet Sensi fragrance that the herb had had on Dolphin Hill and hoped that it had retained its freshness. As I untied the inner plastic bag in the duffel bag, my heart was pounding.

Oh please let the fresh Sensi smell still be there, I thought. The simple smell would boost the price from $1,000 per pound to $1,500 or even $2,000 per pound.

Finally, I opened the bag and bent down to inhale the sweet scent of Sensi. My heart stopped. The blood drained from my veins and I felt faint. The odor nearly knocked me out. The herb had taken on an ammonia smell!

I reached inside to feel the manicured buds, and when I felt between the herb and the plastic, I found a thick and gooey slime coating on the inside of the bag.

"Oh my God!" I said, feeling sick.

I checked another bag and it had the same horrible smell and slime coating.

My knees were weak and I almost collapsed. With tears of frustration, I looked at the entire load in front of me.

Nile sensed my pain and torment. "Look," he said, "we'll deal with it later when we get back to Woodstock. There's nothing you can do about it now."

In deep shock, I retied and closed all the duffel bags, preparing to leave. "Nile," I said softly, "be careful. I don't need any more problems."

"Don't worry. I'll get the load up to you!" Nile replied.

I drove back to the hotel in Savannah, showered, and collapsed on the bed. Virginia and Ari were already sleeping. I passed out soon after I had closed my eyes, but not before I had played back the videotape of the entire operation in Jamaica in my head, trying to locate the exact frame where it had gone wrong.

When had the cargo turned bad? How? Why? All these questions would have to be answered. The problem now was how to pay everyone with ammoniated slime.

During breakfast with Virginia and Ari, I felt isolated, but Virginia didn't seem to notice. After I explained what had happened, she replied, "Don't worry. You'll figure something out. You always do."

We returned to New York. Nile made it back without any problems. His Georgia to New York trip had only one tense moment, when a New Jersey State Trooper had stopped the RV before entering a tunnel.

"Any propane on board?" the cop had asked.

"No," Nile had said.

"Open the side door."

Nile had opened it, but when the cop stepped inside, Nile had held his fingers to his lips and shushed him. Nile had pointed to the box of diapers that I had left on the dining table as a decoy in case he was stopped.

Nile, in a hushed voice, had said, "My wife and baby are sleeping in the back bedroom."

The cop had nodded, smiled, and left.

Nile had laughed to himself and must have thought, *A million-dollar operation saved by a box of diapers.*

Chapter 8

DESPITE the ammonia stench, I managed to make enough money on the disastrous mission to set up my own operation. After dealing with a few key contacts, I had set myself up to cut out the middleman and take the growing end of the process into my own hands.

Sometime later, a guy I knew named Miami Jay came up to Woodstock. I met him at the Little Bear Restaurant and we discussed a deal I'd cemented to build my own ganja farm in Jamaica that I'd decided to call Mountain Spring Farm. Jay was excited. He was building a 50-foot *Mariner Marine*, a high-powered speedboat worth $500,000.

In an excited voice, Jay explained, "It looks like a cigarette racing boat. It's capable of traveling from Jamaica to Florida nonstop, in 30 hours with three men on the bridge piloting and scanning with night vision goggles. It has a completely empty hull for storage. The capacity can be as much as twenty thousand pounds, man! This is the ultimate smuggling machine."

We agreed that I would do the farm deal and grow the product, and Jay would run all the transportation. I now needed equipment to run the farm. I didn't want to ask Daniel for the money, so I called John. I'd sold my landscaping company to him in 1979.

"Invest the equipment in the project and you'll get five-to-one on your investment," I told him. "Determine what everything is worth and we'll go with that figure."

Once it had been secured, John and I made preparations to send the equipment to Jamaica by ship. A powerful ham radio was set up for communication between my new farm and the U.S.

Captain Damian was in his glory. Most of the time, he was on the farm, wearing an Australian hat, baggy plantation-owner pants, and a loose shirt. The first week there, he put the word out in Cambridge that Mountain Springs Farm was looking for workers. About a hundred men and women showed up, and Damian filed them into jobs accordingly and had them fitted for Converse sneakers.

We had worked out a deal with the Army major who was in charge of the National Narcotics Agency – the equivalent of the U.S. Drug Enforcement Agency. I had also worked out a deal with the Superintendent of the Police in Cornwall. We would pay them every month for protection. The major owned a security agency, so we hired guards from him, one at the house and one at the gate.

It didn't take long for life to develop a routine on Mountain Spring Farm. We raised chickens for eggs and for slaughter. And, of course, we tended to the fields.

The farm was running well on a gravity-based irrigation system. The ganja had been planted and was being cared for by my head horticulturalist, Joel. By the time he was ready to transplant, we had 40,000 plants that were fifteen inches high with healthy root systems.

Every day, it rained at approximately 3:00 PM and everyone stopped work. I would sit in the great room every afternoon as it rained and open the shutters. Then I'd roll a spliff of ganja and smoke. I would sit by the open window to watch the rain and the hummingbirds hover over the orchids and hibiscus flowers.

The days flew by. I would often meet with the Army major and Police Superintendent to discuss the security problems that were occurring fairly frequently. Some disgruntled employees that Joel and Daniel had fired or insulted started fires on the border of the farm. But the real serious problems were those that were instigated by our old friend Dylan Hayes.

The Police Superintendent also warned me about a young street hood who had made quite a reputation for himself. The hood was calling himself "the Rock" and had assembled a gang that specialized in terrorizing the ganja trade.

I fired Joel because I had caught some of his contacts driving up the road to my farmhouse earlier that day. Apparently, they were on their way to see Joel about doing some export ganja business – and my cardinal rule for my employees was that they were not to do any ganja business while working on my farm. Any transactions of the sort would compromise our security. In addition, Joel had proven ineffective as a grower. He had even attempted to get Miami Jay to cut ties with me by spreading lies about my competence when it came to growing herb, as well as my loyalty to the project as a whole.

I knew the act meant losing some of my better workers – only those who were loyal to Joel – but it was worth the risk. To his credit, the underhanded back- stabber went quietly.

One night, at about 3:00 AM, I woke up to a knocking sound. In the chair next to my bed sat a guard with his shotgun. Both of us got up. The guard lit a lantern. I was still thinking of the dream that I'd just awakened from. At the door were two men who I did not recognize.

"Who're you?" I asked.

"I am the Rock," the taller man said. "This is my associate, Ben."

I was a little lost as to what to do. On the one hand, I'd just been told that this man was a notorious gang leader – so it wouldn't make sense to invite him into my home. On the other hand, if I managed to get on his good side and maybe swing a deal that would be mutually beneficial, he might leave me alone. Either way, I knew that he was coming in, whether I liked it or not.

"Come in," I said.

The two followed me in and we all sat at the long dining room table. The flicker from the lantern made the Rock's shadow dance on the old yucca walls. They kept their voices at low tones, so as not to wake anyone. The guard sat in the corner next to me with his weapon across his leg.

I began to tell my guests about the dream that I was having at the time they knocked on my door.

"Tell us your dream, Mista' Mac," the Rock said, and both he and Ben folded their hands in anxious anticipation.

I explained how I was in this very room and that here, on the floor, was a small baby wrapped in a blanket. The baby was crying very hard and all of us – my men and I – just stood around as the little baby cried. No one knew what to do or how to help this baby. And then I was woken up by the knocking on the door.

Ben and the Rock offered long, detailed theories about the significance of this dream. In fact, their discussion about the dream went on until sunrise, when they finally left.

Ben and the Rock never said why they had come at such an odd hour, but I knew that it meant the project was doomed.

The next day, Daniel's man from New York wanted to know what the Rock had wanted. I told him that he didn't say, but that he seemed to believe he was entitled to a cut of our business.

"Well, you better make up your mind as to what you want to do," Daniel's contact said, "because Daniel wants to withdraw his investment."

It was a hot, sunny day when I had a meeting with the major at a secluded villa in the mountains. While I was at the meeting, the Rock came to the farm ranting and raving, trying to start trouble with the workers. Finally, his 250-pound sister, Josephine, a woman who worked for me, threw him out of the house. He left while mumbling something about bringing the Army to destroy the crops.

The major informed me that Hayes had paid him a visit earlier that day. He was told that he wanted $250,000 from me or he would go to the newspaper *The Daily Gleaner*, which was essentially *The New York Times* of Jamaica. He would tell them that there was an American in Cambridge growing ganja on a 300-acre farm.

The major looked at me. "Brother Max," he said, "this is not good for you or Jamaica because it will hurt your effort to develop Agro Fuels. You know, I was in Kingston last week and I spoke with people in the Ministry of Industry and they are excited about your project. Your friend Captain Damian made a good impression on them."

The major, of course, was referring to a concession I had made with his government. In return for unimpeded use of Jamaican land for my ganja farm, I would launch my effort to grow sweet potatoes island-wide for an alcohol refinery. This product, added to gasoline, would change the economy and end the island's rampant poverty.

Police Superintendent Sinclair arrived and sat down. "Sorry I'm late," he said. Sinclair had a large build and was sweating in the midday heat. "That Rock fellow . . . he has some bad boys working for him. You know, you should be careful."

The major leaned closer and said to me, "It's over, Max. You can't grow ganja on your farm now. We'll try to work something else out, but right now, the ganja has to go. Military troops from an area outside our jurisdiction are coming to eradicate the fields. I, of course, will be with them. I was notified and asked to accompany the unit. I want you to burn your fields so they can't arrest anyone. This way, it'll look like a false report and they'll leave you alone."

I felt a sinking feeling in my chest. I'd had a bad feeling that something would go wrong for some time, but I had hoped that we would be able to harvest at least the first crop. I was devastated. The money, the project, the work – all gone!

~~~

I wasn't there the day the soldiers came, but Chandler told me what happened.

"When the long line of Army trucks and Jeeps came up the road to the main house, the major spotted me and gave me a wink," he began. "I winked back. The soldiers searched everywhere, but they couldn't find a single ganja plant. After several hours, they left. No one spoke to any of us except the major – and he just quietly asked if we were all right. So, it's over. The ganja fields are gone. Only the irrigation system is left."

"Good work," I said. "Maybe now we can grow our sweet potatoes for Agro Fuels!" Chandler and I laughed at the calamity of it all.

The money that Daniel had invested could have put Agro Fuels – my proposed legitimate business venture and gift to Jamaica's wavering infrastructure – on the road. But Daniel was an herb man. He never invested in anything but the herb business.

During the time of the great ganja burn at Mountain Spring Farm, I was busy procuring another spot of land that could conceivably serve as an alternate growing area on another part of the island. Once the invasion on Mountain Spring was over, everyone seemed to think that the new growing area was my ace in the hole. In reality, it was a diversion. I was making other plans – plans that could salvage all our losses.

At Mountain Spring, we kept the housekeepers but let the farmers go.

What happened after Nile, Chandler, and I left the farm was incredible, I'm told. One night, while we were away checking the new planting area, a huge Leyland truck loaded with at least 30 Jamaicans with machetes and sticks arrived at the gate. The truck was too big to cross the bridge at the gatehouse safely, so it was parked at the bottom of the hill. Men with torches walked up the long driveway to the top.

One of the men from the gatehouse radioed Daniel's man and the other occupants at the house to warn them. He asked the guard in the house if he was prepared to shoot to kill. The guard said that he was not. He asked him for his weapon, and the guard handed it over. They set up barricades and prepared for the attack.

When the mob arrived at the house, the Rock stood in front, yelling and screaming for Mista' Mac to come out. Someone yelled from the house that Mac was not there, and out from the darkness came Rock's sister, Josephine. She stood on the front porch with her big hands on her hips, her eyes focused on her rabblerousing brother and the men behind him.

"You dunoh des people like I do," she said. "Des all goud men and da fair mon. Da problems you caused dem are bad for me and for you! You bra-da! You are wrong! You messen up dare farm business. It tis da work of da devil, mon. You leave dis farm now, fore I myself break all ya bones!"

The members of the mob looked at each other nervously before turning and slowly walking back the way they had come. One giant Jamaican woman stood down 30 men and her crazy brother.

I rented a villa outside Montego Bay. The Rock was still looking for me – presumably either to kill or kidnap me for ransom.

Later, through a deal that I was secretly striking with Raymond and Builder, I learned of the recent fates of Miami Jay. The enterprising drug runner had built his $500,000 high-performance racing boat. It had a payload of 20,000 pounds and was equipped with night scopes, radar, high-tech radio electronics – everything. Builder worked out a deal with Joel, who sent for Jay in Miami to come to Jamaica and pick up a 20,000 pound load supplied by a man named Quacky.

When the big night came, Jay's maiden voyage would be a non-stop excursion. The 50-foot powerboat floated off the coast of Saint Ann's Bay. With more than half the load on board already, Joel went below the deck to talk to Jay, who was making sure that the cargo was stacked evenly.

Suddenly, a hard thump was heard from under the hull. Jay looked up, startled. Then came another thump – only this time, it was louder and forced the big powerboat to list to one side.

Jay ran up to the bridge. By the time he got there, the third wake had caused his brand new boat to heave up farther onto the hard, deadly coral reef below him. The boat was now listing over at a 30-degree angle.

Jay was frantic. He started both giant engines and slammed both throttles down in reverse at full power. The propellers ground down to round steel nubs against the unyielding coral reef. By the sixth wake, the *Mariner Marine* was fully on one side, taking on water.

Jay and Joel had to abandon ship and swim to the shuttle boat for help. The Jamaican lookout was already safely on board, smiling in amusement. Jay sat in the shuttle boat crying as his new $500,000 prize rolled over the coral reef.

By morning, nothing was left. One of his workers handed Jay the steering wheel as a souvenir. The project was a total loss.

Karma . . . bad karma and a good lookout, I thought as I smoked a spliff in my newly-rented villa.

My final trip would do it, I realized. It would straighten everything out and clear the books. I was physically and mentally exhausted. Trading the farm equipment for the latest four thousand pounds of cargo had been the only way to salvage the project.

Nile and Junior had developed a new offload site in Georgia. They had located two cabins on the Crooked River off the intra-coastal waterway, and we had a powerboat to meet the *Cool Breeze*. Our plan was to offload the bales onto the powerboat. We would then bring the bales to shore, where the offload team would carry them into the cabin and then into the camper for transport north. John and Nile would man the powerboat. Captain Damian and his first mate would sail the *Cool Breeze* from Jamaica to the offload site. Four other men and I would carry the bales from the powerboat to the cabin.

Quacky, fresh off his failure with Miami Jay, introduced me to a Coast Guard captain and a couple of police detectives that were in charge of the area that I was working in. At the meeting, we agreed that the Jamaican Coast Guard would load the *Cool Breeze*. We worked out the logistics and security with the police.

I carried a handheld radio so I could communicate with Captain Damian when the *Cool Breeze* arrived for the loading procedure. I emphasized to Captain Damian to stay clear of the coral reef.

"Of course," Captain Damian said. "Everyone knows that!"

"Well, not everyone," I said with a chuckle.

The night for loading the *Cool Breeze* had arrived. As always, the scene was intense. The balmy weather felt hotter and the fear of treachery thicker. I had the sense that time was moving too slowly and the feeling that things were not going well. I tried to tell myself that it was all in my head because, in spite of all the fears and the stress, the large, powerful Coast Guard boat transferred the cargo to the *Cool Breeze* without a hitch.

I stayed with the police all night, making sure there were no surprises. After the cargo was stowed away into the hull of the *Cool Breeze*, Captain Damian radioed me to bid his farewell. As the vessel sailed away from the Jamaican coast-line, the radio signal weakened. Captain Damian and I spoke to each other like the close friends we had become. The conversation was heartfelt, and when the signal finally died, I threw the radio into the Caribbean Sea.

"Farewell, Damian. See you on the other side!" I called out. I stood in the dark, on the edge of the vast star-covered ocean, with Chandler's hand on my shoulder.

I left Jamaica the next day. I don't know why – maybe it was some sort of sixth sense – but I felt that I was leaving for good.

Chapter 9

I had only been home for a few days when, on October 8, 1981, Virginia went into labor and my second daughter, Arli, was born. She was beautiful with her multi-colored hair and kaleidoscope eyes. I found love in the little bundle of blankets as I held her.

Before I even realized what was going on, Virginia was pregnant again. I blinked my eyes and found her giving birth to my third daughter, Ali.

In response to my rapidly-growing family, I moved us all from Staatsburg, New York to Milford, Pennsylvania, 90 miles west of New York City. Milford was a small Norman Rockwell styled town – no traffic, no crime. It was peaceful and safe. I purchased six acres of rolling hilltop land in a pine forest. I then designed and built our four-thousand square foot dream home. Virginia, Ari, Arli, Little Ali, and myself were now living the American Dream. My little Ali was beautiful. I loved her so much.

I have to retire, I thought. *I have to spend time with my daughters.*

It was fall of 1983 when I sat by the fire in our living room, contemplating the big picture. I flashed back at the operations; the Hudson project, the Cessna 310 trip with Eric and all the subsequent attempts, the crashed Queenair trip, the three Cool breeze trips and the final one when Nile got shot out of the boat into the intracoastal, the Jamaican farm project, the Dolphin Hill project, and all the other life threatening moves I had made when I was the guy on the front line. I felt it was time to blend into society, and to maybe start a business. I was getting low on cash, so whatever I did, it had to be soon or I'd be tapped out.

In Bangkok, Thailand, Sam and Bob Übel and their bosses, Bob Lietzman and Mike Farell, were experiencing changes in their lives, too. The Übels' plan to take over the marijuana and nightclub business from their bosses was unfolding on the other side of the world, far from my family in Milford.

Meanwhile, I was enjoying fatherhood. I finally settled on a more legitimate career – selling real estate. Virginia didn't care what I did as long as I made enough money.

I felt a little out of place when I spoke to a real estate broker friend of mine and he said, "Sure! Go to night school, get your license, and then you can work in my office."

So I took a shot.

Real estate wasn't what I'd thought it would be. I was immediately bored. Where was the challenge? The obstacles to overcome? It seemed pointless. All the sales people in the office were backstabbing each other, too – and I couldn't handle being involved with such petty bullshit.

I had already half-heartedly spent about two months in my new line of work when I received a call from Sam Übel.

"I'd like to see you when I arrive in two weeks," he said.

"No problem," I said. "We can meet at my house." I gave him directions. *Here's my chance*, I thought. *I've been out of touch with these guys for too long and Daniel was always pushing me to do business with them.* "I'll have something for you that should make your bosses happy," I said.

"All right. Sounds interesting."

We set a date and time.

"I'm looking forward to seeing you," I said.

"Yes, I'm looking forward to seeing you too."

I sat next to the phone, thinking about how I somehow knew that they had to contact me sooner or later. I didn't have the sincerity money – which I guessed would amount to about $100,000 – that I would probably need to get back into business, but I had a gut feeling that I could raise it in time.

In response, my brother and I met with Daniel at an exclusive health club called the Vertical Club in New York. That day, I pulled no punches. I had no idea if Sam would work with me. This was a total gamble, but something inside told me to go for it – told me that I could make a deal.

Daniel had the money I would need. That wasn't the problem. He had over $4 million in a box that was collecting dust. I told him that Sam had contacted me, and that if I could raise a deposit, I would be in on the next project. With $100,000, I could make the deal.

After selling him on the idea all day, Daniel finally said he wouldn't do it. I was driving him back home to Brooklyn in my car when he announced his decision. I knew he was doing this because of the money he had lost on the farm project.

I didn't back down. I really needed the money. By the time we reached his neighborhood thirty minutes later, Daniel had agreed to lend me money. No strings attached.

Now came a much more difficult negotiation, however. I had to convince Sam to do business with me.

What I didn't know was that Sam and his brother Bob had put into motion a coup against Lietzman. They took his nightclub, his marijuana connections, his political connections – everything. Mike Farell had to go with the brothers, or perish. Farell and the brothers now owned the nightclub known as The Superstar and the highly-profitable herb export business that Lietzman had formerly led.

Sam arrived at my place with his wife Seok Bee, a pleasant Singaporean girl. While she and Virginia spoke in another part of the house, Sam and I were together in my study. I knew that I had to be cool, so I pretended that it was my own money and that I was okay if he didn't work with me.

I handed Sam a strong box with a key placed in it. He took hold and turned the key, carefully opening the box and coolly viewing the hundred-dollar bills stacked neatly inside.

"It's a hundred grand," I said. "I hope this makes you look good to your bosses over there in the land of smiles."

"Yes, it will," he said. "And this will be good for you also."

Sam closed the box and set it down on the carpet. I was already pouring two cognacs from a crystal decanter. Sam relaxed and scanned the memorabilia surrounding us in my study. The years of sailing and flying missions through the Caribbean afforded me some sentimental artifacts that I enjoyed displaying.

We talked for hours. Now that my confidence had been established, I was able to communicate on a level playing field. We brought each other up to speed on what had transpired in our lives. It didn't surprise me – as we both never stopped believing in ourselves – how we both took control of our lives and forged forward, he in Asia and me in the Caribbean.

Sam set down his glass, leaned forward, and folded his hands. "Arthur," he said with a slight British accent, refusing to use my nickname for the first time since I could remember, "you realize that you have to come to Bangkok and meet with Mike and my brother. These days, Mike, my brother, and I all control every aspect of our international operations. As you know, Lietzman is out. What we've discussed here is only a fraction of what we're engaged in.

"We are now deeply involved with the military and, as always, we are coexisting in the intelligence community."

Sam locked his eyes onto mine and spoke carefully. "My friend, your life is about to change in a way you cannot imagine."

I hid my excitement. Inside I was ecstatic, but on the outside, I remained calm and in agreement with his offer.

Sam went on to explain our next mission in a military fashion. "The next operation that we do, you'll be our man on the ground in the States. You'll handle the offload, trucking, warehousing, and distribution. You will also have the final word on quality control. Obviously this aspect will be handled in Southeast Asia. We did well on our last project. We used a 250-foot freighter called the *Cape Elizabeth*. After the project, Mike purchased a 125-foot yacht and totally renovated it in his lavish taste. At some point soon, we will meet on the *Delfino II*—probably somewhere in the Caribbean."

The meeting ended abruptly and I found my entire body filled with a numb kind of intensity. I was blown away. Before Sam and Seok Bee departed, my new business partner and I developed our itinerary. We were both charged with the excitement that comes from the realization that a project was coming together.

That night, secluded at my mountaintop home, I stood under a canopy of stars on my sweet-smelling, freshly-cut lawn and wondered where my life was heading.

My mind was racing with thoughts, scenarios, and possibilities. Asia would be a new experience for me. I couldn't afford to make mistakes. I also couldn't show any exuberance to Virginia because she would only dampen the event with her negative behavior. It was unfortunate that Virginia and I didn't get along. We both knew that we were not in love and were only waiting for our children to grow up so we could divorce.

My plan was to send my brother Junior to Bangkok before I sat down at a meeting with my new group of partners. I had to remember who I was dealing with. These were not the kind of people that would show their cards up front. If I was to cut a fair deal, I had to know their position.

I met Junior and he agreed with my plan. He was close enough to Sam to go to Southeast Asia and live with him in Bangkok – the world's most exotic city.

Junior lived in Bangkok for six weeks. He contacted me regularly and briefed me on the situation there. There were various issues that were important for me to know before I negotiated with our new business partners.

At our previous meeting, Sam had never disclosed to me the fact that, when they cut Lietzman out, they also cut out their distribution network in America. The key to making the coup successful was to replace Lietzman's distribution network. I fit the bill perfectly. It was risky for them to go to Lietzman's people and work with them because Lietzman could find out and drop a dime. Then the U.S. DEA would be waiting for them. The brothers needed me.

I knew that, as long as Lietzman was alive, I would be in the driver's seat. *Shit*, I thought. *If I'd known this earlier, I could've saved myself a hundred grand.*

~~~

The next day, I met Captain Damian in New York. He had been away for a year doing time on some old pot charges when he'd decided he'd had enough, and then escaped from the federal prison camp in California. Considering his troubles, he looked tanned and healthy. It was good to hear his New Zealand accent and see his familiar face.

As he talked, I was looking at him in a different way. I started to laugh.

"What's so funny?" he asked.

"I just noticed that you look like an old friend of mine," I said. "When you move your eyebrows up and grin, you look just like him."

He stared at me, clearly wondering where I was going.

"I have an idea for a new passport for you," I said. "It would help you lay low for a while, just until your legal worries clear up. I'll get some photos of him so you can study them and make the necessary changes to your hair and facial expression. You can then take photos of yourself looking like him. I'll give him your photos and he'll go to the passport office and get a passport in his name with your photo on it. You're close in age and build. I think it'll work."

Captain Damian smiled. "Man, it'll be great if you can pull this off."

I handed him $10,000 and said, "This should hold you. I'll meet you here in three days."

The photos turned out great, and I met Captain Damian for dinner a week after my old friend had made a visit to the passport office. We were sitting in a quiet restaurant in New York City's SoHo neighborhood.

I handed him his new passport. "You're all set," I said.

Captain Damian beamed with joy. "Man, Max! You fucking did it! You pulled it off!"

We ate and drank. I told him about my new adventure in Southeast Asia with my old military comrades. He asked me if there was a spot for him somewhere in this new operation.

I looked at him for a moment and then said, "Damian, you and I went to hell and back in the Caribbean, you've still got sand on your feet from your escape, and now you want to go with me to Thailand to do another operation?"

Captain Damian said, "Max, I wouldn't do this with just anyone. But as long as I know you're involved, I know things will be done honorably. I'll go. Just tell me where to meet you."

I was shocked. "All right. Meet me in Southeast Asia. I'll give you an exact date and place to meet me once I'm in Thailand."

My plan was simple. I would introduce Captain Damian to the Übel brothers and Farell. I knew they would love him. He was a worldly seaman with a British education and had a confident way of carrying himself. They would definitely agree to hire him. Then Captain Damian would be my inside man. Information in this business was very valuable, especially when working with the Übel brothers.

My brother Junior returned from Bangkok. I debriefed him and found that he had fallen in love with a different Thai girl every night. Apparently, he had kept out of trouble because he was always in bed. The information he'd collected was extremely helpful, especially the information about the unraveling of the coup against Bob Lietzman and its repercussions.

Soon after Junior's return, Sam Übel contacted and invited us to the Caribbean for a get-together on the *Delfino II*. Mike, Bob, and Sam would be there.

"We have something important to discuss with you," Sam said, "and it's better to meet in this hemisphere rather than in Bangkok."

My brother left ahead of me for Nassau in the Bahamas.

From the *Delfino II*, my brother contacted me using the satellite phone on board. He explained how the brothers needed to speak to me and that they would have the ship's helicopter waiting for me at the airport to shuttle me out to where they were anchored.

"You're not going to believe your fucking eyes," my brother exclaimed. He gave me an itinerary and I was off.

After a good half-hour of flying over the Caribbean Sea, I was taken aback by the awesome sight of Farell's creation, the *Delfino II*.

"Holy shit!" I said in a low voice. The pilot glanced over at me and smiled.

The yacht was anchored approximately one mile from the Berry Islands in the Bahamas. We were going to land on a round pad located on the stern of the ship's upper deck. I listened to the pilot and captain of the *Delfino II* exchange their approach-landing data, which included the wind speed, direction, and the height of the waves at that moment. We hovered over this magnificent, world-class yacht and slowly descended to a smooth touchdown.

I disembarked the chopper as the propellers over my head continued to spin. I was greeted by a half-dozen uniformed seaman dressed in white. One of them relieved me of my leather bag while another directed me down a wide set of carpeted steps to a railed deck located mid-ship.

There I discovered Michael Farell lounging in a high-back wicker and cushion seat with a five-foot-long birdcage hanging on each side of him. Inside the cages were large tropical birds. Michael sat cross-legged between them, holding his ever-present cigarette and its onyx holder in his upturned hand.

He looked up with his clean-shaven, distinguished face and long, thick, brown hair and said in his perfect British accent, "Oh, Arthur, so good of you to come."

I could hear the James Bond theme song playing in my head as I approached his elevated throne.

I stayed on board the *Delfino II* for several days. Mike's professional crew of ten saw to it that I was never in want of anything. This was not just a luxury yacht; it was a creation of perfection. Mike had spared no expense. The yacht was capable of circumnavigating the globe without stopping for fuel, water, or provisions. From its space-age, computerized control room to its immaculate power plant, Mike had taken care of every detail.

Even the bath fixtures were made of eighteen-karat gold. The staterooms, salons, and dining rooms were exquisite. There must have been a half million dollars worth of artwork tastefully located throughout the interior.

Mike Farell, the Übel brothers, Junior, and I gathered in the main salon for an informal meeting. With drinks in our hands, we sat comfortably in the plush surroundings.

Sam started off by saying, "I don't know if you've been following the news regarding the political unrest in Thailand lately, but a military coup has occurred in Bangkok. People very close to us were involved and our services were requested. As you know, we are very close with the Thai army. We also work with their intelligence division and provide training and consulting services. The coup was in part successful because of our efforts."

I was listening and wondering how I was going to fit into this political scene. I also noticed Bob and Mike judging my reactions. Sam spoke for half an hour about running guns into Laos and Cambodia and taking photos of Da Nang's ports in Vietnam. Finally, he got to the point.

"Arthur, we need your help here in America on a related matter." He explained how a powerful Thai general who was important to our mission wanted to send his daughter to the University of San Francisco. "The general needs a sponsor so his daughter can stay in America and attend the university," Sam said.

I considered their request and thought to myself that Ed Posner, my latest lawyer, would make a good choice.

Sam explained how a strong financial statement was necessary and how secrecy was a must. Mike, Bob, Sam, and my brother looked at me, waiting for my answer. I suggested Posner.

"You all know of him, I'm sure," I said. "And I'm also sure that he'd be able to handle this for us. He'll charge us, of course."

"No problem," Sam replied. "We'll pay him well for his services."

Bob asked if Posner would be willing to get together with us here on the *Delfino II* so that the matter could be put to rest before their return to Thailand. I told him that I would find out.

I used the ship's SatCom to call Posner. The following morning, the lawyer was landing on the helicopter pad of the *Delfino II*. He was paid $50,000 in cash to sponsor the Thai general's daughter.

Problem solved, I thought as I smoked a joint of fresh Thai stick on the bow with my brother under the Caribbean sky.

Upon my return from the 007-style meeting, I tried to cheer Virginia up. I told her about the trip and showed her an aerial photo of the *Delfino II*.

"Nice," she replied, walking off. "Just make some money."

~~~

It was the fall of 1984. I left from JFK Airport in New York for Hong Kong. There, I would have my first meeting with Sam and Mike in Asia.

The novel *Noble House* by James Clavell was popular at this time, and the

story was based in Hong Kong. Like in the novel, my meeting was scheduled to
be at the Peninsula Hotel. Now I would be in the same lavish landmark, having
a meeting with a real life Tai-Pan, Michael Farell.

Upon my arrival in Hong Kong, I immediately checked into a hotel not far
from the airport. Tired from my trip, I rested for an hour and then showered,
shaved, and dressed in a light tan suit with a gold tie and handkerchief. I remembered how Sam had informed me about how important it was to dress the part
of an international businessman from now on.

I had been working out daily, so I felt good as I entered the lobby of the
Peninsula Hotel. I was facing a spectacular, curved stairway under a high ceiling
in the grand entrance. In a raised seating area in the lavish lobby, Sam Übel and
Mike Farell sat at a golden table in gaudy armchairs. The chandeliers sparkled
and, as usual, Übel and Farell were dressed to perfection.

Sam and Michael stood and greeted me with solid handshakes.

"I'm glad to see you made it," Sam said. "I was worried that you wouldn't be
able to decode my last message correctly regarding where and when to meet."

"It was no problem," I replied as I took my place at the Victorian table.

Drinks were delivered and Mike, who held his cigarette holder in his
upturned right hand, said in a perfect British accent, "Arthur, we are concerned
about Lietzman spotting you here with us. If he sees you, he'll know that we're
working with you and that won't be good. So we'll talk for a short while here and
move on to a safer location."

We finished our drinks and Mike suggested that we continue our meeting
at the Mandarin Hotel restaurant. This was one of Hong Kong's finest Chinese
cuisine restaurants.

When we arrived and were seated, Sam said, "We'll get together in Bangkok
to discuss your roll in the organization. I'm sure you will agree to our offer."

That night, after my meeting, I returned to my hotel. The itinerary was set.
The following day, I would fly to Bangkok.

~~~

Bangkok was a happening place. Its entertainment district, Pat Pong, was
divided into three parts called I, II, and III. Pat Pong I was where the Superstar
Club was located.

Mike Farell checked me into the Dusit Thani, one of Bangkok's finest hotels.
It was within walking distance to the Superstar in Pat Pong. I relaxed in my lavish

suite, surrounded by teak furniture with silk coverings, a king-size bed covered in mauve-colored silks, and tasteful Thai artwork that decorated the room. I also had a private butler.

I slept for two days in order to shake off my jetlag before starting my pilgrimage.

My first encounter was with Bob Übel. He picked me up at the hotel in his white Mercedes Benz to take me to dinner at his beautiful Thai-style home located on the outskirts of Bangkok. A young Thai man opened the gate for us to enter the property. Bob commented on how he liked strong young men with well-built bodies working for him, which I thought was odd because his wife Well was a sweet and kind lady.

All of us, including Bob and Well's children, sat on the floor for dinner. After dinner, Bob and I went outside and sat on his lawn area and talked. He was different from his brother Sam even though they were identical twins. Bob was more serious. We spoke about how much had changed since we had first met five years earlier in 1979.

"I'm impressed with how you've maintained control of your distribution network," he said. "I've never heard of anyone who could move as much product as you're able to."

"It *is* amazing," I said. "Herb is a natural product and it's here to stay. I'm surprised our government keeps it illegal. It's not logical."

"We should be glad they're too foolish to see that. Its keeps us in business."

We finished our cognac after we toasted, "Chock dee!" or "good luck" in English.

Finally, Bob said, "Come. It's time for you to see the Superstar."

As Bob's driver drove us down to Pat Pong Street, all of the clubs were pulsating with loud rock 'n' roll music, strobe lights, and exotic girls. As we approached the Superstar, I noticed that it was the classiest club in the area. They had valet parking out front at the curb.

As we pulled up to the club, Bob said, "Arthur, I owe it all to you. If it wasn't for you, my brother and I wouldn't be in this position."

Bob and I walked into the Superstar, where we were greeted by Sam. Andrew Pill (aka Harley), Terry Boland (aka Long John), and Jimmy – Sam and Bob's right-hand men – also greeted me. Fifty or sixty beautiful dancers gyrated to the great rock music on a stage above the oval bar. Booths on both sides of the main room were lined with customers who were all drinking and talking to the sexy young ladies.

The girls on stage wore bikinis with numbered tags. If a customer liked a girl, he would simply notify one of the hostesses or the Übels as to which girl he wanted to meet. If he liked her and she liked him, he paid the club for permission to leave with her for the night. This fee was called a "bar fine."

The lights, the music, and the sexy, tanned beauties were captivating. I sat with Sam and drank gin and tonics. I felt melancholy without knowing why. I felt happy for the brothers and about the operation at hand, but also felt a deep sadness that I couldn't explain.

After several hours of drinking, Bob informed me that Lietzman had been spotted in the area, and for security reasons we had to leave. Everyone shook my hand as I was ushered out the rear door to Pat Pong II. Sam and Bob had reassured me that everything was under control, but there was simply no reason to take unnecessary chances.

"No problem," I said. "I still have jetlag and could use the rest anyway."

Long John and I jumped into a tuk-tuk, a three-wheeled taxi, just outside of the club's rear door. We went to the Montian Hotel located only two hundred yards away, and entered through its front door. We walked through the hotel to the rear exit, which led us to another street where we took another tuk-tuk. My hotel was within walking distance from the club.

All these cuts just to throw off Lietzman, I thought.

Long John returned to the Superstar, and I walked through the opulent Dusit Thani Hotel to my suite. I approached my hand-carved teak door and used my key to enter.

The lights were dimmed and the scent of fresh flowers and fruit were in the air. As I stepped inside the foyer, I stopped in my tracks when I noticed a beautiful Thai girl kneeling in the wai position – the position the Thais use for greeting others – on my silk-covered bed. Her long, dark hair, exotic face, and shapely, tanned body took my breath away.

"Sawasdee, sir," she said in a sweet Thai accent as she looked up from her wai. She slowly moved off the bed, knelt before me, and then removed my shoes, replacing them with slippers. She stood up and held my hand, saying, "My name is Noi. You take shower now." She led me into the granite and glass bath. As she removed my clothing, she said, "I take care you," and proceeded to wash my entire body. She then trimmed my fingernails and toenails and combed my hair.

Noi somehow made me feel young again. Her sweet smell and wonderful body was incredibly arousing. Noi lay down next to me on the king-size bed and looked longingly and warmly into my eyes.

"You very handsome man," she said as she nestled her small face into my chest.

~ ~ ~

The next day, at the Dusit Thani, Mike's favorite hotel in Bangkok, my new business partners surrounded me with food, drink, and conversation. Eventually, we got down to brass tacks.

"We will pay you one million dollars for your offload services," Bob said, "and you'll earn on the distribution."

"I'll need an exclusive," I replied.

"Of course. You're our man on the ground in the States."

After reviewing the logistics, Mike asked, "How's the market in your corner? What's the demand?"

I told them that they couldn't supply me with enough to satisfy the market.

"Well, how much are you talking about?" Mike asked.

"I could move 100,000 pounds in nine to twelve months, depending on its quality and the market at the time," I replied. "If the price is right, I could blow it out faster than you could count the money."

"If you can move the amount you say," Sam said, "we'll make history as the largest marijuana exporters out of Southeast Asia."

There was a moment of silence. I broke it by bringing up the subject of Captain Damian. I figured I could strengthen my position by bringing him on board.

"I'll have Captain Damian flown here to meet with you," I said.

"Fly him to Singapore," Mike said. "You and I are going there anyway. After we meet with Captain Damian there, Sam can meet him in Batam, Indonesia, where Sam is scheduled to be at that time."

I walked back to my suite with a feeling of relief after my successful negotiation. *A million bucks plus distribution*, I thought. *Not bad!* I calculated the time back home and called Virginia to see if everyone was all right. It was late there, so I knew that the children would be sleeping.

Our babysitter answered the phone. She said that Virginia had gone out and would not be home until later that night. "Virginia told me to sleep over and not wait up," she said. Our sitter was an elderly woman who the children regarded as their grandmother. "The children miss you, Art," she said. "I advise you to come home soon." There was a note of warning in her voice.

Chapter 10

MIKE Farell and I safely arrived in Singapore. The country seemed very orderly, and when we exited the terminal, the beautiful landscape impressed me.

This is not a poor country, I thought as Mike's driver greeted us and handled our luggage.

I was impressed with Mike's multi-million dollar home. It had a modern design with a smooth, white masonry finish. It was located in an exclusive area of Singapore's tree-lined suburbia.

Mike's wife May met us at the front foyer. May was a beautiful Singaporean woman who had elegance and good taste. I sensed her sizing me up as we walked into the impressive great room.

As we casually walked from one area of his mansion to the next, Mike would stop at pieces of Asian artwork or ancient Chinese vases to point out their rarity and worth. "This vase, Arthur, is worth over thirty-thousand dollars if you can find one," he said in his classy, well-controlled voice.

The following day, I called home. Virginia answered and I relayed how well things were going.

"Good!" she said. "Make lots of money and don't forget to bring home gifts."

"Don't worry," I said. "I'll find something for everyone."

Later that day, I asked Mike where I could go to buy a piece of jewelry for Virginia.

"Right here in my home," Mike calmly responded.

That afternoon, Mike and May sent for their personal jewelers. While sitting in their home, I chose a diamond and two red rubies from a selection that any jewelry store would have been proud of. The jeweler would return with a custom-made ring in twenty-four hours.

That afternoon, Mike took me shopping for gifts that I could bring home to my three daughters. I filled up a new suitcase with beautiful things – silk pajamas and robes, dolls, fancy hairpins and little handbags.

I relayed to Mike that I was going to retire early that night and would meet him for breakfast the next morning before picking up Captain Damian at the airport. I felt that I was keeping Mike from his family, and I didn't want any animosity to build up. Mike agreed, and we set a time and place to meet in the morning.

Captain Damian arrived on schedule. The three of us drove back to our hotel from the airport in Mike's Jaguar.

We talked while Captain Damian unpacked his clothes in his hotel room. It was apparent that he had jetlag from the long trip, so Mike made plans to pick us up that evening for dinner. Soon, my old friend and I were alone and we discussed how far I had come along in this new Asian venture.

That evening, Mike arrived at our hotel on time. The three of us – in our hand-tailored suits and silk ties – headed to an exclusive British club for dinner. The steaks were delicious. After dinner, we savored cognac and smoked Cuban cigars that were delivered to us in a teak humidor. We talked for hours. I could see that Mike and Captain Damian were connecting.

Phase one, I thought, *is a success.*

Captain Damian and I left the next morning to meet Sam. We crossed the Strait of Malacca in an 80-foot passenger cruiser. Ships from all over the world crossed our stern and bow throughout our journey to Batam.

Batam was a quiet tropical island that seemed to have stopped in time after World War II. Sam checked us into a Polynesian-style bungalow resort. We each had our own little dwelling. Sam and his wife Seok Bee also stayed in a bungalow near us. Each cottage was beautifully ornate and unique.

That evening, Sam brought us to a casual beach restaurant. We sat at a table while barefoot in the sand, eating delicious barbecued prawns. Across the strait, "The Emerald City," the Republic of Singapore, glowed under the starlit sky.

After dinner, we all walked on the beach together. Seeing Sam and Captain Damian standing by my side made me feel like I was partaking in something historic. I felt that I was orchestrating a mystical union. This was where east and west met.

I cannot describe the euphoric sensation – the natural high – that I was experiencing. I loved creating projects and the project at hand carried high stakes leading to rewards which could very well create a legacy for even my children's children.

Back at the bungalow thirty minutes later, there was a knock on my door. Sam entered the room hyper and red-faced, as if he had been containing this pressure all night and was finally letting it all out.

"Shit, Max, he's fucking perfect!" he said. "Where do you find these people?"

"The same place I found you," I replied. "You all come to me."

Sam was beside himself. "Well, my friend, he's on board with us."

"Listen," I said. "He's one of my best men and he's my friend, so treat him right."

"Oh, don't worry about that," Sam said. "He'll be one of my trusted officers. He'll have a very responsible position on my ship and in our organization. Is there anything I should do to consummate this relationship?"

"Yes. You can give him an advance payment. He has a family that depends on him back home."

"No problem. I'll contact Mike and have him handle it. He's perfect. You never cease to amaze me, my friend."

~~~

The next day, Captain Damian and I returned to Singapore. We met Mike, May, and her sister for dinner. We dined that night on drunken prawns – live prawns swimming in brandy that are later cooked in it at the table.

Mike whispered to me, "Stay clear of May's sister. She's a real dragon-lady. She'll rip your eyes out."

I nodded.

We agreed to meet the following morning before Captain Damian's departure for Europe. I would continue on from there to America to prepare for this historic operation.

Captain Damian commented on how May's sister looked pretty.

"Yeah," I said. "Too bad she has a thing for eyes."

Captain Damian gave me an odd look and I laughed.

After some time in Nice, Greece, and Rome, we headed off to New York.

On the plane, I sat in awe of the experience that was unfolding. My love for my family was the motivating force that kept me focused. As such, security was important. If anything were to happen to me, my children would be devastated. I knew all too well what it was like to lose a father at a young age, and I was determined to avoid putting them through the same experience.

I felt like a product of my generation. Art, music, herb – I was raised on them and they left a lasting impression on my life. I was part of the Woodstock generation. When I was seventeen, I drove a red 1948 Willys Jeep. I had spent the summer of 1969 at a commune outside New Paltz, NY with the "mushroom people." It was a great time to be young and free.

Now, unfortunately, the others' convictions were quite the opposite of my own. Their Machiavellian positions were in contrast to my own lifestyle.

I must be careful, I thought. *I'm navigating in dangerous waters now.*

Junior sent one of our drivers to pick me up at the airport.

Finally, I had some time to be with my family. The fall was a great time to be at the Mohank Mountain House, so we all took a vacation there before I became busy again. I would hike the many mountain trails with my children and teach them about the wonders of nature. I was always happiest when I was alone with my three little daughters.

Mike and Sam arrived in New York a few weeks before Christmas. A limo brought them to my home in Pennsylvania. Seok Bee stayed in New York City at the Palace Hotel. Mike and Sam slept in our guest rooms.

The following morning, Virginia made breakfast while we had coffee in our living room by the Christmas tree. Mike cut out a series of angels from folded white paper, pulling his creation apart for Ari, Arli, and Ali's amusement. When he was finished, he told the girls to hang them on the tree. I could tell that he missed his own children.

Chapter 11

IT was February of 1985 and time to meet my Asian partners again.
I met Sam and Mike in San Francisco at the Mako Hotel in the center of the
Japanese complex. My trusted friend, Jamaican John, lived in San Francisco
with his son. I needed someone who knew the area well and John, always polite
and soft-spoken, fit the position perfectly. With his small build, white beard, and
cap on his bald head, he came across as a humble, trustworthy man.

That evening, Mike, Sam, and I met to discuss the mission. There was tension
in the air as we sat in Mike's suite. Mike was writing out a deposit check for the
amount of $1.2 million toward the purchase of a $3.5 million ship called the
Encounter Bay.

This mission would involve an engineering feat that had not been tried before.
Our challenge was to position the *Encounter Bay* approximately 80 miles off the
coast of San Francisco. There, weather permitting, the crew of the *Encounter Bay*
would launch two 40-foot-long, high-powered, cigarette racing boats into the
Pacific Ocean.

Would the integrity of the powerboats' hulls, loaded with a manned crew
and tons of Thai herb, hold up against the impact when they hit the sea? Would
the 1,200-horsepower engines start after being submerged in salt water? If not,
then the powerboats would surely be damaged by being smashed against the iron
stern of the *Encounter Bay*.

If the launch proved successful, a high-speed trip to the coast would be next.
The tremendous banging of the hull against the waves would test the endurance
of the crews of both vessels.

The offload procedure would be an overt illusion. Both racing boats had colorful logos of Geisha girls painted on their sides and bows. Mike's boat was named the *Kimono,* while Sam's was named the *Mariposa.* The purpose of this was to create the impression that our intention was to run time trials for our prized boats. The uniforms that the crew would wear would be the white jumpsuits having the same logo of the offload personnel on shore.

Both boats would race underneath the Golden Gate Bridge and then split up. One would go to the San Francisco side of the bay, while the other would go to the Oakland side. They would dock at separate launch ramps, where my offload crews – with their new, logo-clad, white pickup trucks – would stand by with extra heavy-duty trailers, compensating for the extra tonnage on board the racing boats. Junior would man the Oakland side and Jamaican John would be on the San Francisco side. Bob and I would stand watch, overlooking the Golden Gate Bridge and San Francisco Bay.

That night, while I rested in my Japanese-style suite, I reflected on the events of the day. I recalled sitting at the Mako bar with Sam. He was boasting to the bartender and the others around him about how obedient his wife was.

"Despite the fact that it's 11:30 and my wife is already sleeping," he said, "I can call her on the house phone and tell her to bring me my sunglasses from our room upstairs. Obviously, it's an item that I could not possibly need at this hour of the night."

"Don't bother her, man," I said.

"No, no! You don't understand. It doesn't matter. The fact that I'm telling her to do this is the point. It's obedience." Sam asked the bartender for the house phone. He called his room and told Seok Bee to run his ridiculous errand.

Seok Bee arrived moments later with the sunglasses. Sam thanked her, then put the sunglasses in his pocket and resumed drinking. He totally ignored Seok Bee, treating her like she was a servant. Seok Bee looked at me and I could see the hurt in her eyes as Sam's small audience reacted coolly to his show of authority.

Sam, half drunk at this point, then proceeded to explain to me how Mike's alias would from that day forward be "the Fox." His brother's alias would be "J.T." His own would be "Haig," while mine would be "the King."

"The King?" I responded.

"Oh yes!" Sam said. "It's been like this for quite some time now. You'll always be King Arthur to us, my friend."

Although we all laughed about it, I couldn't help but feel unsettled about my alias. I didn't like to be high profile. It was an alias the government could use to portray me as "the kingpin." Despite my hesitation, the name would stick for decades to come.

~ ~ ~

It was the spring of 1985, and the *Encounter Bay* was based in Indonesia where it was going through extensive outfitting. Haig made sure that his super-ship would possess the most advanced computer and electronic equipment available. He even had a special base constructed under his elaborate captain's chair in the control room. At times, the base of the chair contained hundreds of thousands of dollars. Haig was a big Star Trek fan and Captain Kirk was his idol. Was it a coincidence that the *Encounter Bay* resembled the *Starship Enterprise*?

As we would later discover, the Übel brothers hadn't just been modifying the *Encounter Bay* during the months that would follow – they'd also been using it to run intelligence-gathering operations in Southeast Asia.

Chapter 12

MAY 1985

THE *Encounter Bay* steamed across the Gulf of Thailand under a dark new moon. Haig was meeting with an 80-foot, trawler-style fishing boat that contained over 5,000 pounds of high-grade Thai herb.

In order to blend in, J.T. was dressed like a Thai fisherman. The powerful radar on the *Encounter Bay* detected the Thai vessel, and soon, the silhouette of the fishing boat would appear on this ancient trade route.

Haig sounded the alarm. Papillion (formerly Captain Damian), Long John, the Fox, and a dozen Indonesian crewmembers went to their stations while a captain named Juperee controlled the ship. The tension was thick enough to cut with a sword. Haig organized his men and, two hours later, the cargo was transferred from J.T.'s fishing boat to the *Encounter Bay* without injury or incident.

Haig navigated the ship across the Pacific Ocean through a northerly route near the Alaskan Coast. He would then steam southeast to a point 80 miles off the coast of San Francisco.

While in its northernmost position, Haig experienced a setback when the fuel lines congealed due to the freezing temperatures. The ship floated powerless for days while Haig and his officers tried to solve this deadly problem. Dumping the cargo overboard and calling the Coast Guard was established as a last resort.

Luckily, before they were forced to do the unthinkable and lose all of the cargo, the current moved the ship south into warmer waters. When the temperatures rose, the diesel fuel flowed again and the mission was back on track.

On June 25, 1985, the *Encounter Bay* was stationed off the coast of San

Francisco. The anxiety intensified as the crew prepared to launch the *Kimono* and the *Mariposa* into the Pacific Ocean. Timing the waves was crucial. The powerboats needed to clear the transom and engage in motion immediately upon hitting the ocean.

Haig and Long John operated the *Mariposa*, while the Fox and Papillion operated the *Kimono*. Papillion described the event to me with vivid detail only hours after our mission was complete.

The rush of adrenaline exploded in the bodies of both crews of the racing boats as they were separately launched over the high transom of the *Encounter Bay*. The boats hit the ocean and, for a moment, were submerged – only to pop up above the waves and power away from the iron transom.

"The eagle has landed," Haig said over the radio as the *Mariposa* cleared the wake of the ship.

Both the *Kimono* and the *Mariposa* raced side by side eastward toward San Francisco. J.T. and I received the message of the successful launch on our SatCom. The two of us were focused and excited as we stood on the overlook facing the Golden Gate Bridge.

Suddenly, the *Kimono* and the *Mariposa* thundered under the bridge in plain view. My heart started to pound.

J.T. and I radioed the two land crews and prepared them to accept the racing boats. Two hours later, J.T. and I stood in a warehouse next to the dripping wet *Kimono*, which was strapped to the trailer carriage. My 20-foot-long freight truck was parked, ready to be loaded with our Asian cargo and then packed full of furniture and boxes to cover them in case the truck was stopped en route to the East Coast.

J.T., John, and I spent the day packing up 35-pound packages of Thai herb. Each featured Styrofoam sides in case one of the boxes was punctured. Meanwhile, my brother Junior drove the *Mariposa* to his safe house outside of Oakland where he unloaded and stored the precious cargo for distribution on the West Coast.

Later that evening, I connected with Captain Damian and debriefed him. Apparently, the trip on board the racing boats was rough. The constant hammering of the hull against the ocean and the salt water spray hitting their faces was difficult for the crews to endure. Over time, the white salt started to build up on their eye shields and, at some point, they could no longer see where they were going. They finally went without the eye shields, but that meant that their faces and eyes were fully exposed to the salt water spray. This explained why Mike's eyes were nearly closed shut when I saw him after he made landfall.

Captain Damian and I were tired, but not too tired to feel the glow of success. I was overwhelmed with emotion, but strangely didn't feel like celebrating. Whenever a mission was completed, I usually felt melancholy. I've never been sure why.

While sitting in a trendy-looking pub in San Francisco, Captain Damian gave me his opinion on Sam, Bob, and Mike.

"They're all crazy megalomaniacs in some way or the other, so always be prepared for surprises." He leaned forward and added in urgently, "These Übel brothers are very capable guys and I have a lot of respect for them. I just want you to know that you should be careful. They aren't like you. I don't think they possess a heart between them. Mike's not like them, either. I'm just saying this because you're an easy-going guy. These twins are all business."

"I appreciate your concern and feel the same way about them as you do," I said. "I guess we both have to be careful."

The following morning, Captain Damian left early for Europe. Meanwhile, I arrived at Mike's townhouse in San Francisco for a scheduled meeting with Sam. He was waiting for me with both barrels cocked. No sooner had I entered the room when he started to rant and rave.

"The cost of the operation has doubled! Doubled! Why? So we could do it right! So I could accomplish my mission! I did my part. I ran the gauntlet. Now the whole fucking project is in your hands and failure is not an option! You're going to sell the cargo at the price we set. You'll earn your percentage and that's it. There's not a dime on the ledger for the offload, transportation, or warehousing. Nothing! Everything comes out of your end."

"That's not the deal!" I fired back. "I bought in, remember?"

"That's the deal!" he said.

I knew the type that I was dealing with here. These guys put on a big show and then, in the eleventh hour, their true colors showed. My first impulse was to say "fuck you" and walk out, but that didn't make any sense. I had men in hotels here, safe houses all over the place, and even the truck was loaded.

"You know you're wrong," I said to Sam. "You know the deal we made. Now you want to own the load and give me a percentage to move it for you. Is that it?"

"That's it," Sam snapped back.

I had to choose my words carefully. I made up my mind. "Fine," I said. "I'll see you in New York to transfer funds. Junior or John will transfer funds here in San Francisco. Here's $100,000 that I picked up from my West Coast distributor as a deposit. You and I will keep the books. From now on, it's your load. You own it."

I turned and left. I walked to the corner and hailed a cab. As I traveled to my hotel, I thought to myself how important it was to keep my head straight.

Right now, I had a huge responsibility on my hands. I had to move half the load – 3,000 pounds of Thai herb – across the country from coast to coast past numerous cities and towns, past scores of police stations and patrol cars. Unlike the Pacific Ocean – where there is nobody – the U.S. was filled with potential pitfalls.

If we made it across the country, then the task of storing the herb and selling it safely would be tremendous. I told the driver that, in the event he was stopped and asked about what he was hauling, he should say that he was moving his sister back home after her messy divorce. I also told him to make sure there was a lamp-shade ready to fall out of the rear door for when it was opened at checkpoints.

Everyone was ready. The load would travel over major highways 90 percent of the time. I also had a support car following the truck in case there were any problems. I coordinated with Junior, who was doing an excellent job.

I had an apartment on West 74th Street and Columbus Avenue in New York City. That was where Sam, Bob, and Mike would come to collect their cash.

Five days after the truck left San Francisco, it arrived in Woodstock. The driver, who worked for a friend of mine, explained how the furniture-laden truck, the sister story, and the falling lampshade worked well at the checkpoints. I paid him $50,000 in cash and another $50,000 in herb. I never saw him again.

Instead of selling the load to one or two major distributors, I broke it up and sold it to ten different distributors. This way, I would receive a higher price per pound and I could compensate for Sam's eleventh hour bullshit.

I returned from the West Coast while the load truck was still on the road. I was euphoric over the success of the project. I would finally be together again with my loved ones when I joined them at the Lake Mohonk Resort. I was so happy to see my family that I even managed to relax after being under so much stress.

There was just one small problem: Virginia was very angry. I remember sitting next to her on the beach of the crystal-clear lake, experiencing her wrath. She blasted me for leaving her with the children for so long.

"You have childcare services here," I said. "They have arts and crafts, horseback riding, and storytelling for them. And what about all of the maids? All your meals are prepared. They wait on you hand and foot!"

Virginia argued with me loudly. She embarrassed me in front of the other guests. I later found out that she'd been hanging out with a guy from New York City. This guy worked in the jewelry district on West 46th Street.

I couldn't believe it. I spent over $60,000 on an incredible vacation, where she could be close to her friends, and here she was implying that I was having an affair. Nothing made sense to me about Virginia. I just thought about how insane all the fighting was. Every time we went out to dinner, we fought. Every time we were in the car, we fought, whether the children were there or not.

We returned home to Milford, Pennsylvania. It was getting late. Virginia and her mother – who was visiting at the time – stayed up to watch TV in our den.

My home was in the middle of a pine forest on top of a quiet hill just outside of town. I never received many guests. So when I saw headlights coming in through my large picture-window in my living room, I immediately went to grab my Walther P38 pistol. I had stored the handgun behind the painting above the fireplace.

Suddenly, a group of men appeared on the deck at my front door. One of them knocked and said, "Open the door. This is the FBI."

Fuck, I thought. *Figures. The first time my mother-in-law visits, I get raided by the Feds.* My stomach was in knots, and my mind raced. *Maybe they're thieves pretending to be the Feds.* I held my licensed gun and yelled through the door, "How do I know you're the FBI?"

The agent stuck his I.D. up against the long window next to the door. Virginia was standing next to me, while her mother stood behind me. I handed my pistol and briefcase to Virginia and told her to get them out of sight. My herb records were in the briefcase.

I opened the door.

"Arthur Torsone?" the voice commanded.

"Yes," I replied.

"You're under arrest."

"Do you have a search warrant?"

"Yes, we do."

"Under what name?"

"Your name."

"Well, that search warrant won't do you any good here. This house is in my brother's name."

I don't know if they were lying about having a warrant because they never searched the house.

As my mother-in-law stood in silence, I asked the head agent why I was being arrested.

"For narcotics distribution."

I was angry and prepared to deal with this bullshit right there and then. "What narcotics?" I asked him.

"Cocaine," he replied.

"Cocaine? I've never bought, sold, or carried cocaine in my life!"

"You'll see."

"I'll see what?"

"You had lunch today in New York City, didn't you?" the agent asked coolly.

"Yeah, I did. I ate lunch with my lawyer and a friend. So what?"

They smiled at me like this little fact mattered.

Virginia had returned. I whispered in her ear, telling her to burn my records and call my lawyer, Ed Posner. Little did I know that Posner was already in jail. I told her to take my money to my neighbor Billy who was a good friend of mine. I could trust him with the box containing $200,000 in cash that was hidden in my closet.

The following morning, Virginia took the cash over to him and then burned the documents within a three-inch-thick business plan that had cost $50,000 to develop. She left the herb records intact. After I had returned and discovered this, she said, "I didn't know what you meant by records."

The FBI agents took me away that night. On our way to Scranton, PA, the agents in the car tried to con me.

"You know, Art, all your friends are saying it's you. They're all talking about you."

"I don't know what the fuck you're talking about," I said. "What friends?"

They didn't answer.

I spent five days in the Scranton County Jail – a real pigsty. Because of the holiday, my new lawyer, Maurice Sercartz, couldn't make it for three days.

Finally, upon his arrival, he showed me telephone transcripts between Posner and Gary Fadona, an old friend of mine who was always looking to do business with me. Both of their phones had been tapped by the FBI. Their conversations could have been interpreted as drug business. Then he showed me a transcript from when Posner had called my home and talked about six girls. The Feds chose to interpret this conversation as code for six quantities of cocaine.

"Christ! This is why they put me in jail?" I wailed to Maurice. I quickly explained to him how I had asked Posner for his help locating some girls for Sam Übel and our Thai friends when they were in town.

"First things first," Maurice said. We arranged my bail.

My family had Thanksgiving dinner at the Lake Mohonk Resort without me. I was so angry. The judge could have given me bail, but the prosecutor lied and told the judge that I had a prior conviction.

The Übel brothers didn't come to my aid. They acted like nothing was wrong.

Meanwhile, the newspapers printed a big story. The headline read, *Torsone Arrested in International Cocaine Operation with Organized Crime Figures and Famous "Prince of the City" Lawyer Ed Posner.*

Great, I thought, *now everybody thinks I'm a coke dealer!*

Maurice Sercartz was a very good lawyer. The case finally ended in 1987 with a global plea. Everybody had to plead guilty or there would be no deal. I was the only one who could walk on the matter. But if I went to trial, the global plea was off and Posner and Fadona, plus twelve others, would be facing big time. In the end, I was forced to plead guilty to conspiracy to distribute a small amount of marijuana. I was pissed off. I pled guilty to something I didn't do just to help a bunch of guys I hardly knew.

The Übel brothers didn't care about what had happened. All the money I had lost over this cocaine arrest bullshit was complicated further by the fact that I now had a conviction on my record.

The judge gave me four years probation and a $50,000 fine. The sentence came as a surprise since I was sure that I was getting some time. Though I'd lost a great deal of money on the whole affair, and, in truth, was scraping to get by near the end of it, I at least still had my freedom.

Chapter 13

I T was 1987, and we were ready to bring in another load of Thai herb. Most of my meetings took place in New York City near my lawyer's office.

One such meeting with Sam Übel took place in the Gold Room at the Palace Hotel. Sam held a snifter glass of Louis XIII cognac in his hand as he briefed me on the new project. He also updated me on how the marijuana trade in Southeast Asia was keeping the balance of power tilted in our favor.

"The hard currency being generated by our efforts is directly affecting the way the poor farmers in Laos and Cambodia live," he explained. "They're not apt to go the way of the Communists when their rice bowls are full because they're planting herb. These poor farmers really don't care what government is in control of their country. They only want food and their own land to farm and live on. Government officials try to avoid contact with these people.

"The feedback that we're receiving from the intelligence community is to resume our efforts. Of course, because of our sub-contractor status, we can't go back to our people for help if we run into problems when we're on a mission."

"See no evil, hear no evil," I said.

"Yes, you might say that," Sam droned. "The *Encounter Bay* will now be used as a staging platform to facilitate my crew in preparing the herb for shipment. The ship will remain anchored in a desolate cove near my base in the Indonesian island chain. This is no man's land. There are thousands of islands in the Philippines and Indonesia. Not even aircraft fly over where we're working. On the *Encounter Bay*, we will fill steel cylinders with pre-packaged herb. The ends of these cylinders will be welded shut and then placed into the center of steel drums that, in turn, will act as a spool to hold several tons of half-inch-thick steel cable. Each spool will weigh approximately ten tons. I will then ship these spools from country to country using a company that I purchased that has an established track record for this sort of equipment. Eventually, the equipment will be shipped to Elizabeth, New Jersey. There, Papillion, who, by the way, will be thoroughly trained before he leaves in how to act in the customs receiving office, will accept the equipment and have it trucked to his company warehouse."

"Great plan," I said. "I see that my old friend Captain Damian has become quite valuable to you."

"Yes," Sam replied. "He's a very capable man."

"You enjoy this business, don't you?" I asked.

"It's my life. But the next project after this one will be our last. Just recently, Mike, my brother, and I were approached by an acquaintance of ours in Bangkok. He has a load that he'd like us to move for him. I can't say right now, but the load will be the largest we've ever handled. Don't worry, the next chapter in our lives will be anything but boring and you will always be a part of our ventures."

Since I was still on probation, I knew that I would have to take a back seat on this one. Junior would now be the one to handle all the logistics.

As we waited for the project to take off, I decided to take my family to Orlando for a vacation. Of course, I now had to receive permission from the probation department in order to leave. So far, my probation officer was happy with me. A construction company that I'd set up was busy, and I had two cedar homes being built on spec on a lake not far from my home. My probation officer would stop by about once a month to keep track of my progress.

It was while I was on vacation when I received a call from my lawyer, my brother had got busted speeding up interstate 95 in New Jersey, with $500,000 worth of herb from Jamaica. Now Junior would be out of commission.

Sam contacted me soon after Papillion had accepted the steel spools in the Elizabeth, New Jersey port. The project was ready for distribution. He also explained to me that Bob Lietzman had died. He had been killed in a helicopter crash near his ranch in New Mexico. Apparently, his Thai houseboy had taken off with $500,000 in cash from the poor bastard's house.

"Since your ability to operate is substantially hindered by your probation," Sam explained, "I decided to give a large part of the load to Lietzman's old distributors. I have part of the load here for you. I'm certain that you will appreciate my decision."

"No, I don't appreciate your decision," I snapped back. "You used my man,

Captain Damian, to do this operation, and you know I need the work. You should've spoken to me before you made these changes!"

I figured that part of the load was still better than nothing, so I swallowed my pride and caught my breath in anticipation of the next project – one that would break world records.

~~~

On June 28, 1988, the sleek, 3,250-ton Coast Guard cutter *Boutwell* slipped from her mooring at Pier 36 in Seattle. Soon, she was surging out into the Pacific Ocean at twenty-nine knots.

On board were crewmembers, a helicopter, and several small boats. The 378-foot cutter was armed with two 25-mm machine guns and a 20-mm phalanx weapon system for firing shells and tracers. On her bow was a 76-mm gun used primarily as an anti-aircraft weapon.

Meanwhile, 720 miles away, Sam Übel gazed down from the bridge of the *Encounter Bay*. Our vessel was fitted with an ice-breaker bow, and even in heavy seas, it could maintain a speed of sixteen knots. She also had a back deck the size of a tennis court, ideal for carrying 72 tons of quality Thai-Lao herb. Of the four days it took her to get ready for sea, it took most of one day to load the *Encounter Bay* with bale upon bale of packaged herb in Da Nang, Vietnam.

Mike had purchased the ship for $3.5 million in the name of the Royalville Corporation, a Panamanian company incorporated in London on behalf of Fox Marine International which was based in the Cook Islands. Fox Marine had a satellite Hong Kong office in care of a company called Trade Max. These were all front companies set up by Mike to cover his tracks.

Lucky for Captain Damian, he was not on board the *Encounter Bay*. Because of a falling out with the Übels that occurred after they had reneged on their deal and paid him a fraction of what he was originally promised, he took what he had and left for Europe.

The *Encounter Bay* had antennas hidden in the mast and sophisticated electronics that helped her move undetected across vast expanses of the ocean.

By mid-afternoon on June 30, the ship approached North America. When Haig glanced up, he saw an orange, blue and white striped plane circling the *Encounter Bay*. Haig knew that what he was looking at was a C130 Coast Guard surveillance aircraft. Instantly, he changed course and notified his engine room that he wanted full power. But it was too late. An hour and a half later, he saw a ship on his radar screen.

At 4:22 PM, the *Boutwell* appeared on the horizon. Soon, she was 100 yards away and closing. Over the radio, her skipper ordered the *Encounter Bay* to stop.

Sam's response was terse and dismissive. "You have no authority. I am a Panamanian vessel in international waters."

Once again, *Boutwell's* skipper ordered Übel to stop and prepare for boarding. By then, the cutter was traveling alongside the *Encounter Bay*, but she showed no signs of slowing down. Back at the Coast Guard office in Seattle, a request arrived from the *Boutwell*: "Permission to fire cannon over her bow."

Minutes later, Haig learned the response when a large explosion shook the *Encounter Bay*. Still determined, Haig held his course for Vietnam where he'd be safe. The *Boutwell* inched closer and another shot thumped past the *Encounter Bay's* bow. Haig kept going.

Finally, just before 7:00 PM, a warning rang out across the water from the *Boutwell*. "Get your personnel out of the engine room. We're going to disable your ship."

Haig checked his fuel level and settled on the idea that there was enough to get him to Vietnam if only they could hold out that long. At that moment, round after round of armor-piercing shells punched holes in the *Encounter Bay's* port side and ricocheted inside the engine room.

Haig's chief engineer ran up the outside stairway to the bridge to plead with Haig to stop the ship before someone was killed. Haig opened the exit door to the bridge and kicked the man in the chest, sending him flying down the steps.

"Maintain your station," he yelled, slamming the door.

Between a personal debriefing with Sam and the documented actions of the Coast Guard, I can feel pretty confident that this story is accurate. I even reviewed a Coast Guard video of the entire catastrophe. There was even a *Reader's Digest* article on the story.

Mike was home in Singapore when Sam called him on his satellite phone.

"Michael, they're shooting the life out of us!" Sam told him. "Any minute, they're gonna hit the engines. You don't believe me?" To make his point, Sam thrust the phone outside. The sound of gunfire was ear-splitting. Sam pulled the receiver back inside. "Now do you believe me?" he asked, but the line was dead.

The engine room and bridge of the *Encounter Bay* were raked with hundreds of rounds of gunfire before Sam finally surrendered. On July 13, the crippled ship was hauled into Tacoma Harbor located south of Seattle. Übel and his crew were taken into custody. Days later, agent Larry Bont – a man who had once posed as one of the Übel brothers' runners – stood on top of 72 tons of Thai-Lao herb wrapped in blue, waterproof nylon bags. Each carried the stamp of a blue eagle above a line of bold red type that read *Passed Inspection.*

Ripping open one of the bales, Bont found a layer of clear polyethylene. Underneath this was a cardboard box. Inside the box were 81 kilogram packs of prime-grade Laotian marijuana. After being loaded onto U.S. military trucks, the marijuana was taken to the Army's firing center in eastern Washington. The bales took five days and nights to burn.

Bob called me at my home in Milford, PA. "King, have you heard?" he barked.

"Yes," I said. "Are you all right?"

Bob was calling from a car in Bangkok. "Well as can be expected," he said nervously. "I'm not sure what to do here. If I turn myself in, I'll need a good lawyer."

"Let me know," I said. "If you do, I'll send you a top New York attorney."

Bob said he was going to meet with Mike later and that he would decide then what to do. As he continued to ramble on about nonsense, I began to think that he was drunk so I closed the conversation.

Bob never called back. The DEA picked him up that afternoon in Bangkok. They placed him in the immigration office holding room at the airport in Bangkok instead of bringing him to a Thai jail.

Sam and the entire *Encounter Bay* crew were in custody in SeaTac. Mike, his wife May, and their two children left Singapore and went on the run to avoid being arrested.

In my office at home, I sat alone, surrounded by a decade of memorabilia – photos of the *Delfino II* (which Mike had sold at a loss to pay for the now-seized *Encounter Bay*), swords from Thailand hanging on the wall, trinkets gathered from all around the world. All my mementos from the great globe-trotting era suddenly looked historical.

I started shredding papers and faxes that might damage anyone.

I sent my friend and lawyer to visit Sam while he was in the Danbury Prison. Sam and I were able to communicate in a coded memo.

It's over, Sam wrote. *We can't legally get off. I'll see you when I get out.*

Sam and Bob were sentenced to ten years each.

It was the fall of 1988. I thought long and hard. My family was the most important thing in my life and, as such, I knew that I had to change. I had to move on. I had to retire from the herb business.

Chapter 14

MY life, my crazy life. I tried to kiss my old ways goodbye. To a degree, I succeeded. But no matter how many homes I built or real estate deals I made, there was never enough money to do everything I wanted to do.

When the residential housing market collapsed in my area, I started a new company called Affiliated Concrete Foundations, Inc. It started off great, and I thought that I really had a winner. Then we did some big jobs for which we never got paid.

I was sinking fast. I would watch the Money Store commercials on TV with my beloved Phil Rizzuto pitching second mortgages. I loved Phil Rizzuto, so I borrowed $250,000 from the Money Store, and before I knew it, I had a crippling overhead. Somehow, I hustled and worked like a dog to cover my monthly responsibilities.

At night, I would stand on the wooden deck outside my master bedroom with my faithful dog, Bell, and look at the stars while I smoked a joint. I would ask myself, *How am I going to continue to pay my overhead? What should I do? How can I find peace?* It seemed that the harder I worked, the more money I lost.

Daniel would bring people to me who wanted to use my offload services, but nothing ever panned out. Every time I saw him, he would hassle me. "When are the brothers coming back?" he would ask. "I want to do another Thai trip."

I would remind him that the Übel brothers were still in prison and that I didn't think they could do much from there.

It never failed. He would pressure me to contact them to find out when they were returning so we could work again.

I thought he was crazy. I pacified him by letting him think I was interested, but in reality, I couldn't stomach going back to the old life. I was just buying time, hoping that my construction business would pick up again.

I loved my home life – our barbecues by the swimming pool, the times I would play on the baby grand piano. I would sing and play all the old Beatles' songs and other 60's music.

But it wasn't easy. I was having a hard time making ends meet.

~ ~ ~

It was spring of 1993, and my family and I were having dinner in our sunroom that overlooked the mountains and the Delaware River. We always had dinner together – it was a family tradition.

The phone rang.

"Hey, Haig here," the familiar voice said.

"Sam! Where are you?" I bellowed. In the four and a half years he was away, he'd never called once.

"I'm home," Sam said.

"Holy shit! When did you get out?"

"Not long ago," he replied. "Can you come to see me at my parents' house?"

"Sure. I'll see you tomorrow at 12:00 hours."

"Very good," Sam said, "See you then, King!"

I hung up and returned to the table.

"Who was that, Dad?" Ari asked, always the perceptive one.

"That was Sam. Do you remember him?"

"Yeah, I remember him. Everything all right?" she asked.

"Sure, sweetheart. Everything's fine."

I looked at Virginia as she sat at the opposite end of our table. She pretended not to care, but I knew that in her mind she carried mixed thoughts. She thought of different possibilities – the possibility of returning to the old lifestyle, the possibility of losing control of me, and the possibility of becoming rich again. Whatever the case, she remained silent.

~ ~ ~

Sam and I sat together in the living room of the home that he and his brother grew up in on Barker Road in Springfield, PA. This tree-lined, blue-collar suburban street with its Cape-style brick homes gave no indication that, in one of these houses, men with extraordinary abilities dwelled.

Sam hadn't changed a bit in the time he'd been away. I asked him how he and his brother were able to come back in such a short time, considering that they'd been given a ten-year sentence.

"Well, when you have a world-class lawyer like Howard Witzeman and CIA connections, you get results."

I was so impressed that I laughed. I've known at least 40 men who have done time, and not one ever caught a break like this.

I asked about Mike, and Sam's face flushed red as he sat back and folded his hands. "Michael's wife May turned him in," he said in a dry, matter-of-fact voice.

"What?" I said.

"Yep. She ran off with Mike's lawyer and stole his assets, then turned him in."

"I can't believe she'd do such a thing. My God!"

Then a shadow silently appeared, and suddenly Bob Übel stood by my side, projecting the same dangerous presence that he always had. He gave me a strange smile as we shook hands. I noticed that his eyes hadn't changed. He still looked like he wanted to kill you just for the fun of it.

"Welcome home," I said.

He didn't reply. He just took a seat next to Sam. Now both Übel brothers – the death-defying twins – sat facing me. Their extraordinary personas made me nervous.

After I had answered their questions regarding what I had been up to since that fateful day on the Pacific Ocean, Bob announced that he'd be living in Bangkok from now on, and that if I wanted to see him, I'd have to go there. Sam explained how he had bought a historic home around the corner in which he, his son, and Seok Bee would be living.

Bob excused himself, while Sam directed me to the memorabilia room that he kept in his parents' house. There, encased in large glass cubes, were exact replicas of all the ships that we had used over the years. In a special spot was the *Encounter Bay*. The room had the feel of a mausoleum. Sam viewed his pride of the fleet with pain and anger on his face. It was almost as though he was viewing a casket that held a loved one inside of it.

"I'll have a special room built in my new home for these pieces," Sam said.

Later, Sam acted disinterested when we spoke about Captain Damian. It was bad luck how, shortly after the *Encounter Bay* seizure, Captain Damian was caught by Interpol in New Zealand while he was flying there from Europe. He now had to serve a three-year sentence, in addition to a year in a federal prison in Arizona for his escape.

I tried to interest the twins in several different businesses – a resort in Jamaica, a $110 million port project in Poland, a condo project in Upstate New York, a jewelry business, a computer and Software Company, a consulting firm, a magazine distribution deal, and a project to develop a casino resort with Bob Guccione from *Penthouse* magazine.

Sam would attend the meetings that I organized. He would gather the information from our potential business partners, but then would seldom respond. As such, I was losing face with all my contacts.

After our meetings, Sam would invite me to dinner or out for drinks and it would always be the same scenario. He would ask, "So, when are you going to be ready to work again?" or, "When do you think you can procure funding for a Thai project?" Sam would entice me on one end as Daniel pressed me on the other.

Finally, I decided to ease the pressure and connected Daniel directly to Sam. *Let these two work it out*, I thought. *And if they succeed, maybe they'll back me in a legit business project.*

Meanwhile, a large housing development that I'd begun constructing in the Bronx was having problems. With no chance of collecting my accounts receivable, I needed to make a change before I lost everything.

At home, things were no better. At night, I couldn't sleep. Virginia would say, "I need money for bills." I would tell her what was going on. She'd respond, "That's not my problem. That's your problem. I don't want to hear about it!"

One time I said, "You might have to help out by getting a job."

Virginia fired back, "I can't. I work out and give aerobics classes."

"You only earn $35 a week. That's no help!"

Virginia grabbed her gym bag and left. When I pictured Virginia in my mind, I saw her walking out the front door with her red g-string over her black tights, with her gym bag in hand. She wouldn't even look at me when I spoke to her in those days.

~ ~ ~

It was freezing cold in the Bronx on Christmas Eve of 1996. Snow was falling and traffic was extra heavy. I had just enough money for the toll. I even skipped lunch that day. Inside a small, plastic bag in my pocket was the gold jewelry that I had taken out of my jewelry box that morning. I had never worn it.

An old black man on the job told me to go to Fort Lee, New Jersey, to sell my jewelry. Since it was on the way home, I decided to take his advice. I parked on the street because I didn't have enough money for a garage. I remember walking down the sidewalk with the ice-cold wind stinging my face. Inside one of the many jewelry stores in the area, there were dozens of happy holiday shoppers. They all seemed so carefree, and their smiling faces and rosy cheeks seemed so alien to me. I felt out of place. They were buying gifts for their loved ones, while I was there to sell my old jewelry for money to buy gifts elsewhere.

I looked around for a salesperson, but they all seemed busy with paying customers. My chest hurt as I held the bag in my pocket. I turned around and walked out. I couldn't do it – I was too proud.

This had always been a bad time of year for me. I remember the Christmas season of 1963 vividly. I was already a troubled eleven-year-old boy. My bouts with depression started early, for reasons that were seemingly out of my control.

It was New Year's Eve, and my parents were going across the street to a neighbor's house for a party. My two younger brothers, my sister, and I were left at home alone and we all went to sleep shortly after our parents left.

Later, the silence of the house was shattered by my mother's wild screaming. The sound felt like a nightmare in an audio form. Our mother was screaming in the hallway next to the bedroom which my two younger brothers and I shared. The bedroom was lit with lights shaped as candles that sat in the windows. The room glowed with an orange hue.

My brothers and I sat up, frightened now, in each of our beds.

Being the oldest brother, I turned to them and said, "I'll go see what's wrong. Stay here."

Still hearing my mother's screaming and crying in the hallway, I could make out the sounds of other voices. They were also crying. I stood up and walked slowly to the closed door. When I carefully opened it, I saw that the whole house was filled with people – friends and relatives of my parents – all crying in a state of confusion.

My mother walked up to me and held my arm, saying, "Come here into my room. I want you to see your father."

My hero, my idol, my mentor was dead. He was lying there like he was sleeping. He seemed to have a slight smile upon his lips.

Aunt Toni, a tall, dark, thin Sicilian who was standing to the right of my father's bed, looked at me with hauntingly chaotic eyes. Uncle John and Uncle Guy stood on the other side of the bed.

I stood in silence, looking at my father. In the midst of all the confusion, I suddenly felt calmness. Everything surrounding my father and I faded away. The sounds coming from the crying people in the room all disappeared as my father and I connected. I could feel him looking at me although his eyes were closed. All went quiet and a tunnel formed between us both. Like a warm summer rain, I felt his love pouring over me.

My mother brought me back into reality when she took my arm and walked me out of the room. I left her and walked across the hall to my room. My brothers were still there. No one had spoken to them yet.

I sat on my bed and said, "Dad is dead."

They both turned around and buried their heads in their pillows and cried. Just then, relatives came in to care for them. My sister was now crying in her room with other adults who were trying to comfort her.

I saw my hysterical mother on the floor receiving an injection from Dr. Perino, a family friend who had also been at the party. I walked into the living room. Everyone was in shock. I stood next to Mrs. Perino, who sat on the hearth of the fireplace. She neither spoke nor looked at me – she just sat there holding her drink.

~~~

I stood in the cold winter wind in Fort Lee, New Jersey trying to build up the courage to walk into another of these bright, festive jewelry stores. I turned and kept walking because I knew that I had to do this transaction soon or the stores would close. I walked down a side street where I noticed a small jewelry store without any customers inside.

This is it, I thought, *I can talk to the owner without any distractions.* I walked in and was greeted by a guy about my age. After our ten minute conversation that had to have left him wondering why a man with a construction business in the Bronx needed to sell his jewelry for Christmas. However, he offered me a good price. I walked out with over $800.

From there, I drove to a shopping mall on my way home. I bought presents for everyone, and even had them gift wrapped.

On my way home, I was in pain. I closed my eyes on Route 15, a road notorious for surprise deer crossings. While my eyes were closed, I found myself hoping I would crash. As I drove, I thought about my huge life insurance policy. I knew that my family would be better off with me dead than alive.

When I entered my front door, everyone greeted me. They hugged and kissed me. Even Bell, my faithful dog, jumped up on me. I handed out presents to my loved ones and they put them under the tree.

I sat next to the warm fireplace and the Christmas tree. My children were so beautiful and so wonderful. I worried about how I was going to keep the house, having already missed several huge mortgage payments.

A few days later, my brother paged me. He informed me that an old friend, Greg Antacrockas, had just been released from prison and wanted to see me right away. I agreed, and the following day, I met with Greg for lunch.

He hadn't changed much in the six years he'd been away on marijuana charges. He explained how while he was in prison, he had befriended people who could load us with herb from Thailand. For $200,000 down, we could receive as much as we wanted.

A couple of days after my meeting with Antacrockas, I received a call from Sam.

"Can you meet me at the Plaza Hotel?"

"Sure I can," I replied, and we agreed to meet that afternoon.

On the way to the meeting, I made up my mind to go forward and accept money from Daniel, Skip, and Woodstock Willy – a good friend of Chandler's – to use in organizing a Thai project. My backers agreed to fund me while I put all the pieces of the project together. This funding would cover my monthly overhead, and if I was awarded a construction contract, I could always step aside and have others finish the Thai trip. If I didn't get lucky and win a contract, I would complete the project myself.

What did I have to lose? If I succeeded, I could pay off all of my debts, save my home, and have money left over for my family's future. If I failed, I could always go through with my suicide plan.

At the Oak Bar in the Plaza Hotel, Sam sat adjacent to me. He worked it out so that the sun shining through the windows facing Central Park would be in my eyes and not his. He gave me a speech that I would never forget.

With his precise vocabulary, he said, "Arthur, if we can do a project, you could earn enough money to create a legacy for your family. You'll also be doing good and important things in Southeast Asia on a political level. My brother informs me that we are in a historically pivotal time and that we must work soon or we'll miss the opportunity to complete our mission. When you get over there, we'll brief you on the details." Sam leaned forward. "This is your big chance, my friend!"

Later, Woodstock Willy, Daniel, and Skip all agreed to send me to Southeast Asia to purchase a sailboat and work with our new supplier, Bob Ratner – Greg Antacrokas' contact – who would procure a ten thousand pound load of "Grade A" herb. Sam wanted a $2 million deposit. Ratner wanted a total price of $200,000. Sam would now be our backup supplier if Ratner failed.

Chapter 15

I headed for Southeast Asia in early February of 1997. It was time to launch the operation that would salvage our lives.

Sam had said, "You must have your project ready to go by the Ides of March."

As usual, leaving my family was heartbreaking. I had a job to do though. My task was to procure a new vessel for our operation. When I was finished, I needed to hook up Ratner with the access to the ship. I would get it done and return home.

Before leaving, I spent as much time with my family as possible. When I told them that I had to go overseas to work or that we would lose the house, my daughters cried and said, "Okay, Daddy. We love you. Just come home fast!"

They had no idea what I was doing. If they had, they would have tried to stop me, I'm sure. My sweet daughters were teenagers now and could sense my pain. I didn't tell them of my suicide plan. I was determined to send them to college and give them a life of dignity. I wasn't going to let them live like I had had to.

I gave Virginia enough money to last several months. If she needed more, my backers would send her what she needed. After twenty-one years of marriage, one would have thought that I'd be upset about leaving her for an extended period of time, but I found myself feeling relieved to be getting away from her, knowing that I wouldn't be fighting and arguing anymore. Not having to worry about being attacked or humiliated in front of people was comforting. At the same time, I would look at her and feel sorry for her. She had a good heart and meant well. She was tough and was a good mother to our children. I think that if she hadn't developed a drinking problem, she wouldn't have had these demons that seemed to control her.

My first order of business was to meet with Bob Ratner. He was a decorated Vietnam vet who had spent several years in Thailand. Greg Antacrockas had met him in prison where Ratner had been doing time for bank fraud. Apparently, he was a crazy wheeler-dealer who had been busted for scheming millions from banks in New England where he was from. His Cape Cod accent was noticeable. He stood at 5'4" and had blue eyes and short brown hair. His heavy body gave his face a look that reminded me of Jabba the Hutt.

Before my departure, Ratner handed me a business card. "This is your contact person," he said. "Her name is Minh. She owns a travel agency called Minh's Travel Service. It's in Pattaya, Thailand. If we get separated, we'll use her to find each other. Anything you need, she'll take care of it. But remember, she doesn't know anything about what we're doing, and I don't want her to know. If you need hotels, car services, flights, phone calls, messages, storage boxes, or advice about the area, Minh can help you. After you and Skip arrive, I'll be right behind you. Then I'll show you a sample of the cargo."

We shook hands and parted. The next time I would see him would be in Bangkok.

BOOK TWO

CHAPTER 16

I was eager to get to Bangkok. The trip would take approximately twenty-four hours, including the change of planes in Tokyo, so I had plenty of time to reflect on what was happening.

I thought of how I had been happiest when things had been going well on the Bronx construction project. Even Virginia had seemed to mellow out during that time because a check had come every month to pay the bills. I had left every morning and had returned home for dinner every night.

Regardless, everything seemed to be driving me to Thailand. It was as though I had no choice in the matter. As the jetliner leveled off at 30,000 feet, drinks were served. I looked out the window at the snowy white clouds and thought about how no one was trying to stop me. People were happy to give me money to attempt this project which would support me and my family during the entire process.

It had been twelve years since I had last been in Thailand, but as soon as I cleared customs, received my luggage, and stepped outside, it all came back to me – the heat, the smells, and the sounds.

Sawasdee, Thailand, I thought as I searched for the white Toyota service car that I had hired to take me to the Montian Hotel in Bangkok.

Late that night, I checked into the Montian. It was exactly as I remembered it from twelve years before. After checking into the room, I showered and collapsed on the bed.

I woke up mid-morning on the following day, and lay there for a moment to gather my thoughts. Normally, I worked out in the morning, but that morning I was hungry and decided to get my bearings and check out the old neighborhood after a quick Thai-style brunch.

Once I was out in the Asian morning heat, the vibrant activities of Bangkok hit me. There were so many motorbikes, people, and cars. I wandered into a side street off of Pat Pong and settled down in a local restaurant.

No tourists here, I thought.

Sixties music was playing, and the place looked like it hadn't changed since the Vietnam War. I ordered several small dishes and tasted each one, slowly savoring my favorite spicy food.

Boy, I've missed this, I thought.

Grace Slick belted out, "Don't you want somebody to love / Don't you need somebody to love . . ." It gave me goose bumps.

The Birds, the Stones, Creedence Clearwater Revival, the Young Bloods, Jefferson Airplane, Hendrix, Dylan, Rare Earth, and Buffalo Springfield played. I was drinking cold Singha beers and absorbing the music. After several Singhas, I didn't know what year it was when I staggered out into the hot, sunny street like a drunken American GI.

Jetlag was kicking in, so I returned to the Montian Hotel and crashed until the phone rang.

Skip's voice was loud and clear on the other end of the line. "Hey, it's me," he said. "I'm downstairs."

"Shit, you woke me up," I groaned. "Come up."

He laughed and hung up.

When I got up, it was dark. I had slept through the whole day. Skip and I sat in my suite and bullshitted. Skip said he needed to see a sample of Ratner's product before allocating more funds. Ratner, however, wasn't due until the following day, so Skip and I left the hotel to check out the Bangkok nightlife.

It really hadn't changed. The girls were still the most exotic creatures on Earth. Their perpetual tans, ultra-smooth skin, small facial features, full lips, sexy eyes, and long, full manes of hair that flowed over their tight and fit bodies were only half their allure. The way these girls treated you was the other half. If you found the right girl, it was easy to fall in love.

Ratner showed up the following day. We all met in my suite to discuss our game plan. Ratner said he'd be back in a few hours with a sample.

"Great," Skip said. "I'll catch a flight out tonight. Max, you can then go and check out that sailboat."

My experience in acquiring loads of herb told me that Ratner wasn't playing with a full deck of cards. How could he get a sample in a matter of hours? As a rule, they didn't keep large loads for export in Bangkok. The herb stayed in country, in Cambodia, or in Laos.

At 1:00 AM, he finally returned and dumped a small plastic bag onto the table in my suite.

"What the fuck is this?" I wailed. "This looks like something you bought from a street dealer!"

Skip picked up one bag and began to open it.

"This is shit," I growled. "I've thrown away better weed than this garbage." I knew Ratner wasn't in the business, and I wasn't going to let this cheap conman get away with trying to put one over on us. "This is an insult. If this is your idea of a joke, I'm not laughing."

"Listen," Ratner said. "My partner's contact is in Pattaya, three hours away. You're right. My partner picked this up locally. He was too lazy to drive to Pattaya and back."

"Look, Ratner," I snapped. "This is no game we're playing here. If you and Greg want four million dollars, then do your fucking part."

Ratner was shaken. He didn't expect my easygoing demeanor to possess such anger, but I was pissed. Skip sat silently, observing the exchange.

"Look," Ratner finally said, "to do this right, we need to go to Pattaya. From there, my partner will go into Cambodia and return with a true sample. But this'll take time."

"How long?"

"A week . . . maybe two."

Skip shook his head. "I can't stay that long."

"I'll go to Pattaya and view the sample," I said. "I'll take photos and send them back to you."

"Fine," Skip said. "I'll leave tomorrow for New York."

As Ratner walked to the door to leave, I said, "Tell your partner that if he tries to cut any more corners, we'll find another broker."

"Don't worry," he replied as he left.

In the car on my way to Pattaya, I reviewed the information that I had received from the yacht broker in Phuket. The specs the broker had faxed me were detailed. The sailboat's overall length was 60 feet. The beam was fourteen feet wide. It had a special hull construction system called tri-ply, in which three layers of heartwood were woven with resin. It was a very strong and flexible design. The power plant was a 110-hp diesel Isuzu engine which had a lot of hours on it. Apparently, the vessel had won many races in Australia. Its desalinization plant and wind generator made this vessel ideal for our purposes.

My biggest obstacle was the price. My backers didn't want to spend more than $150,000, and it was going for $330,000.

The capable load my partners and I set was ten thousand pounds. At $1,500 per pound, that equaled a wholesale value of $15 million.

The broker was named Jon Jenkins and he was originally from Amsterdam. He was married to a Thai woman and had two children who attended a private school in Phuket. I learned all of this through my phone conversations and faxes with him. Jon, pronounced "Yon," knew me as "Al Tori."

As instructed by Ratner, I checked into the beautiful Siam Bay Shore Hotel once I was in Pattaya. It was within walking distance to Minh's Travel Service and everything else I could possibly ask for.

The view of the Gulf of Thailand from the hotel was magnificent. The blue water, the small green islands, and the colorful Thai fishing boats moored all around the shoreline were all picturesque. Pattaya Beach was the party capital of the world. This was where thousands of sailors from the American, British, and Australian navies made their port of call for R and R. Sailors in their early twenties arrived and cut loose here every year. And when the navies weren't there, tourists from all over the globe were. Of course, 99% of the visitors were men and 99% of the locals were women.

Not many men entered this land of bliss and left in one piece. These sweet creatures were capable of ripping out your heart and dropkicking it over a fence before you realized what was happening to you. Like the song back in 1985 said, "One night in Bangkok makes a tough man tumble."

After I had showered, changed, and unpacked, I called Minh. "Hi Minh," I said. "This is Max, Bob's friend."

"Oh yes, Max," she said. "I've been expecting your call. Can you come down here so I can meet you?"

"Yes," I replied. "I'll be right over."

After I had hung up, I sat still, numbed by the wonderful voice that I had just heard. Minh spoke with the most unusual Thai-English accent. Now I was curious to see what she looked like. I knew that she was off limits so I wouldn't allow myself to lose control. Ratner was in love with her, but blew his chance to win her heart when he was arrested seven years prior.

I walked down the narrow beach road that led to Minh's office. I noticed on my way the volume of go-go and beer bars, restaurants, and outdoor café bars. During my time there, I would come to know Pattaya as a cauldron of desperate humanity. Crippled beggars, some with missing limbs, crawled on the filthy streets. Huge elephants slowly lumbered by as their Maha handlers charged tourists 50 baht to feed them. There were monkeys and boa snakes wrapped around the necks of camera-toting street hustlers, shoe-shine boys, and three-year-old girls in pretty dresses selling Chiclets gum. All this was stirred in a stew of go-go dancers and drunken tourists staggering to the boom-boom beat of the dance club music.

Minh's travel agency was sandwiched between go-go bars and clubs. When Minh greeted me, she was as lovely as I had expected her to be. She wore a business suit, jacket, and skirt. Besides being beautiful, she looked very professional.

Minh's business catered mostly to the local girls who worked in the clubs and bars. She later told me that she had to tell the girls who worked for her to treat these local girls with the same respect as the tourists. Minh was right to say so. I came to learn that many of the foreigners treated these girls terribly.

I asked Minh if she would like to join me across the street for lunch. There, she could watch her office from the window table that I could see was available. Minh hummed and bit her lower lip slightly. Eventually, she agreed to join me.

We sat so that Minh was facing her office. The street was so narrow that she could see much of what was happening inside her office from our table. Minh and I talked about everything except my real purpose for being in Thailand.

I told Minh that Bob Ratner and I were in Thailand working on a real estate deal. I also told her about my life in America, about my children and Virginia. She tried to quickly educate me about Thailand and Pattaya.

As she spoke, I observed her dignified, serene movements – she had a controlled calmness about herself. Her long, dark hair, rosebud lips, and eyes that were always in a state of passion, were all very arousing.

Minh went on to tell me how she had left her home in the north of Thailand to make money in Pattaya for her family. She was fifteen years old when she came to Pattaya. She had danced for a place called "Baby Baby Go-Go." The owner had been a German man named Uli. He had 450 girls working for him at the time and owned three go-go bars. Minh said that she became his special girl. Years later, he had married her.

"Uli and I are still married," she said.

I asked her how old she was.

"I'm twenty-five now." Minh explained how she tolerated Uli's wild lifestyle. "I told Uli not to bring me any problems or embarrass me," she said. "I don't want to know or see the girls he's with." She looked down as she spoke about the subject. "When I was young, I didn't understand. I thought and lived like a Thai girl. But now I know better. I think like a Westerner. I can speak and read English. I taught myself. I know things now that I didn't know before. Someday, I will leave Uli and start a new life with someone who respects me."

Minh returned to work after our lunch date. I was touched at how quickly she had opened up to me. I felt close to her already.

I knew that I had to wait for Ratner's partner to deliver the sample, so I had time to kill. After I had seen the sample, I would call the yacht broker and notify him that I was in Thailand. I would let him know that I planned to visit him and see the vessel. When the time came, I'd have to fly to Phuket from the U-Tapao Airport near Pattaya.

After several days of exploration, I settled on the Blessing Bar to drink iced tea in the late mornings and BJ's Bar for beers and meetings in the evenings. Both were within walking distance of Minh's, which made things easier for both of us.

Every morning, I would walk in the hot sun to the Golden Gym to work out. I don't know how this gym stayed in business because I seemed to be the only customer in the place.

I'm not sure if it was the excitement of the project or my new environment, but my depression had disappeared. I'd never felt better in my life. I was supporting my family and working on a venture that could net me as much as $4 million – an amount that would set me up for life.

Ratner's partner hadn't arrived with a sample yet, so I smoked the herb I had picked up from one of the girls at the bar. The sticky, potent stuff and the cold Singha kept me in a mellow state. The sexy girls, meanwhile, kept me aroused.

At the Blessing Bar, the girls would softly massage my hands, arms, and shoulders while I made Singhas disappear. They had adorable faces, beautiful long hair, and wore perfectly fitting jeans. At the Blessing Bar, the girls were a fifteen on a scale from one to ten. They could turn on a dead man.

Looking at the photo album of my life in America, the girls were all taken aback by how beautiful my daughters were. They would laugh and carry on about how lucky I was.

One afternoon, Minh waved at me and called me to come to her office while I was at the Blessing Bar. Her sign language told me that I had a phone call.

I picked up the phone in Minh's air-conditioned office. It was Ratner. He explained how, that evening, his partner would drop off a gift-wrapped package to Minh. I was to collect it, review it, and call him back with my response. If the sample passed inspection, he would connect with my brother to collect his deposit money.

That evening, my hotel suite phone rang. It was Minh. "Hi, Max. I'm here in your hotel lobby with a gift for you. Can you come meet me?"

Oh, that voice, I thought. "Sure I can," I said. "I'll be right there." I knew Minh wouldn't come to my room. The hotel staff all knew her and, as such, she wouldn't want to be seen going to a farang's, a foreigner's, room alone.

Minh was sitting in the lavish lobby with a beautiful gift on her lap. She had an excited expression on her face in anticipation of me opening the mystery box.

"Hi Minh. Thanks for coming over," I said as I sat down, facing her.

Minh handed me the gift like it was my birthday. I had to think of something quickly because I couldn't open the box in front of her, but I could tell that she was dying to find out what was inside.

"Oh, Minh. Listen, I'm expecting a phone call from New York. I have to run back to my room. Can I call you later?"

"You can always call me," Minh said with a noticeable sadness in her voice.

We stood up and gave each other a customary wai. I waited until she had left the lobby before I retreated to my suite.

Poor Minh, I thought. *She's still like a child in many ways.*

The sample turned out to be excellent – the best Thai herb that I'd ever seen. I snapped photos of the buds. Some were a foot long and heavy with resin. I smoked the dense, multi-colored bud and was completely satisfied with the taste and the aroma. *The folks back home will love this,* I thought. *This is the Cuban cigar of weed, the Cristal of ganja.* I spent the rest of the night smoking and munching from the snack bar in my suite while I watched Thai TV.

I contacted my partners in the States and prepared them to receive the DHL package with the photos. Everyone back home knew I was a connoisseur of herb and felt confident that the product was as good as I claimed. I informed everyone that my next task was to make arrangements to purchase the ocean-going vessel that would carry our precious cargo home.

Funds were released to Ratner. He transferred the money to Thailand to Minh, who still thought that Ratner and I were doing a real estate deal. I told Ratner that I didn't like the idea of transferring money to Minh – that it was a potential problem for her if the situation fell apart.

"Don't worry," he said. "I know what I'm doing. You do your part, and I'll do mine."

I knew that herb like this would be worth a fortune in America. I really didn't want to do it, but I had to throw away the three pound sample. I couldn't fly to Phuket with it, and I couldn't leave it at the hotel. I could only save a small amount for my personal use. I thought about giving it to one of the girls at the bar. They all sold herb on the side, but nothing as good as this. They would have loved me to death if I gave this to one of them, but that would have been a security breach and I had to maintain a businessman front.

Chapter 17

I T was time to fly to Phuket to purchase the vessel that would sail our Cambodian cargo home. Minh arranged my car service and flight. In the car on the way to the airport, I thought about how Jon Jenkins, the yacht broker, had said that he had two sailboats for me to look at. Both were large enough. Both were ocean-going and qualified for such a trip across the Pacific. One needed work while the other was in class "A" condition.

The flight to Phuket was short. During my trip, I took the time to read a short novel that I had picked up at the airport bookstore. The title of the book was *Tarutao*. It was about a prison on an island in the Andaman Sea that was transformed from a Thai prison into a POW prison for the occupying Japanese during WWII. It was a great story about how the starving prisoners and the prison officials became pirates in order to survive starvation and the lack of quinine to fight malaria.

At the Phuket Airport, I rented a white Toyota Land Cruiser, threw my bags into the back, and took off to find a place to live. I explored the coast of Phuket and found a cottage for rent that was perched upon a rocky cliff overlooking the Andaman Sea. It was not far from town, so I would have the post office, international calling booths, restaurants, and anything else I needed nearby.

The waves below the veranda of my new temporary home crashed on the rocky cliff and sometimes sprayed salt water as high as I was standing. The sun, the wind, and the shimmering blue water were exhilarating.

That day, I called Jon Jenkins. We met at his office in Phuket. He was a likable fellow in his late thirties. In many ways, he reminded me of my old friend,

Captain Damian. His easy-going style made me feel comfortable as we talked about Thailand, America, sailing, and his present inventory of yachts.

I reinforced my position by reminding him that I was buying a sailboat for my wealthy brother in America. This way, I had the option of making or not making a final decision on the spot. If I wasn't sure about the deal, I could always say that I had to consult with my brother regarding any decisions. This could buy me precious time for negotiation.

After a long and friendly conversation, Jon and I agreed to meet the following day to inspect the two sailboats he was brokering. I returned to my cottage. This seaside place reminded me of Citronella in Jamaica – a world sixteen years away. The hypnotic sound of the sea coupled with the cool breeze from the ceiling fan soon relaxed me into a state of blissful sleep.

I awoke that night at about ten o'clock, wanting to go out and grab a bite to eat, as well as check out the Phuket nightlife.

That evening, I walked the busy streets of Patong Beach. This tourist district was not like Pattaya and certainly nothing like Bangkok. European, middle-aged couples and families moved about the town and beach area. There were large luxury hotels, restaurants, and gift shops. The discos, go-go bars, and beer bars were few, and were concentrated in one area at the center of town.

I walked from the beach area to the center of town, crossing side streets and tiny alleys where locals huddled in nearby makeshift eateries. Some of the best Thai cooking was found in these out-of-sight hideouts where the food was inexpensive and served quickly. I hadn't eaten yet, so I headed toward a place I'd seen earlier.

I found a club known as The Rock Hard Café on the corner of a busy inter-section – easily the best location in town. I walked in and immediately realized that someone had dumped a lot of money into it. There was an elevated stage to my right, where exceptionally beautiful girls danced in bikinis to the outrageous sound system.

I struck up a conversation with the manager. He was from New York City and was also the head cook. By the looks of him, Big Bill liked to eat.

"The owners are wealthy Americans," Big Bill said. "Sons of major stock-holders in Coca-Cola. Old money. This is their playground."

"Can't blame them," I replied.

After talking to Big Bill for a while, I decided to leave. It was getting late and I was beat. But I knew I would be back.

At my cottage, I lay in my soft bed and thought about how the girls of Thailand were so respectful. They always wai the temples or spirit houses. Even at the Blessing Bar every morning, the girls put out offerings of tea and food to Buddha at the little shrine they had. They would burn incense and say a little prayer. They had such strong family ties and respectful customs.

How could they accept the abuse from some of the foreigners? Even some of the Thai men abused them. They were second-class citizens, yet they endured. It seemed as if these kindhearted creatures had no place to go for protection.

Poor Thai girls, I thought as I smoked a joint and dozed off to the sound of the surf below me.

The next morning, I met Jon at his office. We drove in his car to Ao Chalong, a large bay where the two boats were moored.

"First, I'll show you the *Oktedy*, and then the one that needs work," Jon said.

So we motored out to the *Oktedy* on a Zodiac raft. *What a beautiful sailing vessel*, I thought as we approached the majestic looking *Oktedy*, moored about a half mile offshore. We climbed on board beside the cockpit in the stern. Her sleek lines made it look like she could cut through seas in any weather.

We started in the bow and worked our way to the stern. I imagined the amount of space that I would need to stow away my cargo. There was more than enough. The crew wouldn't have to be hampered by a lack of living area.

I already knew what I had to do – I needed to buy the *Oktedy* with owner financing. *I'll just make him an offer he can't refuse*, I thought.

I asked if there were any banks in the area that offered financing.

"There is no financing in Thailand for luxury boats," Jon said.

Of course, I already knew the answer to my question, but it set me up for my next statement. "I'm sure my brother will pay the full asking price of $330,000. In a few months, he's liquidating part of his company. In the meantime, he'll pay you $100,000 and the balance of $230,000 in ninety days. If he defaults, you keep the $100,000 and the *Oktedy*."

His expression told me that this was totally unexpected.

We went over the details of the deal and I further explained that, after we allocated the $100,000, we would like to stay on the *Oktedy* to do some sailing. Also, we would insure the *Oktedy* in case of damage or loss.

"You'll be totally covered," I reassured him. I could tell that he had a strong interest in my offer – after all, he had nothing to lose. Yet I realized that Jon would need time alone to think it over, so I suggested we return home.

I spent the next morning at the international calling booths in town. I called all the yacht brokers in Singapore and Kuala Lumpur. I didn't call the broker in the Philippines because Sam had advised me to stay out of that area because of its reputation for selling "hot" vessels. So I touched base with my list of brokers. Nothing in our price range had come in since I had last called.

I contacted my partners and told them to start getting Ratner ready to return so he could begin preparing the load.

"As soon as you make the deal on the sailboat, we'll release the funds to Ratner," Woodstock Willy told me.

My next call out to Virginia revealed that the money I had left was holding out. She wasn't lonely, either – she had plenty of guys around her at the gym. I had seen and heard enough to know that she wasn't without physical attention. I just hoped that she didn't embarrass my children any further. My daughter told me that Virginia had gone drunk to her school concert, and had acted in an embarrassing way. Virginia acted very promiscuously when she was drunk, so I could just imagine what went on.

I planned on giving Virginia $1 million when this latest operation was completed, and then I would say goodbye. No matter what happened, our marriage was over. I knew that if I went to jail, she would never wait for me even though she had promised me many times that she would.

In a week, I received the call I'd been waiting for.

"Good news, Al," Jon said. "I've decided to accept your offer. I'm drawing up the agreement now."

"Great," I said. "I'll transfer the hundred thousand."

I immediately contacted my partners and notified them of the good news.

"We've got ourselves a world class sloop!" I said. "Send the funds and send Ratner. Timing is crucial now!"

It was early May of 1997. The sooner we loaded the *Oktedy* and set sail for America, the safer it would be. We could avoid the storm season and arrive in Seattle when there would be plenty of sailboats to blend in with. As such, we had 90 days to complete our mission from the time we signed the agreement, and the voyage across the Pacific would only take 45 to 50 days. Within 48 hours, Ratner would be in Pattaya, preparing his Cambodian people for his end of the operation.

The following day, I flew to Pattaya.

I checked into the Bay Shore Hotel, and it felt like home. The funds for the herb and the *Oktedy* were being wired to Minh in Pattaya.

The following day, Bob Ratner arrived, as well as over $350,000 needed to purchase the herb in Cambodia and the *Oktedy* in Thailand. I explained to Ratner the importance of procuring the load as soon as possible. Ratner told me that he had Thai Navy and Cambodian military partners who were connected to powerful government officials in both countries. He explained how Cambodia was extremely volatile at the time and how the country could fall right back into a civil war at any moment.

At this time, Pol Pot was being held under house arrest in northwest Cambodia, not far from the Thai border. The Khmer Rouge, who had been Pol Pot's Communist-backed army, was slowly being dismantled as the world's human rights organizations were pressuring Cambodia's Prime Minister, Prince Norodom Ranarith, to put Pol Pot on trial for his war crimes and genocide against the Cambodian people. Cries from the survivors of the killing fields demanded justice and a trial in Thailand. Millions had been tortured and killed during this dark time in Cambodian history, and it seemed that Pol Pot's days were numbered.

I told Ratner to make arrangements to get us into Cambodia to verify the load. The following day, Ratner's Thai partner, whom he called "the Old Man," and a group of six serious-looking Asian men met in Pattaya to discuss the project. Ratner kept me separated from everyone. That day, I watched him and his Asian entourage from a distance. Some in his group were well dressed while others were obviously bodyguards.

Maybe Ratner really is connected, I thought as the group walked with an authoritative presence down the main street in Pattaya Beach.

After a couple days of meetings, Ratner informed me that we could go into Cambodia in about a week, depending on the situation at the border crossing and the in-country security factors. In the meantime, I would head down to Phuket with Jon and test sail the *Oktedy* to the ocean marina.

My partners in New York had allocated $350,000 to Ratner, who informed me that he had transferred $200,000 to his Thai and Cambodian partners as payment for the cargo. The remainder was for the *Oktedy* purchase and expenses.

I told Ratner that I had to return to Phuket to deal with the sailboat, but that I would be back in Pattaya in time to travel to Cambodia to verify the load.

"I'll take care of my end, and you take care of yours," Ratner said in his Cape Cod accent.

~ ~ ~

It was mid-June of 1997. I arrived in Phuket late that night and rented the same white Jeep that I had before. The next morning, I met Jon as planned and the two of us took a short trip to the *Oktedy* in a Zodiac raft, which gave Jon just enough time to brief me on what was happening.

"Great, Jon," I said. "I've got the money for you. I stopped at the bank on my way here and withdrew 400,000 baht." That was approximately $10,000 – the "sincerity" money Jon had asked for.

"Oh, Al, that's perfect," he said. "Thank you. I also suggest that we replace the engine and do some upgrading."

That was fine with me. "No problem. Let me know how much you need."

"Al, you're a pleasure to do business with."

I laughed and added, "Just keep some cold beers on ice."

"Ahh! You bet, my friend."

Once I saw the *Oktedy* again, I had full confidence in her ability to make the trip across the Pacific Ocean with our precious cargo and crew.

That day, we sailed the Andaman Sea that borders the west coast of Thailand. The sea was an emerald and turquoise mosaic, and the sun reflected off of the water like shimmering diamonds. Ancient rock formations emerged vertically from the water, creating castle-like structures. The weathered stone and tropical vegetation leant them a prehistoric look. Some even had archways large enough to navigate a small craft through.

Jon and I stayed outside in the cockpit. The blue canvas cover shaded us and Jon's cold Singhas cooled us in the ocean breeze. As we sailed, he explained how this magnificent sailing vessel was run. It was surprisingly simple. Everything was automatic.

"The key to avoiding problems," he said as he held on to the five-foot-diameter chrome steering wheel, "is to be prepared before and during a storm. The *Oktedy* was designed for blue water ocean sailing."

I was sunburned and half-drunk by the time I set foot on the dock at the ocean marina. I called a taxi to pick me up after I said my goodbyes. Off I went to retrieve the Jeep.

That night, I called my partners and brought them up to speed as to how things were progressing. My friend in New York, who had family in Newfoundland, was ready to send his cousins, the captain, and the first mate to Thailand. We needed a second mate and Ratner informed me that his Thai partner, the Old Man, had a good seaman for the position.

Over the next few days, I visited Jon a few times. He had completed the survey and had started working on the replacement for the diesel engine. Ratner informed me that we would soon be able to enter Cambodia so he wanted me to stay nearby. I told him that I would be at the Bay Shore Hotel in Pattaya on the following day.

Only hours after I arrived in Pattaya, I came down with a high fever and a stomach virus. During my illness, Ratner informed me that the green light was given for us to cross the border and inspect the quality of the herb. I told him to postpone the trip until I could travel. I had to run to the head so often that it would be impossible for me to be in a car for hours on end with no place to relieve my aching stomach.

"We can't postpone," Ratner said. "I'll go and tell you what I see."

I thought about it and decided that there was no other way. Ratner left the following morning after I briefed him on what to look for. If the cargo was anything as near as good as the sample, we would be in good shape – at least in better shape than I was in.

Late that night, when Ratner returned, he sat in my suite as I questioned him about the trip into Cambodia. He looked like he had seen a ghost.

"That's one dangerous place," he said. "There are guns and soldiers everywhere. But I saw the pot and it's all there – over ten thousand pounds of it."

"Relax," I said. "You don't have to go back."

It was the end of June of 1997. A few days after Ratner returned from Cambodia, we were sitting in a small Thai restaurant. He explained to me how tense the political situation in Cambodia was and that his contacts were preparing for something.

"Something big is going on over there," he said. "But I'm told not to worry. The military will maintain control of our cargo no matter what happens. We're almost ready to go. But, last night, I had a meeting with my people, and we need another $200,000 for the in-country security."

"What!" My scream was held at a whisper so no one would hear me. "Are you crazy?"

"Listen, Max. You'll get your load. It's just that with all that's happening in Cambodia right now, they need money to take care of our people."

I looked at this fucking guy, remembering that I'd told myself something like this would happen.

"If we don't step up to the plate, we won't get our load and that's it," Ratner said with finality in his voice.

I stayed calm. "I'll call my people," I said as I stood up and walked out.

That same night, I called my partners from the international calling booth at Minh's. After several calls and two hours of conversation, the decision was made that the $200,000 would be wired to Minh's account within 24 hours.

"When it looks close, I'll come out there," Skip told me.

"Great," I replied. "I could use an ally over here. This Ratner is a fucking piece of work to be around."

The money was transferred to Thailand, and Ratner informed me that he would allocate the funds to his people in Cambodia. During this time, I stayed in touch with Jon, who told me he was looking for a new engine that would fit the engine mounts on the *Oktedy*. I made sure that he knew I was anxious to sign the contract.

"No problem," Jon said. "Al, you can call me anytime."

Every night at 10:00 PM, I called a predetermined phone booth in the States to update my partners and my brother on our progress. I also called my family. They were all busy with their lives, so I was far less stressed about things on the home front. I just missed them terribly – and it broke my heart to hear my daughters' voices.

~~~

11:00 AM: JULY 5, 1997

It was blistering fucking hot. Due to my illness, I still felt very weak as I walked from the Bay Shore Hotel to a little restaurant not far from Minh's place for breakfast. Something was odd. I noticed that there were small groups of people huddled around radios and TV sets in front of cafés, restaurants, and beer bars, listening to the broadcasts.

I had a flashback to the Kennedy assassination in 1963. *Something's wrong*, I thought. I could feel the blood in my head throb.

I started to jog down the empty street and detoured into Minh's office. "What's happening?" I blurted out as I entered.

Everybody was solemnly listening to the radio.

"Max!" Minh cried. "Commander Hun Sen of Cambodia has attacked the central government in Phnom Penh. It's a coup, Max." She had a very worried look in her eyes. "The Thai army is now on alert at the border in case it spreads to Thailand and becomes another war."

Minh's voice broke up when she said "war." Some of the other girls in her office were refugees from Cambodia, and they were visibly upset because they still had family there.

"Minh!" I said. "Where's Ratner?"

"He's looking for you. Try the breakfast restaurant."

As I ran down the street, my head was spinning. We already had $700,000 invested in this project, and the country we were working in didn't exist anymore! I was sweating and trying to catch my breath as I ran up the steps to the open-air restaurant, where people were grouped together in front of the TV. Ratner was sitting alone at a round table in the corner. He had his reading glasses on and was reviewing the morning paper. He didn't say a word as I took the chair opposite him. Ratner acted calm, as though nothing was going on.

"I just spoke to our people," he said nonchalantly. "We won! Hun Sen declared victory this morning."

I stared at him in shock. "What do you mean we won?" I felt like I was in the middle of a weird dream.

"Our man rolled his tanks into the Phnom Penh Airport, surrounded the capital, and assassinated over a hundred government officials. Prime Minister Norodom Ranarith has fled to France, and Commander Hun Sen has taken over the country in a bloody coup. The good news is that he's our man, so the load is yours! You actually picked a very good time to launch your mission. Congratulations!" Ratner calmly smiled as he looked over his reading glasses.

I was still sweating from running. I turned to the black and white TV on the rear wall of the restaurant and could see images of Hun Sen's tanks firing shells, as well as plumes of black smoke rising in the distance. The cameraman was obviously running from the shooting as he tried to film the scene. It became impossible to interpret what was happening in the chaos. Footage showing

Cambodian people running through the streets in confusion and fear was also presented.

I turned back to Ratner, who smiled smugly as if he was responsible for what I was watching.

"Relax," he said, with a new confidence lining his voice. "Prepare your crew to depart."

Chapter 18

BY July 20, 1997, Jon Jenkins had located a new engine for the *Oktedy* and was preparing to remove the old one. My contact in New York, who was related to the Newfoundland fishing captain, informed me that the captain and the first mate were on standby to fly to Thailand. I had allocated two payments to them already, totaling $10,000 – more than enough to get them there. The Cambodians reassured us that the load was safe and that they would give us notice when it was ready to be moved.

There were two major political parties in Cambodia: Hun Sen's party known as the Cambodian People's Party, and Prime Minister Norodom Ranarith's party known as the Funcinpec Party. The world was now watching to see how the bloody coup would unfold.

Hun Sen was taking a lot of heat for his bold action. The Voice of America radio was denouncing him and calling for his arrest for war crimes during the Pol Pot regime. He'd been a commander in the Khmer Rouge before he joined with the Vietnamese Army to overthrow Pol Pot and his soldiers. The VOA demanded his arrest for the killing and beating of opposition party members and other human rights violations.

The last thing that Hun Sen needed was a security leak exposing his party's involvement with our operation, so high security and caution was imperative.

That night, back at the Bay Shore Hotel, Minh called me from her office.

"Max, I noticed on your passport that today is your birthday. Come on, get dressed. We go out for your birthday. In Thailand, your birthday is a special day and you shouldn't be alone."

I wasn't in the partying mood, but Minh's enthusiasm sparked something in me. We walked through the Bay Shore Hotel to the plush lobby. This was a central area in the hotel with tables, chairs, palm trees, and a piano.

Minh turned to me and said, "Let's sit here, order a drink, and listen to the piano music before we go out."

She was so cute in her attempt to make my birthday special that I needed to remind myself that she was off limits. After a few minutes of listening to the music, Minh said that she had to go to the ladies' room.

I relaxed in the sunken lobby area, listening to the piano and reminiscing about the days when I had played the piano and sung with my daughters. I realized that, despite my frequent absences, this was my first birthday separated from my family.

Minh returned, followed by three female employees who brought me a beautiful birthday cake with the words "Happy Birthday, Max" written on it.

"Ah, Minh," I said. "You're the best!"

Minh had such a loveable smile, and she was genuinely happy to make me feel special and loved on my birthday while being so far away from home. We cut the cake and shared it with the hotel personnel around us. Everybody was so friendly and, by that point, I recognized most of them.

The piano player was now playing a song I used to play called *Unchained Melody*. I told Minh how I missed playing the piano.

Minh lit up and said, "Max! You play! I sing *Unbreak My Heart*."

I felt a rush. I wasn't sure if I should bring more attention to myself, but then I figured that it was a good front. I told Minh that I would play. Minh spoke in Thai to the piano player and he handed her the sheet music. It had the chords printed on top of the scale and the words underneath for *Unbreak My Heart* by Toni Braxton.

Minh had a beautiful voice. People stopped and watched us and the hotel employees beamed and smiled over our performance. Minh rested her hand on my shoulder as we performed. When we finished, she buried her face into my shoulder and hugged me. Everyone clapped. I then began to play some old Beatles' songs I knew, and Minh stood behind me with her arms draped loosely around my neck.

Chapter 19

WHEN I contacted Jon, he informed me that the *Oktedy* was ready to go and that I should stop by to pay the $100,000 and sign the contract. I told him that I was in Pattaya and that I would be in Phuket in about a week – as soon as I closed on a condo I was buying.

"Okay, Al. I'll be here waiting for you," he said.

The next day, at my 10:00 AM link-up, I received word that our new vessel would be piloted by a man named Captain Jim "Jimmy" Bower and that the Cambodians were ready to move. It was now just a matter of time until this phase of the operation would be complete.

The next day, I headed out of Phuket for the airport. I would fly to the airport in Bangkok, meet Skip at the terminal, pick up cash from him, and immediately head down to Singapore to connect with Captain Jimmy and see him off. Everything went like clockwork.

On the flight to Singapore, I thought about the pain Virginia had caused me in my life. Now I was alone on the other side of the world. *Once this operation is complete,* I thought, *I'll set aside enough money to take care of my children's needs for the rest of their lives. Then I'll take a hard look at what I should do. Why can't I meet someone who loves me as much as I love them? Somewhere out there is the right woman for me.*

Jimmy Bower met me at the Singapore Airport as planned. It had been thirteen years since I had last set foot in this strict Asian republic. It had been Mike Farell and Captain Damian who I had met then.

The more things change, the more they stay the same, I thought.

Captain Jimmy and I dined at a trendy restaurant on the riverside in the heart of Singapore. I told him that I wanted to check out the *Oktedy* after he had bought all the items on the checklist. Bower explained to me that Jon was still there and that he would leave only once the *Oktedy* had left.

"If he sees you, he'll know that something's up," Bower warned, and he was right. For security reasons, Captain Bower purchased the *Oktedy* the day after I notified Jon that I was not able to go through with the purchase. I had told Jon that I needed to return to the States for personal reasons. The yacht broker did not know that Captain Bower and I had worked all of this out previously, or even that we knew each other. Now I could not be seen near the *Oktedy*.

John, our first mate, was already on board and Ratner's friend Tobling, who would be our second mate, was due to fly into Singapore after his meeting with the Old Man. If the provisions, the generator, the SatCom phone, the life raft, the new radar, and all of the other equipment and spare parts were purchased and installed on the next day, the *Oktedy* could depart for the Cambodian coast on the following morning.

I informed Bower about the exact latitude and longitude in which he was to position the *Oktedy* in the Gulf of Thailand. Our supplier, the Thai Navy captain who worked with Ratner, had faxed this data to him and Ratner had relayed it to me. The exact date and time to meet the Cambodian army would be relayed to the *Oktedy* when she was 100 miles from the transfer point. Bower estimated that it would take seven days from this point to position himself close to our transfer target.

I mentioned the very real problem of pirates. The South China Sea and the Gulf of Thailand were notorious for high-sea pirating. I explained to him how the Thai captain would give him an AK-47 when they transferred the load.

"But make sure you throw the gun overboard when you leave the Philippine Sea and enter the South Pacific. It's only for your protection, anyway," I explained.

Captain Jimmy and I stood outside on a wooden pier in the twilight of a Singapore sunset. I had already allocated $60,000 in cash to him, which he had used to purchase the remaining equipment and provisions. In the humid night air we stood facing each other. We knew what was ahead of us.

We shook hands and I said, "See you on the other side, Captain."

"Don't worry, I'll make it," he replied as he disappeared into the crowded Singapore nightlife.

~ ~ ~

SEPTEMBER 6, 1997

The vessel *Oktedy* departed the Republic of Singapore for the west coast of Cambodia, near Kompong Som in the Gulf of Thailand. Between that point and the time that they would meet with the ship of the Cambodian army, they would be unarmed and extremely vulnerable to pirate attacks.

I departed Singapore on September 7 on Thai Airways. Before my plane took off, I made contact with Captain Jimmy via SatCom. This satellite link-up was transferred via a land-based antenna in Australia. While in flight to Pattaya, I reflected on how, in the midst of all this funding and logistics, I found myself alone. The sound and pressure in the jet's cabin slightly deafened my hearing.

A most unusual woman's voice spoke over the PA system. It reminded me of a song I knew.

"I'm not in love," the woman's voice was saying. "Requesting quiet, requesting quiet, requesting quiet."

I felt emotionally and physically spent. We had overcome so many obstacles and now, finally, the *Oktedy* was on her way.

In Pattaya, Skip and I were crazed with anxiety. Skip had gone there after we had met in the Bangkok Airport to transfer the cash that Bower needed. Ratner was still in the States and was communicating with his people in Cambodia. He would then relay messages back to us in Thailand. I would then forward any information to the crew of the *Oktedy* by SatCom.

On September 13, Captain Jimmy informed me that he was in position 100 miles from the target, waiting for further instructions about how to proceed.

Ratner was telling us to be patient. He explained that the Cambodian gunboats would be departing at any moment.

"But I'm surrounded by pirates!" Captain Jimmy barked.

I contacted Ratner again and pressured him to get the Cambodians on target.

"Be patient. They should be there tomorrow," Ratner replied.

"There might not be a tomorrow!" I fired back. "The crew's surrounded by unfriendlies and they might be dead by then!"

"Please!" Ratner cried. "Tell them to hold their position!"

I relayed the information to Captain Jimmy.

"I'll hold for another twenty-four hours," he told me. "Then we'll have to come into our emergency position."

He was referring to a location I had given him in case there were any problems during the loading phase of the operation. The position was a marina located not far from Pattaya.

Twenty-four hours later, there was still no sign of the gunboats.

"I'll abort mission," Captain Jimmy said. "I'll be at the emergency position within eight hours."

"Roger," I replied and contacted Ratner.

Ratner agreed to connect the Thai Navy captain directly with our captain to simplify the communication channels. "I don't want you or Skip to meet the Thai captain," he said. "You're the money men. If he meets the money people, then money will become an issue. Just let the two captains meet and work out the logistics."

I set up a time for a meeting of the two captains at the Bay Shore Hotel in Pattaya. Captain Jimmy brought the *Oktedy* into the emergency marina near Pattaya and we met at the hotel just before his meeting with the Thai captain. I briefed him about the meeting.

Bower was an intelligent man, and he understood how business and negotiation worked.

"Just stick to the subject of the military operation to move the cargo from the Cambodia gunboats to the *Oktedy* and we'll be back on track," I informed him.

Captain Jimmy agreed and then went to another room in the hotel to meet the Thai captain.

Skip and Tobling sat in my room while the two captains met. Tobling was Indonesian and also a sea captain. Back in 1993, he was the captain of a ship called the *Golden Venture*. This ship's ill-fated journey from China ended up in New York, where the *Golden Venture* ran aground on Coney Island. The cargo of 300 illegal Chinese aliens had mutinied after waiting over 30 days at sea with little food and water. They had tied up Captain Tobling in the wheelhouse after it became apparent that the boats to shuttle them to shore were not coming. Many of the Chinese passengers had drowned when they tried to swim ashore. Tobling did three years in a federal prison.

Tobling, having some knowledge of the other side of the operation, said, "Hun Sen just raised his right arm and signaled his officers to move out." He demonstrated by raising his own arm and waving it forward with only his index finger pointing upward. Tobling had been in Cambodia with the mysterious "Old Man" before he had flown to Singapore to meet up with Captain Jimmy.

After the meeting, Captain Jimmy entered my room and gave the thumbs up as he walked up to us and shook our hands. "We're on!" he said with a smile.

I knew this was it, and a pang of fear rushed through me. I knew that, once the load was stowed away in the *Oktedy*, we were committed. There was no turning back. If we failed, I would go to the place where the angels sing.

That night, under my watchful eye, the crew of the *Oktedy* cut loose. They all drank, watched kickboxing fights, and enjoyed the beautiful Thai girls.

The following morning, I gave Captain Jimmy more money for diesel fuel and provisions, and by noon, they were sailing to Cambodia to meet their destiny.

Skip and I had been drinking heavily since the *Oktedy* had left Singapore, and now we were totally out of control. Stoned and in an altered state of mind, the penetrating music of the dance club absorbed me. I would watch the Thai dancers before me while I listened to songs like *God Is One of Us* and *Unbreak My Heart*. I was lost in one way. I had shed my Western self and had now become Asian in my heart. By then, the Thai way of life had become my own. Without thinking, I would speak and respond to all the Thai customs as if I had been born and raised there.

While Skip and I waited for the *Oktedy* to be repositioned, we spent our days and nights stoned and drunk. We knew that we were leaving soon and so we lived as if there were no tomorrow. Skip was in love and got married to Sow, a beautiful northern Thai girl. Meanwhile, I was spending time with the girls from the Blessing Bar.

I was starting to unravel. In my delirium, I tried to maintain communications with Captain Jimmy. He would call Minh at her office and leave messages for me. Minh would contact me and I would call Captain Jimmy directly. Minh had no idea where he was calling from.

Three days had passed, and the Cambodian army gunboat had not arrived. Again, Captain Jimmy was under siege.

"I'm surrounded by pirates!" he yelled. "What's going on?"

A flurry of calls went out to Ratner. He called the Old Man.

On September 19, Captain Jimmy contacted Minh at her office at 7:30 AM. Minh called me at the Bay Shore Hotel.

"Captain Jimmy called. He said everything is under control and he'll see you in America."

"Thank you, Minh. I'll need a service car to Bangkok Airport tomorrow morning."

"I'll take care of everything, Max," Minh said in her captivating voice.

Skip was sitting on a chair next to me.

"It's done," I said to him. "They're on their way."

Skip stood up to high-five me, but I wasn't up for it. I just held up my hand out of courtesy.

"What the fuck is wrong with you?" Skip growled. "You just pulled off an impossible operation and you're depressed."

"I'm always depressed when I succeed."

"You're fucking crazy!" he said and left me alone in my room.

This was my last night in Thailand. This phase of the mission was over. *Rep-Roy-Lao*, I thought. It's over. That night, I walked on the strip that I had come to know so well. Sweat ran from my face. I hadn't slept in two days.

I passed by Minh's office and saw her standing by her desk through the large glass window. She was staring right at me with a look of hurt and worry in her dark, Asian eyes. She knew the girls from the Blessing Bar. She knew how I had been living.

I kept moving. Music blared out from the clubs on both sides of me. The narrow street was packed – a scary, sub-human circus. Street touts pushed their wares, snake heads and cheap necklaces, up to my face. All stood in front of me with outstretched arms, begging for a few baht. I kept walking. I hadn't eaten and had only been drinking and smoking Thai herb.

Suddenly, I felt someone tug at my arm, pulling me backward. I thought I heard my name, but the music was so loud and my head was spinning. I turned around and there was Minh. She pulled me out of the crowd to an outdoor barstool in front of a beer bar. The pink, fluorescent light made her face glow.

Minh gave me a deep wai and said, "Chan Sue-Sud-dor," meaning "I will be loyal to you" in English.

"Pom lak koon (I love you)," I replied. I saw a sudden reaction in Minh's usually calm persona before she turned and disappeared into her world.

I was lost and fragmented when I left Thailand on that sweltering day on September 22, 1997. Surely, only a shell of a man was departing, although the *Oktedy*, together with her courageous crew and precious cargo, had made it out against all odds. I left in my wake a part of myself – my shattered heart and the remains of my Western existence.

Chapter 20

RETURNING home, I felt like I was reentering the Earth's atmosphere from another galaxy. I was a mental mess when I landed at JFK. My family greeted me and I couldn't stop hugging and kissing everyone.

"Dad, you look different," Arli said.

"Yeah, you've changed," Ali said. Yet no one explained to me how I had changed. They all just looked at me with astonished expressions on their faces.

Entering my home felt surreal. My dog Bell, the piano, the kitchen – all seemed like duplicates from another life. But they were all real. My home and my children – I had missed them so much. I brought everybody gifts, but they all just wanted to focus on me. I couldn't believe that I was finally back, safe and sound.

The jetlag was murder. I slept on and off for days. Virginia and I were, for some reason, getting along.

My Thai experiences all seemed like a dream at that point. The people I'd met during my time there didn't seem real, but like creations of my imagination. When my daughters wanted to hear about my experiences in Thailand, I felt like I was describing this dream. I couldn't tell them about the gut-wrenching mission to move six tons of marijuana out of Cambodia in the middle of a coup d'état. Instead, I told them about the time when I visited the longneck women of Mai Hong Son near the Thai and Burmese border. I had photos of me with these poor women, all of them held more or less captive in their brass rings by the men in their family.

I spoke about the orphanage in Pattaya, where over 400 handicapped and unwanted children lived. As I showed my daughters some of the pictures I bought that were drawn by the armless children who used their toes to hold the pencil, I explained how I would like to return one day to help this heartbreaking place. I described the many ancient Thai customs that I had experienced and how respectful and spiritual most Thais were. My children listened in awe.

~~~

Time was passing quickly and the mission progressed. Captain Jimmy was facing some serious storms at sea. One typhoon after another swept through the Philippine Sea, the South China Sea, and the South Pacific. It was one of the worst typhoon seasons in recorded history. At my home, I would watch the world news and weather at night. On the television, I could see that the giant, spiral storm systems were directly in the *Oktedy's* path. I could visualize how the crew was battling the stormy sea to keep alive.

I felt helpless, and I began to wonder how long they could endure their daily beatings by one of nature's most brutal forces.

On October 1, we received an S.O.S. SatCom from the *Oktedy* saying that a super typhoon had hit them and caused heavy damage. They needed help quickly.

I was in my car when the radio played *Message in a Bottle* by The Police. *How serendipitous,* I thought.

Apparently, the typhoon had blown out the sails of the *Oktedy*. There was also damage to the navigation lights, which they needed to enter the Strait of Juan de Fuca located west of Seattle. They needed a long list of sail parts, special tools, and mechanical parts. I knew that it would take a couple of days to acquire all of the parts and equipment.

I made a SatCom call to the captain to work out a solution to this serious problem.

Captain Jimmy, in the midst of the storm, explained to me, "My closest landfall is Saipan. I can make it there in five days to a week. However, I'll be totally out of fuel then, and once we lose our power, we'll lose our ability to maneuver the vessel. We could lose her entirely if that happens."

We brainstormed our options.

"You can't come in," I explained. "Customs will want to clear you. I'll have to come to you."

We worked out a plan to meet in the Pacific Ocean, 30 miles north of Saipan. We would both use our Global Positioning Systems for an accurate rendezvous.

In a storm like this, it would have been very difficult to locate each other without this new technology. The other option was to dump the load and contact the Saipan Coast Guard for an emergency airlift. This option, of course, would be our last resort.

I called a meeting with all the partners. There were 12,500 pounds of herb on-board. At $1,500 per pound, the entire load was worth $18.75 million. The thought of dumping the load in the Pacific Ocean was sickening.

All the partners looked to me for a solution. We reviewed the nautical chart and located the *Oktedy's* present position in relation to Saipan Island, which is just north of Guam.

I explained my plan. "I'll take two men with me, a captain and one mate. We'll fly to the island of Saipan. I'll commandeer an ocean-worthy vessel and rendezvous with the *Oktedy*, thirty miles north of Saipan. As long as the ship has SatCom, we can find her. First, we'll purchase the sails and all the equipment needed. I'll bring Captain Kirk with me."

Kirk was an old friend of mine with an unfortunate name and title combination. He had already agreed to join the rescue mission. Captain Kirk was a heavy-tonnage ship captain who worked for a large shipping company in New York City. I would also bring Chandler, who had remained loyal to me over the years.

Twenty-four hours later, Captain Kirk, Chandler, and I were at the Newburgh Airport to meet Skip. He would drive us to JFK to depart for our rescue mission to Saipan Island. Chandler, taking a separate flight, would first land in California to pick up custom-made sails. He would arrive in Saipan a few days after us. We had most of the supplies ready and boxed up to take with us. Ropes, tools, several 55-gallon drums of diesel fuel, and provisions would all be purchased in Guam and Saipan.

I had a hard time sleeping on the flight to Nineta Airport in Japan. I thought about my family and how they'd hardly had a chance to be with me. *If this rescue mission fails*, I thought, *it's over. Really over.*

From Japan, we flew to Agana in Guam. We stayed in Gaum for two days, making phone calls, trying to find a company that chartered or leased boats. We had no luck, as the options were limited on this small Pacific island. It looked like we would have to go to Saipan and commandeer a vessel the hard way.

Captain Kirk and I flew to Saipan on Micronesia Airlines. The low altitude flight was scenic. As the storm system neared, the picturesque environment changed.

We checked into the Hilton Hotel on the north coast of Saipan. There was something about this city that felt very strange to me, though I kept this to myself. We had rented a van at the airport and, on our way to the hotel, I had noticed the relics from World War II. In the water, along the shoreline, were rusty landing-craft left over from the Great War. The concrete pillboxes and bunkers that the Japanese had used to defend themselves from the advancing American naval fleet still remained. Some of the bloodiest battles in the Pacific had been fought right here. I had a feeling throughout my stay in Saipan that I had returned to the scene of violent crime.

At the hotel, we dove into the phone books and discovered that there were no ocean-worthy vessels available without a captain and a crew included. Eventually, we got wind of a man named Manny Blass and his tour boat the *Corral Queen* via some mechanics we ran into near the docks. Blass put us on to a guy named Eddie Flores, who owned boats that we could charter. It wasn't long before we had our hands on a suitable rescue vessel.

Later, Chandler arrived with all the sails and supplies. We spent the next few days getting the boat ready and buying everything we needed to accomplish our task. We had hundreds of feet of half-inch rope, fuel pumps, lights – so many items, so many details. The hotel room had a whole corner filled with boxes of supplies and tools.

Throughout this time, we kept in contact with the *Oktedy*. They were getting near our target location. Captain Jimmy requested 800 gallons of diesel fuel.

"Shit!" Kirk said. "Is he motoring that vessel to the U.S. instead of sailing her?"

On October 10, Captain Kirk, Chandler, and I moved into a different hotel on the far end of the island where it was less crowded. Our new base was called the Saipan Mariana Resort Hotel. By this time, we had a van and a pickup truck to transport all our stuff. Soon, we would need two pickup trucks.

We located a place that sold 55-gallon drums for the diesel fuel. We bought binding straps to hold the heavy drums together and a hand truck to roll the drums from the truck to the boat. When filled, the drums would weigh approximately 400 pounds each. For security reasons, we would only have a few minutes to load the six heavy barrels onto the boat.

All the other supplies and gear would be preloaded onto our rescue boat, which was named *Blank Check*. We would have to load the boat just before our departure in order to limit our exposure in the event that anyone showed up to ask questions about the barrels of fuel and supplies.

The Mariana Hotel was an old World War II prison camp. During the war, it was first run by the Japanese and then by the U.S. military to keep POWs after the final battles. The main hotel was on the beach, but across the road on a high hill overlooking the vast seascape was a row of bungalows that had once housed the Japanese prisoners. These bungalows had been converted into guest cottages. We occupied the end unit, which had a garage next to it. We had become friendly with the maintenance man there, and he let us use this space to store all our supplies and equipment. Captain Kirk and this man got along well.

At one point, the man asked us, "What's all this rope for?"

"Mountain climbing," I answered.

"Oh yes," he replied. "There are many cliffs to climb around here."

The sheer cliffs I saw were pockmarked with artillery shell fire from the war.

The following day, we purchased the rest of the supplies and took our 30-foot cruiser for another test run. We had taken her out only once before – the day that we had received the keys from Herman, who worked for Eddie Flores.

"This boat's all we've got," I said. "We have to make it work."

"These gas engines aren't dependable. If they fail, we're dead," Captain Kirk said in a foreboding tone.

As the target date for our rendezvous with the *Oktedy* approached, the weather worsened. The *Oktedy* only had enough fuel to get into position. Then, after that, she was powerless – no sails, no engines. If it came to this, Captain Jimmy would have a hard time keeping the *Oktedy* aimed into the waves and wind.

Captain Jimmy only had a small window of opportunity to rendezvous with us, and the reports we were receiving from the National Oceanic Atmosphere Agency were not good. A new storm was moving in our direction. We calculated its speed and direction. It would be at our target location within hours of our ETA.

Normally, we could have coped with this problem had the rescue vessel been built for the high seas. A 30-foot, lightweight, gas-powered sport boat was not the vessel to rely on. But Captain Kirk, Chandler, and I were prepared to rescue the *Oktedy*. No one even suggested that we back down.

Standing on the porch of the vintage WWII bungalow, I faced a part of the Pacific Ocean that, at that geographical point, was still called the Philippine Sea.

The waves were growing larger, white caps were everywhere, and the sky was a steely blue-gray.

Kirk stepped outside and stood next to me. "It's not going to be easy," he said.

I felt a draining grip of fear in my chest and throat as I nodded in agreement.

Captain Kirk and I reviewed our plan. That night, we would load the *Blank Check* with all the supplies, and then take the pickup trucks to a diesel station to fill the six barrels. We would haul three barrels in each truck. Kirk and I knew how difficult it was to move these barrels, since each of them would weigh approximately 400 pounds.

Good thing I've been working out, I thought.

The wind was picking up. My shirt was pressed flat against my chest. The sea was white with windswept waves. All around us grew the threatening energy of the storm front. I could feel the turbulence speaking to me, warning me not to fuck with nature.

It was time to go. We all knew exactly what to do. We had gone over our plan many times. The six 55-gallon drums were filled. The load of diesel fuel was so heavy that the two pickup trucks barely made it to the marina without blowing a tire or busting a leaf-spring.

As we pulled into the Memorial Marina area, I noticed how the trees along the coastline were being bent by the wind. The sky continued to darken in spite of the hour. We parked our pickups close to each other near the ramp of the dock where our rescue boat waited. The plan was to move so fast that, if the marina guard radioed for backup, we would be out of the marina before his reinforcements arrived. Now, with the oncoming storm, no one in their right mind would dispatch a vessel to chase us.

Captain Kirk and I jumped out of our trucks and moved quickly to untie the straps holding the barrels. Sure enough, the guard was sitting right there at the dock ramp next to us. I handed him two sandwiches in the hopes that a gift might distract him enough to leave us alone. He must have been hungry because, after his initial confused expression, he quickly walked away to the other end of the marina to enjoy his dinner. He never even asked what the six red barrels were for.

Chandler and I offloaded the heavy drums onto the ground. One by one, we attached them to the hand truck and efficiently rolled them down the ramp to load them onto the boat. We laid a blanket over the edge of the boat so the bright red barrels would not scratch the fiberglass.

In less than eighteen minutes, we completed our task just like we had trained for at our camp.

After parking the trucks in the Memorial Marina parking lot, we cast off and slowly motored out past the night guard as the storm descended upon us.

Chandler and I worked on lashing down the heavy barrels in the flat area on the stern. Captain Kirk was up on the flying bridge, securing the GPS. After we secured the drums, I climbed up to where Captain Kirk was. He showed me the points on the shoreline to remember for our return in case something happened to him.

The humid wind kept increasing in strength. North of us, we could see thunderheads and ominous dark clouds – and it was north where we were going. We tried to reach the *Oktedy* crew on the cell phone and the VHF radio, but we got no response. The waves were now four to five feet high and the chilling, stormy darkness enveloped us. One moment, we were hot and sweating. The next, we were soaking wet and cold.

The storm front hit us like a bus. In a flash, all hell broke loose. There was no doubt any longer what we were in for. Immediately, the waves increased to seven and eight feet high. Captain Kirk maintained his speed of ten knots into the storm. The pouring rain and wind were so intense that we could hardly see thirty feet away. The boat rolled and pitched in the turbulent sea. The wind blasted the rain sideways as I climbed down the pitching ladder to retighten the ropes around the fuel barrels.

I started to become seasick while trying to stand on the rolling deck. I could hardly see as I tried to retie the knots. The ropes were slippery in my hands, and my eyes stung from the rain that sandblasted my face. Chandler was helping me on the other side of the cluster of barrels, obviously experiencing the same confusion.

"I need a flashlight," he called out as he descended into the cabin.

Captain Kirk had his hands full trying to keep the vessel angled so the growing waves wouldn't enter our stern where the heavy barrels caused the boat's transom to ride dangerously low.

"I can't find the flashlight," Chandler yelled from the cabin door.

I ran inside and looked where I thought it was stored and – wham – my seasickness overwhelmed me. I grabbed the flashlight and ran outside.

The storm was screaming now. The boat was rolling severely and the blinding rain and wind hammered us. The waves were now ten to twelve feet high. I noticed how close the waves were coming to entering the stern. If they did, the water would move down to the engine compartment and kill our power. Without power in a storm like this, we were dead.

Captain Kirk yelled for me to come back up. I climbed the swaying, cold, chrome ladder to the top while holding onto the rails for my life. I held back the bile in my throat as I made it to the bridge and sat next to Captain Kirk. The canvas top over our heads was useless. The fierce wind blew the rain in sheets straight into our faces.

Captain Kirk was trying to use the GPS and VHF radio. He needed me to read the numbers from the compass to him, but the wind and the rain were so intense that I couldn't. Finally, I caught a quick glimpse. My head was splitting and the swaying bridge made my stomach turn. I had to concentrate and control myself so I wouldn't throw up.

Suddenly, I heard a rolling sound and then a crash. The boat shook as Captain Kirk and I both turned around to look. The heavy steel drums had broken loose and were sliding violently across the deck. They were smashing against the sides of our lightweight rescue boat.

"Fuck! The sides of the boat are going to split open!" I screamed. I ran down the ladder as the 2,400 pounds of steel barrels slid on the deck before me.

Chandler emerged from the cabin and tried to help me steady the drums. We tried to retie the ropes that had broken loose but we were losing the battle. The waves were now monstrous and towering over our heads, dangerously close to entering the open stern section. Only Captain Kirk's maneuvering prevented our vessel from taking on a deadly wave.

I yelled up at Kirk, "How far?"

"Halfway," I heard him scream over the sound of the relentless storm and the straining engines.

I yelled at the top of my lungs while trying to control the moving drums. "Radio?" I belted as I positioned my hand like I was holding the portable VHF radio.

"No," Captain Kirk called.

Chandler and I were already exhausted from trying to retie the barrels. Some of the fuel had leaked out onto the fiberglass deck, making the surface as slippery as ice.

Captain Kirk hollered down to me. "The barrels are too heavy! They're causing the stern to ride too low! Storm's getting worse!"

Chandler and I barely had enough energy left to stand up. I had to think. The wind and the rain blinded my sight. If we kept the fuel, we stood the chance of losing our boat and our lives. If I threw the drums overboard and met Captain Jimmy, I could still give him all the other supplies and meet him again the next day with more fuel.

I yelled back to Captain Kirk, "I'm throwing them overboard!"

Kirk nodded. The storm was screaming. Chandler was so sick and exhausted that he couldn't help me anymore. His 60-year-old body sat in the dark cabin. Captain Kirk couldn't leave his station. It was up to me to pick up these slippery 400-pound drums and throw them into the threatening sea, or else I would die.

I went to grab one of the moving drums but couldn't get a grip – and my foothold was useless. It seemed impossible to lift them over the side. My nausea was making my soaking head spin. I felt like throwing up when the thought, *I'm going to fucking die out here*, hit me. The ocean reflected the color of the sky, and it looked like liquid iron. The rain continued to pour and the wind was a howling gale. The waves were now mountains.

I started to throw up. I was heaving into the black ocean so violently that I almost choked. Bile was stuck in my airway and I gasped and wheezed for precious air. A bad thought hit me again – *I'm going to drown in the Philippine Sea. Of all the places in the world to die, it's going to be here.*

Captain Kirk threw a lifejacket down to me and yelled, "Put it on! Now!"

I tried to fasten the jacket. I had caught my breath, but was still nauseous and exhausted. I couldn't get the straps undone, and out of frustration, I threw the jacket into the towering waves. I turned to face the barrels. My head was pounding and my nausea was drawing out my strength.

A wave hit the port side and a rush of water came over my feet. I grabbed the barrel closest to me and tipped it forward so I that could wedge my fingers underneath the rim. With all my strength, I heaved the barrel up. The task defied all odds. Gritting my teeth, I summoned a last ferocious burst of strength. My arms and legs quivered wildly as my shoulders threatened to pop out of their sockets.

I heaved once more, and this time, the steel drum flipped over the transom into the black, churning sea.

The remaining five barrels were still sliding back and forth on the slippery deck. Grabbing another drum and getting a hold of it was like trying to grab a slippery shark on a roller coaster. Not being able to get a foothold was making this near impossible. I repeated what I had done when I threw the first one over. Even though my arms and legs felt powerless at this point, I somehow found the strength – and the second barrel went into the sea. *Four more to go*, I thought.

I will never know where I got the power to do this. Gasping for breath and choking down waves of nausea, I grabbed the closest drum and tried again. I couldn't move it up to the edge like before. The heavy drum kept falling back down as I tried several times to raise it.

As the boat spun in the storm, I heard Captain Kirk yell, "I'm heading back. We'll never make it if we don't head back now!"

I was too weak to speak. I looked at the barrels in front of me and knew that we couldn't return to shore with them, so they had to go.

I tipped the next barrel forward and lifted. Halfway up the ledge before me, the sight of my daughters became as vivid in my mind as the storm surrounding me. A spray of salt water broke across the stern, dousing me as I heaved the heavy drum overboard. I heard it splash with a steely sound. Before I could turn to grab another, a sliding barrel roared across the deck and smashed my ankle.

"Fuck!" I screamed.

Captain Kirk saw what happened and climbed down the ladder. Together, we lifted the remaining barrels and threw them overboard.

I grabbed the ladder to the flying bridge and held on, knowing I couldn't go inside the cabin because it would only make me sicker. I wedged myself between the ladder and the cabin. I had no strength left in my body as I peered out into the mountainous, metallic-black water.

~ ~ ~

Somehow, Captain Kirk got us back. We loaded the sail bags and supplies into the trucks in case Manny or Herman came by in the morning.

"We got our asses kicked out there," I said to Kirk.

"We sure did," he agreed. "Let's get a call out to Captain Jimmy and work out a new ETA."

The storm was still raging as we took care of the mess on the *Blank Check*.

No one was around except the Indian marina guard, and he stayed clear of us. The guard's face was a picture of perplexity.

We returned to our bungalow and cleaned up. I felt like a dead battery. My swollen black and blue ankle throbbed with pain. Captain Kirk contacted

Captain Jimmy and told him what had happened. He asked him if he could come in a little closer so we could hit him the following night.

"I'll come in fifteen miles toward you," Captain Jimmy said. "But that will use up all our fuel."

"If we don't find him," Kirk said to me as he held the phone, "he'll be left with no sails and no power. It'll be the end of the mission."

"In this storm, there'll be no chance of being compromised out there. Tell him that fifteen miles south is okay."

Kirk also told Captain Jimmy that we would be bringing him less fuel. Captain Jimmy grumbled, but understood that he had no choice.

"Sail that ship home," Captain Kirk bellowed before working out a new ETA for the following night.

It was late, and we were burned out. Chandler had crashed, and Captain Kirk and I were going over our checklist for our second attempt to find the *Oktedy*. We sat in the old log cabin styled sitting room under a dimly lit ceiling lamp.

The bungalow was shaking from the powerful wind blowing in from the north. The rain was still falling in sheets. I thought about the crew of the *Oktedy* and how they were in the same relentless storm. In eighteen hours, we would go out there again. Kirk checked the weather reports with NOAA and found that the storm system would still be in our path.

The thought of going through this rescue attempt again made my stomach turn. I was totally empty. I'd thrown my guts out into the sea along with barrels of diesel. The throbbing pain of my left ankle was another reminder that this nightmare was real.

That night, I lay awake in my bed and listened to the vintage WWII shelter shake in the violent Pacific storm. I knew that the next rescue attempt was going to be bad, but I had no choice. My family and friends depended on me to come through. When I finally fell into a fitful sleep, I had a bad dream and woke up calling Virginia's name.

On the morning of October 16, I stood on the small wooden porch facing the Philippine Sea. The sky had a pale-greenish glow while the white-capped swells had a cold, metallic cast like pewter. The wind was blowing as hard as it had the night before.

Kirk and Chandler came out.

"Come on," I said. "Let's go buy some fifteen-gallon containers. We'll give them a couple of hundred gallons of diesel fuel. They're getting three new sets of sails anyway. They can sail home and use the fuel to keep the batteries charged."

"Exactly," Kirk replied. "The *Oktedy* is a top-of-the-line sailing vessel. What the hell does he need so much fuel for? We nearly got killed last night trying to deliver him this fuel. And for what?"

The force of the wind made us lean into it.

After a moment of silence, I said, "Let's get on with it."

The marina guard must have thought that we were crazy for going into the same storm two nights in a row. He didn't even come near us this time. He just sat as far away from us as he could without actually leaving the marina.

This time, we had plastic handheld containers that contained fifteen gallons of fuel each. There were twelve containers in all for a total of 180 gallons. We loaded the *Blank Check* and slowly motored out of the marina into the awaiting storm-torn sea.

We all knew what to expect. The differences that night would be the absence of the heavy barrels and our decreased travel distance.

We held our course as we pushed our way into the wind and heavy rain. Two to three miles out, the storm hit us hard as though it were waiting for us, taunting us and enveloping us. The boat rose and fell as we plowed forward.

"Keep an eye out," Captain Kirk yelled. "She may be near!"

We only had about 40 yards of visibility. I looked for the high mast over the towering, black waves while continuously trying to contact Captain Jimmy on the VHF radio.

Captain Jimmy had given us a list of equipment and supplies to purchase. We even bought them food – steaks, fresh fruit, salad, beer and juice. Everything was wrapped tightly in boxes for them.

The rain was falling, driven southward, while the sky remained shrouded and furious. Captain Kirk held his course as all three of us searched for the *Oktedy*. He looked past the bow, Chandler looked on the starboard side, and I looked on the port side.

Like a recurring nightmare, I started to throw up. This time, it was more like dry heaves, but my head still spun and my stomach felt nauseous. I held onto the ladder and kept looking over the mountains of waves around us.

"Where the fuck are they?" Kirk yelled down from the bridge. "We passed the point where we agreed to meet. I'm turning around. Keep looking!"

We turned 180 degrees and headed back.

A few miles later, I thought I was seeing things. "There she is!" I screamed out over the sound of the twin engines and the relentless storm. She looked like a ghostly galleon in the fog and rain. It was only a silhouette, but no doubt the *Oktedy*.

Kirk turned toward the direction that I was pointing and came upon her slowly.

"Captain Jimmy!" I yelled when we were within twenty yards or so.

"Yeah, Max. Is that you?"

"Yes," I yelled. "I'm going to throw you a rope. Tie it to your raft. Attach your rope to the raft so you can shuttle it back and forth. It's too rough to come closer to you!"

Captain Kirk kept the power boat at about 60 feet away from the *Oktedy*. I threw the rope, which I'd tied with a special knot that I'd learned when I was younger.

"Good shot!" Kirk yelled down to me as my toss hit the mark.

"Yeah!" Chandler said as he got the supplies out of the cabin.

As the storm raged, the *Oktedy* crew labored to place their raft into the water. Captain Kirk was having a hard time keeping our boat away from the hull of the *Oktedy*. The wind and waves kept forcing us closer and closer to the larger vessel. Kirk would maneuver the twin screws so the *Blank Check* could avoid a disastrous collision.

The storm blew in fitful bursts that boomed like salvos of great guns firing over the ocean. The rain slanted in sheets that flicked and subsided. I caught threatening glimpses of the tumbling waves as our small craft jumbled and tossed through the unforgiving sea.

The air was full of flying water and the wind screeched. As the boat careened wildly in the towering waves, we were drenched. I became hideously seasick and leaned out over the transom of the boat and retched, clearing my throat – this time, more violently.

The *Oktedy* crew signaled me to pull the rope. In the blinding rain, I pulled. The Zodiac raft skidded across the churning waves to our spinning boat as the *Oktedy* crew held onto the opposite end of our shuttle line. Chandler and I leaned over to load the raft. Our chests pounded against the gunnels.

Once the raft was loaded, I signaled the *Oktedy* crew to pull back. We reloaded twice. One more would do it, but our boat was being forced out of control by the wind and waves. We were drifting into the *Oktedy*.

I yelled up to Captain Kirk. "Kirk, you're going to hit!" I could barely see because of the stinging rain blowing into my eyes. With open hands, I reached out and pushed as hard as I could against the cold, slippery, dark blue hull of the *Oktedy*. Its massive hull reminded me of how powerfully built she was. We missed colliding by five inches as I slowly pushed with all my strength. I could see the towering vessel above me. This angle made the *Oktedy* look tremendous.

Captain Kirk was having a hard time controlling our vessel. "My left engine is out!" he yelled down to us in a frantic voice as he kept trying to restart her. "No go! If we lose the other one, we're dead!"

The turbulent storm continued to blow us around in the area next to the *Oktedy*. The last raft-load was going out.

"Hurry," Kirk yelled, "I can't stay in this position any longer."

Again, we nearly collided and I pushed us off.

"I can't stay here!" Kirk screamed. The rescue boat spun and pounded into the waves mercilessly.

First mate John of the *Oktedy* disconnected our end of the rope. I quickly brought it into our boat so the loose end wouldn't get tangled in our remaining prop.

"That's it!" I yelled up to Captain Kirk.

He responded immediately and moved away from the battlefield next to the sailboat. I held my arms up high toward the *Oktedy* crew and they all returned my farewell. I stood and watched as the *Oktedy* disappeared into the fog and stormy seas.

"See you on the other side!" I yelled into the wind and rain.

Captain Kirk was still trying to start the other engine, but it was to no avail. He yelled to me to check the breakers. "See if one has tripped!"

I went inside the cabin where Chandler sat, exhausted. I slipped past him and checked the panel. My nausea got worse the longer I stayed inside. The breakers, it turned out, were not the problem.

I ran out and relayed this message before I threw up over the side. The remaining right engine began to miss and stall, and then resume.

I climbed up the swaying ladder to the flying bridge and took the seat next to Captain Kirk.

"Better get your lifejacket on," he said.

I climbed down the ladder as the waves tossed us around like toys. *If one wave comes inside, we're history*, I thought. I handed a lifejacket to Chandler and he quickly put it on. I couldn't stay inside. To help hold myself up, I stood wedged between the ladder and the cabin. I held onto my lifejacket in the pounding storm.

The closer to shore we came, the lower the waves became. Soon, Captain Kirk was motoring with the one engine into the desolate Memorial Marina.

Captain Kirk, Chandler, and I left the island of Saipan without any attention. We gave away all our gear to the maintenance man at the bungalow and then disappeared. The following morning, the three of us departed for America, the *Oktedy's* final destination.

Chapter 21

FINALLY, I was home with my loved ones.

"Dad, you look skinny!" my daughters said to me.

It was early November of 1997. Soon, I would have to leave to offload the *Oktedy* in Seattle.

The truth was, every time somebody told me that I had changed this time around, I believed them. I *did* change. My depression was gone – my thoughts of suicide a distant memory. I had a mission that was almost complete. The good things that I would do for my family and close friends . . . I would secretly donate money through Minh to the children's orphanage in Pattaya.

My life will be complete, I thought. After 30 years of endless worry and work, I would finally be able to retire and help my loved ones. My daughters would be able to see the world and develop into bright young women. They would attend the best schools and never have to worry about money like I had worried all my life.

Days later, we received a message from the *Oktedy's* crew. An ETA and a description of their problems were relayed to me via a call from Kirk.

"The engine and transmission are down and they can't charge the batteries," he told me. "So they don't have full use of the SatCom. Their only way of generating power is with the wind generator, and it takes time to build up enough power to operate the system."

"What about the gas generator?" I wailed. "Why doesn't he use that?"

"He doesn't have it."

"What do you mean he doesn't have it?"

"He didn't buy one."

"What the fuck is wrong with him? I allocated the money for one and even had it on the list of items to purchase in Singapore. He could've asked for one in Saipan, too. Was he out of his mind? That's an important piece of equipment! A $23,000 SatCom and we can't even use it because of his fucking bullshit!"

He left an ETA of November 25, 1997, which would put him 100 miles out from the coast of Seattle, far beyond the range that we had agreed upon – and well into some extremely choppy waters that time of year.

Of course, I was the one who would go out to meet the *Oktedy* and transfer a generator and other items that Captain Jimmy had requested in his last contact with our crew. Since Kirk was tied up and couldn't make it this time, I was set up with a capable seaman named Mike. He was over six feet tall, slim, and fit. His blonde hair and blue eyes made him look younger than his forty years.

Mike and I worked out our travel plans and meeting point. I would arrive a day before he would.

"From now on," I told him, "you'll be known as the Bird. I'll be Max."

I explained how our offload site was already manned by a special crew under Woodstock Willy's direction, who would handle the entire offload procedure, even the trucking and distribution. All we would have to do is bring the *Oktedy* into the Straight of Juan de Fuca west of Seattle.

The Bird and I put on our "two guys on vacation from the East Coast" act. We had brought our fishing gear and coolers for beer and food to the charter boat company with us. We ended up renting a 28-foot fiberglass sport cruiser called *Seeker* from Anacortes Yacht Charters that was located about 50 miles northwest of Seattle.

The Bird and I moved the *Seeker* from Anacortes to Port Angeles. We spent that cold, damp night docked at a marina near the U.S. Coast Guard Station in Neah Bay. We listened to all radio signals over our CB scanner and nothing from our lost crew was transmitted. We did, however, hear the U.S. Coast Guard announce a bulletin asking all seagoing vessels to be on the lookout for a 60-foot sailboat that was reported missing. The description was not quite of the *Oktedy*, but it was close enough to cause worry.

As we drifted into the open ocean the following day, the calm, picturesque seas became unforgiving ten-foot waves. During the last communication that we had had with the *Oktedy*, they revealed when they would be at the target location. Captain Jimmy and I had established three possible landings when we'd met in Pattaya – one in Canada and two in the U.S.

The plan was for me to relay one of these points to Jimmy while he was sailing across the Pacific. On his nautical chart were marked three locations – points A, B, and C. Before the *Oktedy* had lost its ability to receive our communications, I had announced his target: point 'C' – the Sequim Bay location near Seattle. Now Captain Jimmy was requesting a change to point 'B', thus putting the burden on me to reach him.

It wasn't long before I found the mighty Pacific pushing me back to shore.

The decision was then made – amidst thorough debate – to call the Übel brothers. They had heavy equipment in Seattle, vessels large enough to cut through the huge waves and find the *Oktedy*. Skip and I agreed to offer them $250,000 for their part in transferring the generator and other important items to our stranded ship.

The Übel brothers knew this area well. This was where they had imported loads in the past. They had mentioned to me how they still kept vessels in Los Angeles, San Francisco, and even in Seattle

I pulled out my coded phone directory and dialed Sam Übel's home number. He answered and the sound of his voice was comforting. He completely understood the dilemma with little explanation and agreed to call me back in ten minutes. He called right on time.

"Well, you're in luck, my friend," he said. "We happen to have a vessel in Seattle capable of handling this mission."

Before I hung up with Sam, Bob spoke up on the other line. "I'd like to be your supplier in the future."

"That's fine by me," I said. "After the *Oktedy* mission is complete, I'll have the working capital to pay the $200 per unit charge that we previously discussed."

"Good. I'd like to do a project with you after this one is complete."

~~~

NOVEMBER 29, 1997

Sam contacted my brother, who was now based in Port Angeles with Skip and Willy. The Bird and I were stationed on the *Seeker*, near Neah Bay. In case the brothers missed our stranded crew, we would intercept them in the strait and transfer a generator and provisions.

Over the phone, Sam read off the list of items Bob had on board his tugboat-style vessel to my brother. Everyone was impressed with the detail and efficiency that the Übel brothers displayed. They had everything from a DC-powered microwave oven with a hundred ready-to-heat-and-eat dinners, fuel, foul weather gear, flags from local sailing clubs, radios, a generator, and more.

"These guys are too much," Skip said.

Junior reminded Skip and Willy that the Übel brothers were charging $250,000 for the operation. Skip and Willy agreed that it was worth every penny.

Sam also told my brother that Bob had moved westward past the Cape Flattery lighthouse at the entrance to the Strait of Juan de Fuca, and that he would keep us posted on their progress. "We will not abort," Sam said. "We will not abort our search."

Everyone, including myself, felt relieved that the Übel brothers were on the team, working to finalize our mission.

To me, the eleventh hour always seemed so quiet. We monitored the radios and stayed off the cell phones around the clock. Everyone was connected electronically, except for the *Oktedy*.

The Bird and I were cold aboard the *Seeker* and the dampness penetrated our bones as we sat in a dark cove on the strait, only a short distance from the entrance to the Pacific Ocean. It was December 1, 1997.

The Bird and I took turns using the night scope to scrutinize each vessel that passed our location. We waited for the call from Sam that would tell us everything was under control. My body shivered while a vague but pervading sense of trouble and depression pressed heavily upon me.

The Bird decided to take the raft and paddle from our boat to shore only twenty yards away to see if we were alone. I stayed focused, watching the strait.

I was watching as the Bird made it to shore and was checking the beach for footprints when I was taken by surprise. It felt like a knife had been thrust into my chest. An explosion illuminated the sky above the entrance to the strait. The sky above the mouth to the strait glowed a fiery red. At the source of the explosion was a vessel, a sailing vessel . . . the *Oktedy*!

"No!" I screamed. I stood in shock on the deck of the *Seeker*. Out of nowhere, a Coast Guard helicopter appeared from the hilly shoreline behind me. The chopper circled around me as a soldier in a harness wearing a flight helmet leaned out of the wide-open side-door and aimed a long black object at me.

The Bird, aware of the confusion, had raced back and boarded the *Seeker*. "What the fuck's happening?" he yelled.

"I don't know! I'll burn the charts and papers. You head out!"

The Bird fired up the two engines while I pulled up the anchor. We moved northeast toward Canada. I threw all our electronics overboard and burned all our data in a steel grill we had outside on the stern deck. The flames blew backwards toward the two white and red striped Coast Guard choppers that followed directly behind our wake.

Two Coast Guard cutters came into view to join the two choppers. I yelled to the Bird to stop. "All the papers and charts are gone. There's nothing left on board. Let them come."

The Bird shut the *Seeker* down and we floated in silence, approximately one mile from Canada. The two choppers moved up and hovered over our heads, blowing chilly wind down upon us.

From one of the Coast Guard ships, they called to us over a loudspeaker. "Prepare to be boarded. This is a routine safety check."

The other ship remained in front of our bow to prevent a sudden escape.

The Bird and I knew that we could have outrun the cutters and that the choppers would have had to end their pursuit when they had reached Canadian territory.

The Bird and I stood at ease as our vessel was boarded.

They thoroughly searched our vessel for an hour, finding nothing. As suddenly as they arrived, they departed.

"Thank you for your cooperation," said the one in charge.

The Bird and I were left floating in the middle of the strait, wondering what the fuck had happened.

We decided to return the *Seeker* to the first marina that we had used, since we were far from the Coast Guard Station at Neah Bay. Our car was parked there and we were anxious to communicate with our partners.

The operation was over. What exactly had happened was still unknown to us.

I was a biological roller coaster – one minute I felt manic, and the next depressed. I needed to know what had happened.

Later, the Bird and I pulled the car over to a spot off the country road that ran along the coastline. We didn't say a word in the car for fear that there was a wiretap inside. When we got out of the car, we discussed our options.

"Maybe we should hide out for a few days," the Bird said.

"No," I said. "First, we have to meet the others. Then we'll decide what to do."

"What the hell caused the *Oktedy* to explode?"

"I don't know. We'll find out later."

It took several hours to drive to the hotel in Port Angeles where the remaining team was based. When Mike and I entered the room, we noticed that the curtains were drawn. It was dark except for the glow of the television set.

My brother, Skip, and Willy were sitting on the beds in front of the TV set. The room was silent except for the breaking news bulletin on the TV showing a video taken by the U.S. Coast Guard of a sailboat burning and sinking to its watery grave. The video shot from a U.S. Coast Guard cutter showed, in plain view, the transom of the vessel as it burned. The name of the vessel was painted on the stern: *Oktedy, Sydney, Australia.* The poor *Oktedy* disappeared beneath the waves.

My heart wept in silence, and I died a little inside when I saw her go down. No one spoke.

The line that struck us all as the most horrifying was, "The crew was arrested when bales of marijuana were found floating to the surface shortly after the vessel disappeared beneath the waves."

Everyone in the room was crushed: all the work, all the effort, all the obstacles that we had overcome, the huge investment – all of it now lay at the bottom of the sea.

"We have to hire lawyers for the crew," I said.

"Contact me in Woodstock when you get back," Willy said. "We'll decide which lawyers to hire."

Skip tore the Buddha necklace off his neck and threw it – a gesture aimed at me. He then said, "I'm leaving," and kissed me on the cheek.

Before Willy left for Woodstock, he took care of securing the offload site. The Bird returned the *Seeker* to the Anacortes broker and the remaining team returned to the East Coast on separate flights. I was anxious to speak to the Übel brothers and ask them what had happened.

~ ~ ~

Junior arrived home a day after me. He brought with him a photo and newspaper article about the *Oktedy.* I sat in my kitchen, surrounded by my family.

I was spent. I had tried to create a legacy for my family and ended up losing everything.

Virginia read the article. "How could this happen?" she asked.

"I'm not sure yet," I said. "Once we hire lawyers to defend the crew, we'll learn the details."

On December 3, 1997, my lawyer, brother, and I met in Middletown, New York at an Italian restaurant. My lawyer read the newspaper article, and when he finished digesting the information, he asked me how much I had intended to earn if the mission had been successful.

"About four million," I said.

"Max," he said, "if I was losing everything and had a chance to make that kind of money moving pot, I would have done what you did too."

His words didn't help, but I appreciated the effort to console me.

"The crew comes first," I said. "I'll communicate with you on a daily basis."

On my way home, I considered my options. It looked like the end of the road.

I stayed close to my children. They seemed to sense my pain and concern for their futures. As the hours passed, my depression deepened and my suicidal thoughts returned.

On December 5, Sam called Junior and left a startling message. "Tell the King that he's not dead. I have a plan that can solve his problems. I want both of you to meet me at the Plaza Hotel tomorrow at 21:00 hours!"

The next day, my brother and I met with Sam in a luxury suite at the famous Plaza Hotel in New York City.

Sam wore a handmade dress-shirt, silk tie, perfectly pressed pants, and polished shoes.

"I have a plan that will solve your problems," he said as he aimed his laser-pointer at laminated nautical charts of the world. He articulated the history of his marijuana smuggling career, breaking it down into five dimensions, claiming that it was time to create a sixth dimension – a pre-carriage position designed especially for me. "I've taken into consideration your abilities and present support system."

Before this meeting got started, I had asked him why Bob hadn't been able to find the *Oktedy*. Sam assured me that everything possible had been done to locate her, but that during the night, the *Oktedy* must have slipped by them. Sam then reminded me that I owed him money for his services even though they had been unable to intercept the *Oktedy*.

To me, Sam seemed a little emotionally detached from what had happened. He seemed totally focused on this new operation that would salvage my life and recoup my partners' investment.

"Arthur," he continued, "you've lost everything. Soon, you'll be indicted. You cannot afford a proper attorney. You'll not be able to support your family while you are in prison. Your only option is to leave this country. Through my six-dimension plan, you'll be able to support your family and even see them from time to time. You can then return to America when you're ready to fight your case with proper lawyers. Through my plan, you'll be able to earn enough money to live for several years in Southeast Asia."

I listened while Sam described my involvement.

"You'll have to purchase a Thai-style fishing boat and supply a captain and crew. This vessel will be loaded in the Gulf of Thailand and your crew will move it to my private island in Indonesia. We'll call this Poppy's Island. Your captain will have no knowledge of where he is going. We will, along his journey, signal to him as to what direction to take. After several sorties and the product are safely stored, I will transport this load to America on my own ship from the island. My crew will handle the offload procedure. My brother will procure the load for you. You'll be relatively safe. However, you will have to raise the capital for the purchase of the Thai vessel and the cargo. We will work on a $200 per pound charge for your load, just as we had previously discussed.

"Tell your friends to dig deep into their pockets. Ultimately, everyone will be indicted for the *Oktedy*. I want you to instruct them to cooperate with the U.S. Attorney and negotiate for a lesser sentence by claiming you were responsible. It ultimately won't affect you since you'll have a good lawyer by the time you return. It will also encourage the others to invest in my six-dimension plan."

For the next hour, Sam used his charts to review our plan. He reminded me that he would use his ship, his expertise, and if I was short, his funding. I was shocked to hear the last bit – the Übel brothers were known to be tight as a drum when it came to money.

"If you think it will help," Sam said, "I'll arrange a meeting with your partners to review my plan. Without funding, this project won't work."

Skip and Willy agreed to meet with Sam in New York. They liked his idea.

"It makes sense," Skip said. "Better to earn while we can and fight this thing with money."

Willy also agreed and said he would fund the operation if Skip also put in. They agreed to support my family while I was involved in Sam's new plan. That was a relief. I could now take care of my family while I dealt with the havoc all around me.

I called my attorney. A week had gone by. I told him my plan and that I would be leaving soon. I also told him how I had spoken to all my partners and informed them to cooperate with the government when they were indicted so they would receive a lesser sentence. I explained Sam's theory that how, ultimately, it wouldn't matter. I'd be away and would only return when all was clear or an acceptable sentence was offered.

My attorney was dumbfounded. He'd never heard of such an idea. "Max, I really don't know what to say, but I'll do whatever you ask."

I met with Bob Ratner and Greg Antacrockas. They, of course, were happy to hear my plan. They only stood to gain by it. Ratner said that he would help raise funds to do this new project at a five-to-one interest ratio. He knew that he had to earn in order to leave the country and live overseas while the case unfolded.

"I have no choice," he said. "I'm looking at twenty years if I'm busted again."

He also told me that Minh was in big trouble in Pattaya. The Thai captain and his partner, the Old Man, were being pressured by Cambodian army personnel who had been involved in the operation. "There's a backend owed on the *Oktedy* project. The money I gave them only got us loaded. Their profit was owed to them after the completion of the mission. That's why we loaded 2,500 pounds extra. That was for them. The problem here is that poor Minh is in the middle of this whole thing. She's the only one that the Cambodians and the Thai can go to. They think she's part of it."

Poor Minh, I thought. *What a fucking mess!*

"Christ!" I said. "Just show them the newspaper article. That should convince them that it's a total loss and that no one made a penny."

"I tried that. They think we had offloaded half the stuff in Canada and that the boat then got busted in America while we tried to offload the second half. They want at least half their money!"

"How much is that?" I asked.

"Forget it. It's over a million."

"Fuck! No wonder they're hot. You can buy Cambodia for that kind of money!"

"Look, Max. You have to see Minh and take care of this problem when you go back over there."

"Me? I don't know these people. These are all *your* people!"

"I can't go back there now. I need to earn some more money so I can invest in your new project. You have to help her. If you don't, they'll kill her. They've already been to her office and threatened her. She sent me a fax."

Skip and Willy were paying the legal bills and supporting the families of the crew while I coordinated their defense lawyers. I even flew down to Miami to pay Captain Bower's lawyer in cash before he flew out to Seattle to meet with him.

While all this was going on, I tried to have a normal life with my family. It wasn't working out. Everyone could sense my dilemma. Virginia knew what was going on, but as long as the money kept coming in, she was in total agreement with what I was doing.

"Will you wait for me if I'm captured?" I asked her.

"Of course I'll wait for you."

I knew that she didn't mean it. I knew Virginia very well. The longer I stayed, the more stressful it became.

While Skip and Willy raised the money to launch the project, I toiled with the realities of leaving my loved ones yet again. I told my daughters that I had to go back to Thailand to work on another project and that when this one was completed, I would retire and they could spend as much time with me as they wanted. On the surface, everyone took it pretty well. I felt that, in six months, the project would be finalized. Then we could all meet in Europe or Asia.

During the *Oktedy* operation, I had returned home three times. This time, it would be different.

~ ~ ~

I met Antacrockas and Ratner at a large shopping mall in Boston where we discussed the new project and the life-threatening position Ratner had placed Minh in. "I might have to bring the Übel brothers into this situation," I said. "They have connections with the military and they know the Thai godfather in Bangkok. This whole thing might get complicated."

"Do me a favor and speak with Minh right now," Ratner said. "I'll call her from a phone booth."

We walked to a phone booth and Ratner used his calling card.

"Don't let Minh know that I'm here," he said as he handed me the phone and put his finger to his lips. I held the phone to my ear and looked down at Ratner, thinking, *What a pathetic man.*

Minh answered the phone in her sweet voice. "Good morning, Minh's Travel Service."

"Sawasdee, Minh. This is Max."

"Oh, Max! I'm so glad you called. Where are you?"

"I'm in America. Are you all right?"

"No, Max. Bob said you would be here already."

I looked down at Ratner and shook my head in disgust for his continuous lies.

"Minh," I said, "I'll be there soon. In the meantime, call these people or tell them when you see them that I'm coming to see them personally. Tell them that I'll take care of everything."

"Oh, Max, it makes me so happy to hear your voice. These men are very angry with Ratner. They have come here many times looking for him. Why he never call them? They say to me, 'If Ratner no come here or send their money by the end of this month, they will start shooting,' and I believe them, Max. I can tell these are dangerous men."

I wanted to reach out through 12,000 miles of phone line and hold this courageous girl. She broke my heart.

"Minh, just give them this message and they'll wait for me. I'll be there in two weeks. I'll call you as I travel toward you."

"Yes, Max. I will do this. Thank you. I feel much better now."

"I'll be there. Bye-bye for now."

"Bye-bye, Max. I will wait for you."

I hung up the phone.

"Great," Ratner said. "That's one less problem I have to deal with. I'll have a hundred grand for you in a few weeks. I'll wire it to Minh for you."

"No!" I said. "Not again. Send it through my brother. The Übel brothers have a way to transfer the funds."

I didn't want to spend any more time with Ratner, but I needed to know what his plans were.

"My plan is to send you one hundred grand, buy myself a phony passport, and lay low in Thailand and wait for the profits to come in from the project."

"Listen," I said, "the brothers are demanding that I get a phony passport. Get me one, too."

Soon, my new identity, Harry Luckenbill, was written on my new license and passport.

⌐⌐⌐

December 23, 1997

I felt as though my life was in someone else's control. Thanks to the Übel brothers and others, I had a new identity and a way to overcome everyone's losses. I was also in a state of deep depression. Having had to leave my family before I had a chance to spend time with them was killing me.

On Christmas Eve, I told Virginia that I didn't want to spend Christmas at home – that the Feds had a warped sense of humor and were likely to show up on Christmas morning to take me away.

With my new task to return to Thailand to take care of Minh and complete a new project, my priorities had changed. My brother and all my partners were encouraging me to go as soon as possible. Even Virginia was anxious to see me leave so I could finalize this new plan.

"Let's all go to the Mohonk Mountain House for Christmas," I said. "They'll have a big Christmas tree and we can have a fireplace in our rooms. We'll bring all the presents and, this way, we won't have to worry."

Despite the rush I was under, everyone agreed. The children were excited.

At the resort, my daughters and I sat next to the beautiful Christmas tree in the 125-year-old great room at the Mohonk Mountain House. I knew this would be my last Christmas with my family in America for a long time. My daughters and I sat close to each other and sipped our hot chocolate while we listened to a happy group of guests singing *Silent Night* by the grand piano. Behind me, the old stone fireplace had a crackling fire going and I could feel the warmth on my back. The contrast between this old-fashioned American tradition and the events unfolding in my life seemed surreal.

I then heard a voice – a voice I knew but couldn't place. I turned around to see the man who was speaking, and there he was. The man my father had loved, the man I loved, the man who played for the New York Yankees and later spoke for the team as a TV announcer, the man who had convinced me to borrow

$250,000 as a result of seeing his commercial spot on television. The Hall of Famer, Phil Rizzuto, was sitting with his wife Cora next to the fireplace on a comfortable couch.

I turned back to my daughter Arli, who was a big Yankees fan and knew all about sports legends. "Arli," I said. "Look! It's Phil Rizzuto."

Her face lit up, and before I could turn back to see him, he was standing in front of us next to his wife with a warm, friendly smile upon his aging face.

"Skooter! Merry Christmas," I said as I stood up and shook hands with him. I introduced my children.

He had no idea what impact he'd had on my life. We ended up spending our Christmas Eve by the towering spruce tree, talking about the Yankees and his own incredible career. Arli had such a good time. She still has a photograph of herself and my youngest daughter Ali standing next to him at the hotel. His room was next to ours and he ended up taking a liking to my children.

On Christmas morning, Virginia, my three daughters, and I opened our presents by the fire in our antique-filled room overlooking the frozen lake.

Ari gave me a writing book for Christmas. "Here, Daddy," she said. "You can write your story now."

Outside, a heavy fog lay over the rocky landscape. In our suite, the fragrance from burning candles that Virginia had bought filled the air. I was upset, but tried not to show it. I'm sure that everyone was doing the same – all doing our best to be brave. But I could sense the pain that they all felt in their hearts.

After Christmas, we returned to Milford. I walked through my home for the last time. *If I fail,* I thought as I stepped out the door, *I'll leave my family with my life insurance so they won't lose this place.*

Virginia and the children were in the Explorer, waiting for me. We drove away in silence.

From Montreal, I would fly to Amsterdam, and from there on to Bangkok, where I was to meet the Übel brothers.

I said goodbye to my daughter Ari when we left her off at Union College near Albany. Virginia, Arli, Ali, and I continued on to Canada. The lousy feeling I had in my chest wouldn't go away. Soon, my life – the close family life that I had enjoyed for 23 years – would be over.

We made it to Montreal late. Snow-flurries were falling. The streets were covered with ice and snow. It was Canada as I had always pictured it.

We checked into a large luxury hotel, and over the next two days we stayed close together. We went out to dinner and checked out the city, but the shroud of pain caused by my impending departure hung over us constantly.

I gave enough cash to Virginia to last her for over six months.

On my last night, I spent time alone with each of my children. We talked and cried and tried to reason out why this was all happening. But no matter what I did to comfort their shattered hearts, the fact remained that I was leaving soon and for a long time.

The following morning came too quickly. The Explorer was parked in front of the hotel. Virginia and I said goodbye to each other. I was still angry at her and knew that our marriage was over, no matter if I won or lost. The lingering animosity between us reminded me of how our marriage had been for 23 years.

I hugged and kissed my daughters goodbye, feeling my heart sink as they disappeared around the corner.

Chapter 22

AMSTERDAM *would be a good place to live*, I thought. I had purchased my airline ticket for Bangkok under my new name on my second day there. The three days I spent exploring the city reminded me of how uptight and controlled America was. There, you could smoke a joint of herb while having a cup of coffee in any number of small cafés.

On my last night there, I dined on spicy Thai food as I sat in an Asian restaurant on a narrow cobblestone street in central Amsterdam. After I left the place, I wandered through the many narrow store and restaurant lined streets.

I found myself in a quiet, dark intersection where one of the small streets curved around. It was cold and damp. I heard an odd sound coming from around the bend in the road. The wind blew frigid air and I held my coat closed at the collar. I was surrounded by unlit buildings when I realized that I was alone, save for this whooshing sound. I continued to walk in the dark toward the sound. Then I saw where it was coming from.

A man standing in front of an old church surrounded by old Dutch-style buildings was twirling a rod that was about six feet long and had flames on each end. I could hear the sound of the flames blowing as he turned the long rod in front of himself. On the stone church, the flaming rod created a display of strobe-like flickers and giant shadows. Only he and I were on this cold, dark street.

I felt a tinge of fear, a feeling that my future was now beginning and that I would be experiencing many strange things to come.

The following day, on my flight to Bangkok, I reviewed the project ahead of me. The Bird would travel to Bangkok when the Übels were ready to use him. The brothers had said they would supply the rest of the crew. The Bird and the Übels' crew would shuttle a traditional Thai fishing boat from Cambodia to Sam's private island. Sam would then transport the accumulated cargo from there to America on his ship. My partners would distribute the herb. My days of moving herb would then be over.

When I arrived in Bangkok, I would purchase a cell phone so I could stay in touch with Ratner, Skip, Willy, my Asian contacts, and my brother. On the personal side, this cell phone would also be the only link with my family.

I entered Thailand through the Don Muang International Airport in Bangkok.

I picked up a cell phone right there in the airport with enough credit on the calling card to last several months. From there, I took a two-hour trip by service car to Rayong.

It almost felt like I had never left this land of illusion. The experience that I had had in the few months that I spent in America had taught me that Thailand was now a part of me. I realized how difficult it had been for me to coexist in both worlds. My body may have been in the States, but my soul was in this land of Buddha and spirit houses.

From Rayong, I took a ferry to the small island called Koh Samet. This was where Bob, aka J.T., had advised that I should live until it was time to move out and begin the operation. I spent a few days there and disliked the tourist environment. I wanted to live in Thailand and live the real Southeast Asian life – not the contrived and pampered lifestyle on Koh Samet.

Sam, aka Haig, had instructed me to fax him once I was in Thailand. I sent a short message to his home in Singapore, letting him know that I was in the country and on my way to Bangkok – and that I would contact him from there within 24 hours.

There were only a handful of peasant workers on board the ferry back from Rayong. I ended up sharing some of my Partagas cigars with this group of old ladies and men while they shared their homemade whisky with me.

This is more like it, I thought as I caught a light buzz on this old Thai steamer with a bunch of toothless friendlies.

I returned to Bangkok and checked into my favorite hotel, The Dusit Thani. From there, I communicated with Haig. We agreed to meet at the Oriental Hotel in Bangkok in one week.

I was curious as to how Haig and J.T. had handled a couple of pressing situations related to the *Oktedy* loss. One important matter had involved Jon, from whom we had purchased the *Oktedy*. I had learned that Jon was having a hard time collecting the insurance money from the *Oktedy* disaster. When Captain Jimmy Bower took it upon himself to sink the vessel in his attempt to bury the cargo, he had possibly sunk Jon as well.

I had found out where Jon was living in Indonesia and called him. I leveled with the poor man and told him how bad I felt about what had happened. Although I wasn't privy to Captain Jimmy's plan to sink the *Oktedy* if attacked, I promised to pay Jon in full for the *Oktedy* from my next project's profits.

"I wish you had told me your plans," Jon replied. "*I* would've made it to bloody America in one piece. I can assure you of that!"

I told Jon that I would send him enough money to hold him until I had completed my next project. He thanked me for my effort to help him and gave me his bank account information so I could transfer the funds to him.

"Good luck, Al," he said. "You're a good man."

Before I departed from Canada, Haig volunteered to deliver the money to Jon and J.T. volunteered to take care of the other problem we had. Skip had stupidly used his credit card at the Bay Shore Hotel in Pattaya. J.T. said that, through his connections with the police, he could have Skip's and my records erased from the hotel's bookkeeping department. I paid J.T. $5,000 to take care of the matter.

I kept in touch with Minh. She knew that I was having a meeting soon with people that could possibly help end her dilemma. She told me that the Thai captain was waiting for me to arrive.

I slept off my jetlag during the day and visited Pat Pong, the old neighborhood, at night. The penetrating rock 'n' roll, cold Singha, and sweet, friendly company calmed my high anxiety. It was good to be back in the land of smiles.

～～～

We met at the Oriental Hotel in room 619 on the following day. The meeting was typical of the Übels – orchestrated and demanding in a military fashion. Also present besides Haig was Andy Pill, aka Harley. I recognized him right off. The last time I had seen him had been ten years earlier in New York City with Mike Farell at the Waldorf-Astoria. He had been Mike's bodyguard and personal valet. After the Encounter Bay event, he had gone on the run for seven years. Now that the Übel brothers were back in action, he had become their gofer. As time went on, I was surprised to see how he accepted the brothers' abuse and degrading treatment.

I could see that he had lost a lot of hair over the years. His dark, reddish-brown hair was now slicked back, exposing his baldness. What hadn't changed were his dark, beady eyes and his handlebar mustache. At 5'9" with a growing pot belly, I always wondered why they considered him a bodyguard. I assumed his ability to endure the Übels' insults and condescending treatment kept him employed. He also lived in Thailand and was, as he claimed, unhappily married to a Thai girl – if that's even possible.

From Haig's suite, we could watch the sampans navigate the historical Chao Phraya River. He brought me up to speed on how he and his brother were making out on the two matters they had promised to handle.

"I personally took care of Jon in Indonesia," he said. "I gave him the money you gave me for him, and he'll stand by for your instructions. My brother has ejected Skip's and your data from the Bay Shore Hotel in Pattaya."

I thanked him for a job well done and began to brief him on another important issue: Minh. Even though I had already made plans to meet Minh's intimidators, my intention had been to seek help from the Übels all along.

After explaining the entire situation in detail to him, Haig folded his hands and said, "Before I can comment on this, I must speak to my brother. He's the one with connections to the Thai police and he has the relationship with the Thai triad boss here in Bangkok. We may have to set up a meeting with these people in order to calm this thing down. Obviously, we can't go forward with our project with this situation hanging over our heads."

Haig then asked Harley, who was sitting quietly near us, to fetch his cell phone and dial J.T. Harley then left to go to the bank to take advantage of the exchange rate, which had hit fifty-to-one. Haig and J.T. spoke for over 45 minutes. I could tell from what I heard on Haig's end that this was going to be complicated.

"Here's the deal," Haig said, exasperated after the exchange with his brother. "Ratner's contact here – the Old Man, as you call him – is obviously a heavy player. We might have to bring him into this dialogue in order to end the threat to Minh and our project. My brother suggested two possible scenarios. The first is that you, the Old Man, and the Bangkok godfather meet and clarify the truth so your people can return to Cambodia and end their suspicions about whether the *Oktedy* had made a drop-off in Canada. Understand that it will cost big money for my brother to engage the Bangkok godfather in this problem. So the second plan may be more attractive to you. You meet the Thai and Cambodian people and communicate the truth to them.

"You have the ability to do this. We feel that this approach can work only if you present an opportunity to earn to them. My brother suggests that you make them an offer: either you pay them a substantial amount of money to lay off of Minh or you place them in a position to earn. I personally suggest that you sit with the principles and offer them a project to work on this year. We will integrate them into our project. Obviously, they are capable of procuring a sizable load, as they proved when they loaded the *Oktedy*.

"By engaging them in a project this year, you'll accomplish two objectives: first, you'll put yourself in a position to become a man with substantial influence, and second, in this new position, you'll procure the load and direct all activities in Cambodia, which would move you into important political circles. There could be matters of historic importance developed here. From now on, you will be our man in-country – our ambassador, so to speak."

Haig paused to let this new concept sink in, and then continued.

"We, of course, will supply security for your meetings. These people are capable of killing or kidnapping you if they feel it's their only recourse. We will not let that happen."

I asked him about his contacts in Cambodia and whether this new development would interfere with their existing relationships there.

"For many years," Haig responded, "our military contracts here in Thailand have handled our procurement of product and transportation in-country, whether it was Laos, Vietnam, Cambodia, or here in Thailand. I don't have to tell you with whom we are allied. Besides the intelligence community, we are connected to powerful Thai army personnel. They are in turn connected to military personnel in other neighboring countries. You remember what we did in the *Encounter Bay* operation.

"You will become our direct contact to the Cambodian military and political powers – a position we never directly had before. I understand that Prime Minister Hun Sen was involved in the *Oktedy* project. So, you see, you're not far from some very important relationships already. Certainly, you'll be working with the provincial leaders."

"I'll call Minh and arrange a meeting," I said. "Where's a safe place to do this?"

"Right here. It's a five-star hotel with excellent security. Plus, my brother and I, along with our people, can protect you by securing the perimeter of the hotel before and during the meeting."

I had already told Minh that I would take care of this problem and would meet these Thai and Cambodian people. Now, I had the Übel brothers in my corner to help me. What I hadn't planned on was this new addition to the project. I would now have to procure the load and go into Cambodia to accomplish the task.

While in Haig's presence, I called Minh. "Sawasdee, Minh," I said. "This is Max."

"Yes, Max, I'm glad you called," Minh said. "The Thai captain was just here. I told him you would meet with him. How do you want to do this?"

"Tell him to meet me at the Oriental Hotel in Bangkok. Call me back and let me know when he can."

"I will, Max. I will call you right back. I know where he is going right now."

"Good, Minh. I'll wait for your call."

Minh called me thirty minutes later. "Max, I spoke to the captain and he doesn't want to meet you at the Oriental Hotel. He wants to know if you can meet him and his people in Pattaya."

"Hold on, Minh."

I asked Haig what he thought about meeting in Pattaya.

"Negative. That's a notorious gangster town and security there would be extremely difficult."

"Minh," I said, "a meeting in Pattaya is not safe. Ask him if he will come to Bangkok."

Minh was silent for a moment, and then said, "Max, I will call you tomorrow morning. By then, I will have a meeting place set."

"No problem. I'll wait for your call." I hung up and said to Haig, "Tomorrow, I'll have a place and time for this meeting."

"Very good!" Haig responded. "You understand my operational scenario then?"

"Yes. I'll direct the meeting into a business proposal so the people from the *Oktedy* project can earn, and I'll be the man on the ground in Cambodia."

The following day, Minh and I exchanged phone calls. We finally agreed to meet at the Dusit Thani Hotel in Bangkok.

Minh explained to me how there was going to be a problem with translation and that she was willing to attend the meeting so she could aid in our communication. "The captain speaks little English," she said. "I should be there."

"No, Minh," I said. "I don't want you involved any further."

"Max, I'm already involved. I have no choice. It is better that I am there to help you. Then there will be no mistake."

Christ, I thought, *I can't keep her away from this fucking scene.*

"All right, Minh," I said reluctantly, "but that is all you will do. After we've made an agreement, I don't want you involved anymore!"

"Yes, I understand. Tomorrow afternoon, I'll meet you at the Dusit Thani Hotel at one o'clock. The Old Man, the Thai captain, and some other people I don't know will arrive around three."

"Okay, Minh. I'll be waiting for you in the main lobby."

∼∼∼

1:00 PM: JANUARY 30, 1998

Minh arrived from Pattaya in a white Mercedes Benz. She fit in with the luxurious atmosphere that the Dusit Thani Hotel projected. Her long, shiny black hair looked beautiful. Her dark business suit made her look professional. We sat together in the library and had coffee while we talked. Her calm, distinguished manner hadn't changed. I was impressed, especially in light of the danger that she was in.

I briefed Minh as to what my plans were and how I would speak to them about the *Oktedy* and the way the operation had unfolded. I would then make them an offer that would overcome their losses from the previous year.

Minh understood and thought it was a good plan. She then surprised me by telling me how the Old Man and Bob Ratner had a bank deal going on while I was working on the *Oktedy* project. She explained how she had found out later that most of the money that was sent to her from my partners had gone into this bank fraud scheme. She described how the scam had failed and how Ratner and the Old Man had lost much of the money that had been sent to them.

After I reviewed the numbers, it was apparent that Ratner, Antacrockas, and the Old Man had stolen most of the money meant for the *Oktedy* project. I made a mental note to call my brother and have him pump Greg Antacrockas to tell the truth.

Right on time, the group of Asian men who had been threatening Minh arrived. Everyone except the Old Man was present. After what Minh had just finished telling me, it was clear that he would lose face if the truth came out. I would soon find out just how much had been taken when I asked the Thai captain how much money he had received from the Old Man and Ratner.

We all greeted each other in the main lobby so my security people could get a good look at who I was dealing with. We exchanged customary Thai greetings before we moved to the Chinese restaurant on the far end of the lobby.

Even though the Thai captain could speak some English, Minh interpreted for me. There were two other men with him, and I could see that the captain was in charge of the meeting. Minh introduced him as Captain Chin. I later discovered that he was a Royal Thai Navy captain, deployed in their intelligence division. He was tall for an Asian man – at least 5'11" with a medium build. He looked about 42 years old and had a full head of curly hair. I noticed that he had a pleasant smile, and like most Thais, perfect teeth. He spoke Thai to Minh in a low, soothing voice. He didn't seem dangerous at all. His companions, however, looked quite menacing and they rarely spoke.

The five of us sat in a private area of the relatively empty restaurant.

Minh and I sat next to each other and I faced Captain Chin. His two companions sat next to him.

I discovered many important pieces of information on that memorable day. I learned that Ratner and the Old Man had given very little money to Captain Chin to do his part of the operation – and that was why there was so much anger and animosity. I learned that Captain Chin still owed money to the Khmer Military – money that he had promised to pay them months ago. There was a Cambodian general, a colonel, a Khmer warlord, various CPP politicians, and security people in Cambodia all waiting for this Royal Thai Navy intelligence officer to return with their much-needed money.

The picture was beginning to come into focus. Ratner and the Old Man had gambled with the *Oktedy* money to do a bank fraud scheme and they had lost. Because of Captain Chin's integrity, he had been able to convince his Cambodian counterpart to work on credit. Ratner had screwed his partners over and had placed Minh in a terrible position. I would not let Ratner know that I was privy to this information – that is, not until the time was right.

Our meeting lasted seven hours. Half of this time was spent reasoning out the facts over the loss of the *Oktedy* and its cargo. It was not easy convincing these three men that the *Oktedy* had never gone to Canada, that everyone was told that the vessel would go to Canada merely for security reasons, and that it would have been a needless and severe security risk if we actually had two offload sites in two separate countries.

"There is double the exposure by offloading twice," I said. "Once is difficult enough!"

There were times when, after Minh had translated my words, the three men facing me reacted with heated responses of disbelief. But the offer to work with me again and pay cash for their cargo and services helped make the meeting a success. J.T. and Haig had been right.

We made plans to meet again. This time, I would introduce the Thai captain to J.T., and later, to Haig.

After the three men had left, Minh and I walked and talked by the tropical gardens in the hotel atrium. I thanked Minh for all that she had done for me.

"Max, you saved my life," she said.

As we walked, I had the urge to hold her hand, but knew this would insult her.

Minh volunteered to translate further. I explained that, since a joint venture had been established, J.T. could interpret now.

Minh, in her wonderful accent, said, "Max, I will be in Pattaya if you need anything – I will be there for you." She faced me when she said this. Her calm, confident expression and natural beauty created an urge in me to embrace her – and to kiss her soft lips – right then and there, but I took a deep breath and controlled my desire.

"Be careful, Minh," I said. "I'll come visit you, and after the operation is over, I'll ask you to help me find a house to buy near the sea."

Minh stood silently and maintained her sensuous eye contact. She smiled.

I was exhausted. Minh left and I returned to my suite. I called Haig from my cell phone.

"It's over," I said with relief.

"Yes. We maintained our security watch the whole time. Are you ready to be debriefed?"

"Give me an hour to shower."

"Very good. I'll meet you in the Dusit Thani's lobby. Then we'll change our location."

J.T., Haig, and Harley listened to the details of the meeting as we sat in a Japanese restaurant in Pat Pong III. Our table was by the window on the second floor of the place so that Harley could observe the street below.

"I'm impressed," J.T. said. "Soon, you'll be integrated into an area of the world that few Westerners are privy to – this is a valuable position that you're in."

"The captain wants me to come into Cambodia to have a meeting with his people," I explained.

Haig asked about the Old Man.

"When Captain Chin learned how much money had been transferred to Minh by my partners for the *Oktedy* project and how little he was given to work with, he decided to disconnect himself from the Old Tiger—as the captain referred to him," I said.

"You realize that we don't need any loose cannons here," Haig said.

"I agree. The Old Man won't be aware of our project. I'll remind Ratner that we're on a need-to-know basis, and if he wants his investment protected, he must disconnect himself from the Old Man."

I was burned out and felt as if I was coming down with something. After my seven-hour meeting, I had had to endure two hours of interrogation from the twins. I was ready to pass out.

"Contact the captain and set up a meeting for tomorrow at the Carlisle Restaurant on Silom Road in Bangkok," J.T. said. "Call me with the time he'll arrive there."

At the meeting at the Carlisle Restaurant on the following day, the captain explained that it might take a few weeks before he could bring me over to Cambodia, where he wanted me to meet his military contacts. He had some pressing Navy business to attend to. He was also the personal assistant to the King's daughter – Princess Maha Chakri Sirindhorn. Whenever she was present at large public functions, he would dress in his ceremonial whites and escort her.

J.T. was impressed. This Royal Navy captain had the pulse of all naval operations on land and sea. He also taught at the Naval Academy.

After Captain Chin left, J.T. told me the captain's prices were less than the prices that he had been paying in Cambodia, and that over the years his people kept charging more and more for the product. By then, the price they were paying was far greater than the numbers we had discussed at our meeting with the Thai captain.

We moved to the Japanese place on Pat Pong III to meet Haig to discuss the new project.

"You will no longer have to shuttle a Thai fishing boat to our private island," Haig announced. "I will be on station with my ship in the Gulf of Thailand where I will accept your load."

"The captain informed me that the Cambodian army will load us," J.T. interjected. "I wouldn't want to be in the shoes of any pirates trying to overtake these guys."

"Bring over the Bird," Haig added. "We'll still need an experienced seaman to be with the load as it's brought out of Cambodia to meet my ship."

Even though I was sick as a dog, I comprehended all the changes that were being made. "I have to go," I said. "I'm not feeling so well."

"Get some rest. I want to meet you tonight at 21:00 hours at the Crown Royal."

The Crown Royal was an upscale establishment where mostly the British community gathered. The owner was one of the famous CIA Air America guys known for their involvement in the Vietnam War. They had run covert CIA operations and had smuggled contraband in U.S. Army aircraft during the war. The brothers apparently knew them well, and had even worked with them on occasion. Haig and J.T. confided in me about missions that they had performed in Southeast Asia for the CIA. Even the *Encounter Bay* had been used at one point. I recall the time when a truckload of guns had been covertly moved over the Thai border to aid anti-Communist forces. This was an area of the world where there were no rules, only missions.

Apart from that little nugget of truth, I couldn't figure out why Haig had invited me to come in the first place. We just ate at the posh place and then went home.

The world that I was entering was rife with history of genocide, political unrest, and military hostilities. Perhaps, at some point, I would be asked to aid the American intelligence community, just like Haig and J.T. Maybe my legal problems would be forgotten if I were to help the U.S. military in this volatile region of Southeast Asia.

Perhaps no country on Earth had suffered as brutally from as many forms of conflict over the past 30 years as Cambodia had: civil wars, border wars, massive bombardment via a superpower's B-52s, genocide unparalleled in its savagery that eliminated a full seventh of the country's population. How could this happen to a former great empire, where extraordinary temples like Angkor still remained as proof of its once-glorious culture?

It was now 1998, and according to the Cambodian guidebook and the Thai newspapers that I had read, Cambodia was one of the most dangerous places on Earth. At the time, it was not uncommon for the remaining Khmer Rouge guerrillas to launch 82-mm mortars and rocket-propelled grenades into Cambodian villages. In one attack, 46 Cambodians were slaughtered in their village by Khmer Rouge marauders in Battembang. Inhabitants in these attacks were usually marched off into the woods and bludgeoned to death as the guerrillas chose to save their bullets for the Cambodian army.

There are millions of landmines still buried throughout Cambodia, waiting for an innocent victim. Children are often killed by these landmines when they are playing by the roadside or working in the fields.

Many of Pol Pot's victims who survived his genocide roam Phnom Penh like zombies, some hideously disfigured, and nearly all penniless.

If only my family and friends knew what kind of a place I was going to be doing business in.

I started to get that sick feeling in my throat, chest, and stomach. I would be in the Cambodian jungle, surrounded by ex-Khmer Rouge soldiers who were now Cambodian soldiers. Because of the upcoming election, I would be exposed to the most chaotic and menacing environment since the Pol Pot regime. To make matters even more foreboding, I would have to trust people who had only recently wanted to kill Minh and me and anyone else connected to the *Oktedy* mission.

Now I had to cross the border without a passport and convince these malevolent Cambodians that the last project was a total loss and that I had returned to try another.

~ ~ ~

That night, while wracked by my mounting flu, my dreams were fearful, disjointed, and delusional. I was afraid, alone, and confused. *Where is my family? Where am I?* The sheets were soaked with my sweat.

The next day, I tried to eat, but nothing stayed in my stomach long enough to energize my body. I felt weak and lightheaded.

Harley called. "Hey! You all right?"

"No," I said. "I'm all fucked up. If I'm not better tomorrow, I'll go to the hospital."

"I just called to let you know that I'll be with Haig at the Crown from 17:00 hours on."

"Thanks. If I have the energy, I'll stop by."

Late that afternoon, the maids arrived to remake my bed. I didn't want to wreck it again, so I showered and left for the Crown Royal.

I entered the room and noticed the women – each of them sleek and well-dressed with sexy bodies, perfect hair, and adorable smiles. Their sensuous eyes pulled me in. I spotted Haig and Harley in the center booth. They had a girl named Eon and another girl between them. They moved to welcome me and it felt good to be around people.

Haig and Harley were already half-smashed. Eon brought me a Singha and walked away. I saw her speaking to a girl that I had never seen before. It was hard for me to see her at first. Then, suddenly, a tunnel was formed in the crowd and there she was – this Thai Aphrodite was staring right at me with her devouring eyes.

Eon returned and said, "My girlfriend wants to meet you."

I never took my eyes off this incredibly beautiful girl as I nodded. Eon spoke to her, and slowly, this vision walked toward me. If beauty were illegal, this woman was manslaughter. Her tan skin, lustrous hair, and curvy, tight body moved slowly in my direction. Her seductive eyes, prominent forehead, and sexy, full lips made my heart pound with anticipation. I stood up and she extended her soft hand. We sat next to each other.

Eon delivered two cognacs for us. Haig, Harley, and their companions were being loud and obnoxious while I asked in a low voice what this unusual woman's name was.

"My name is Ahm," she said while maintaining sensual eye contact with me.

Her voice . . . I wanted to hear this soft, mellifluous sound that came from within her again. "My name is Max," I said.

Ahm was breathtaking. The crowd around us, our friends at our booth –

everyone disappeared in this moment. Only the music playing remained as I absorbed Ahm's presence.

"Mac, you not feel good?" she asked as she placed her hand over mine. I wanted to tell her never to leave my side. We spoke in such low tones – her voice was like that of the ancient sirens, drawing me into her. I don't know how long we remained in this trance. We spoke, we held hands. Her delicate face was not exactly oriental, but carried an exotic, unique loveliness – it was ethnic-less, a beauty beyond description.

I was angry at myself for not feeling well. Ahm wiped my forehead with a cool towel as Haig watched the two of us. He knew me well enough to know how I felt about this woman beside me. My fever was coming on strong now, and I had to lie down.

"I have to go now," I said.

"Ahm," Eon said, "take Max home."

They spoke Thai to each other as Ahm stood up to leave with me. I was weak. Outside, Ahm held my arm and flagged down a taxi. I slumped down in the rear seat as my beautiful new companion held me close to her. She wiped my forehead and ran her soft fingers through my hair. She spoke Thai to the driver as he drove.

"Wait, Mac," she said to me. "I bring you medicine."

The taxi stopped in front of a pharmacy.

Ahm returned to the taxi with a small bag. "You very sick, Mac!" she said as we headed to my apartment. Once inside, she gave me a half-dozen pills to take. "You get in bed now," she said. Then she removed my clothes.

I had the chills, and Ahm covered me with blankets. Only a dim light was on, but I could see and feel her presence in the room.

As time passed, I began to burn with a high fever. Ahm sat next to me on the bed and wiped my hot skin with a cool towel. When I shook with chills, she covered me.

This was my worst night with the Asian virus so far, and Ahm never left my side. I would awake from the heat to find her cooling my chest with a cool towel. I reached out to hold her.

"Don't worry, Mac. I no leave you," she said, leaning forward to kiss me.

The sun was up when I awoke. I heard Ahm in the kitchen. She was cleaning the dishes in the sink. My fever had broken, so I tried to stand up and realized how dizzy I was.

Ahm walked into the bedroom. "Mac, sit down," she said. "I get medicine."

I sat on the bed as she fed me the multi-colored pills.

"Mac, I have fruit for you." She had sliced up some pineapple and banana.

We sat next to each other as I ate.

"I'm sorry I'm so sick," I said.

"Later, you no better, I take you to hospital. You farang. You not ready to eat and drink water in Bangkok. You muss be careful, Mac."

My cell phone rang and Ahm answered. I heard her say, "No, he cannot see you now. He sick. Call tonight after he rest." After hanging up, she told me in an annoyed voice, "That Harley."

She's already protecting me, I thought.

By late afternoon, I was feeling much better. I had slept most of the day. Ahm never left me. We were now sitting on the veranda, only three stories up. The sun was setting and the Bangkok lights were starting to outline the shape of this sprawling city.

Ahm smiled when she saw me move with more energy. My strength was returning. That's when I noticed her incredible smile.

"Thank you, Ahm, for taking care of me," I said.

Ahm spoke to me with her melodious voice. "Mac, I no want to leave you, but my mother take care of my son and daughter, and tonight my mother go to her friend house, so I have to go."

"You're married?" I asked, afraid to hear the answer.

"No, my husband die. I not married."

I was relieved to hear that she was single. We stood close to each other. I remembered her soft lips when she kissed me during the night. We embraced, our breathing quickening as we held each other. Her firm, shapely body formed a perfect fit into mine.

"When can I see you again?" I asked.

Composed, Ahm looked at me before she answered. "Tomorrow, come to Crown. I wait for you."

Soon, she was gone and only her sweet fragrance and the memory of her alluring voice remained.

I stayed in my apartment that night. I slept well and kept taking the medicine that Ahm had given me.

The following day, I felt better and left for the Crown Royal. I called Haig and Harley answered. "Haig had to leave town with J.T.," he said. "I'll meet you at the Crown."

"I'm on my way," I said.

"I'd like to move you to a new apartment," Harley said when I'd arrived at the Crown. "It's closer to where we will be holding our meetings. I'm sure you have better things to do than sit in traffic."

"Sure. When do I move?" I asked.

"In a couple of days, I'll have everything ready."

Since it didn't take long to speak to Harley, I spent the afternoon at the Crown with Ahm.

Ahm introduced me to some of her friends who also worked at the Crown Royal. This was a busy place. Ex-pats from all over the world frequented the Crown and the hostesses that served drinks and waited tables there did well.

Days passed and Ahm and I quickly became close.

At the Crown, we sat alone in one of the booths. I loved her sense of humor. Her eyes glowed and her smile was adorable. A tiny dimple in her cheek appeared when her face lit up. Ahm's lashes were impossibly long and thick. Her big, brown, almond-shaped eyes and her carefully-shaped lips, the color of crimson, begged for kisses. When she slowly touched her tongue to her lips, my heart skipped a beat. Ahm's lustrous, dark hair flowed over her shoulders like a black, cascading waterfall.

I told Ahm about my family in America, about my three daughters, and my crazy marriage. She listened and stayed near me. Evenings, we dined out and returned to my apartment. Ahm and I would kiss, hold, touch, and absorb each other for hours.

"Wait, Mac. We make love later," she would say in her gentle voice.

I couldn't get enough of her. I loved her warm, full lips. Virginia and I never kissed, and now I was with a beautiful girl who loved to kiss me.

Ahm helped me to move into the Omni Serviced Apartment Complex. This was a 20-story granite building that was only a year old. The place was outrageous, and had a new gym, pool, elegant furniture, carpets, and fixtures. There was a large master bedroom with a walk-in closet, bathroom, kitchen, and a large living room.

The nearby Nana Plaza was shaped like a horseshoe and, when standing inside, you could hear the thunderous rock 'n' roll music pounding out of the doors from the nearby bars and clubs.

Ahm was a great help to me. She folded and hung my clothes and neatly placed everything where it belonged. She laid my family photo album on the nightstand next to my bed.

"Here, Ahm," I said. "Look!"

We sat side by side on the bed and I showed her the photographs inside. I pointed out each of my daughters.

She carefully looked at each photo and studied them as if she was searching for something in particular. "What her name? How old she? Where picture taken?" She wanted to know everything about my family. She silently looked at the photo of Virginia.

We checked out the new neighborhood. There were many restaurants, clubs, and stores. Everything I needed was within walking distance. We found an upscale Italian restaurant where we dined by candlelight and drank red wine. I was admiring Ahm's beauty and her sensuous serenity. I was free-falling in love.

Ahm reached over to my hand and held me, saying, "Come, Mac. I want to make love to you."

"Waiter, check please!"

Ahm laughed at my comic gesture. Then we practically ran back to the Omni.

We showered together, and our slippery, soap-covered bodies became one. Ahm slowly lathered my chest, and then worked her way down. She knelt before me and washed my legs and feet. I let out a groan when Ahm applied just the right pressure as she surrounded my manhood with her lips. Her hands slid over my soapy body.

She pulled me into her. When she moaned, I couldn't hold back any longer. I closed my eyes and saw flashing lights. My legs wobbled and I had to hold onto the showerhead to steady myself.

Slowly, I withdrew.

Ahm smiled, "Ah, Mac. You like?"

I lifted her to her feet. "Oh, Ahm, I like a lot."

Ahm dried me with a big, soft towel in the candlelit bathroom. There was a large mirror over the granite walls and I couldn't help but stare at our reflection as we embraced facing the mirror. Our naked bodies looked so natural together.

Seeing this ultra-feminine Asian girl in my arms with her long black hair and baby-doll eyes took my breath away.

Ahm had turned down the blankets on our bed in the luxurious master bedroom. After she lit more candles, she slowly moved in next to me on the soft bed. We lay facing each other, touching and kissing. Sliding my palm over her hip and thigh, I was again amazed at how silky-smooth she was. I drifted my hand over her firm, shapely butt as she moaned. Her full, firm breasts were pressed against my chest. We consumed each other with our mouths. Our lips and tongues were one as we explored each other in ecstasy. Ahm straddled me as we were locked in a deep kiss. I then took her plush lower lip between my teeth as I felt her soft hand guide me in a second time. She gasped.

Ahm's voice became an aphrodisiac. Her face was in a state of passion, her eyes half-closed. Her hair flowed over her face like feathery satin.

As I held her hips in my hands, Ahm ground herself into me and we went over the edge together. She buried her face in the nape of my neck while we recovered, her lips softly kissing me, causing a tingling sensation.

Ahm raised her head. Her hair enclosed our faces in a tent of fragrant, feathery softness. Our eyes were inches apart.

She whispered, "Mac, please no leave me."

I couldn't help kissing her all over her adorable face. In between kisses, I whispered, "Leave you? I want to be with you forever."

Ahm's smile was slow and sweet. It lit her face as she softly ran her fingers through my hair.

"Oh, Mac, you make me so happy."

Ahm and I stayed in our new home for days, leaving only to eat a light meal, and then returning to make love. I had convinced her to stop working so we could spend more time together. Her mother was watching Ahm's children, as is the custom in Thailand. However, Ahm would rise at 5:00 AM to be at her mother's house to get her four-year-old son ready for school, and then return a couple of hours later. She would wake me in her special way.

"Darling, okay I wake you up like this?"

I responded by wrapping my arms around her warm little body and making sensuous love to her.

"Maybe I wake you up like that, too," I whispered.

"Ah, Mac, I go sleep right now, and then you try. Okay?"

We laughed hard.

Ahm placed her soft, warm hand on the side of my face as we lay next to each other. "You so handsome, Mac," she said. "I look at you when you sleep, and I feel . . . mmm, my man handsome."

Time passed, and Ahm became an important part of my life. Her wisdom and experience helped me. The damage to my soul from my dissonant and harsh marriage to Virginia was being repaired by this lovely, perceptive woman.

One rainy afternoon, I sat by the open window in the living room. My brother had called me and informed me of the problems we were having controlling the *Oktedy* crew. He had explained how the amount of money we needed was growing.

"Can Sam and Bob chip in any money toward the project?" he asked in frustration.

"You know how they are," I replied. "They never invest their own money. Now that Mike is gone, forget it." We signed off.

I remained sitting by the open window while the sound of the late afternoon rain danced beside me. I was holding my head in my hands with my elbows resting on my knees. Ahm walked into the room and saw me sitting in this defeated position. She startled me when she suddenly spoke sharply.

"Hey! What you doing? Why you be like that? Come on, don't do like this. You can fix problem, Mac!" She pushed my shoulders back and straightened me upright. "You don't do that! You are . . . you are . . . strong!" Ahm was at a loss for the right English words.

I reached out to her and pulled her into my arms. A surge shot through me as I held her. "I love you, Ahm," I said.

She fell silent as tears formed in her big brown eyes. Her long, dark hair was partially in her face and covered her trembling lips. She looked into my eyes and said, "I love you too, Mac. I love you forever." Her voice carried a child-like quiver.

We held each other as we listened to the warm rain falling outside our window.

Ahm witnessed what I was going through. I would return from my meetings with J.T. and Haig feeling upset because they refused to help fund the new project. This left the entire burden on my partners and I even though they knew that we had just suffered a major setback. Haig would sit in his big armchair and preach.

"If you want to overcome the *Oktedy* loss, you have to come up with the cash," he would say.

When I reminded him that he had offered to help finance our project during our meeting in New York City, he claimed that I must have misunderstood him. There were four of us there. We couldn't all have misunderstood him.

I never told Ahm what dangers I was facing.

"What you doing, Mac?" she would ask when she saw me worried and troubled over the task ahead. "Come on, Superman. Smile. Smile, Superman!" Ahm would say in her sing-song voice, bringing me up out of my pain.

Ahm was a good mother and I felt bad that I was keeping her away from her son and daughter. She explained to me how, in Thailand, the grandmothers helped raise their grandchildren and how she helped support her mother. This was how Thailand's social security system worked.

I asked Ahm if she would like to have her children spend time with us at the Omni. I had met her mother, sisters, and children by that point and I felt close to all of them. Her father had died some time ago.

"Are you sure, Mac?" she asked. "Maybe children give you headache?"

"Let's give it a try," I said.

Ahm and her sister Eng helped me learn how to speak Thai. Their care and tenderness moved me, and the void in my heart was filled.

We spent most of our free time at the Omni. There was no reason to fight the traffic jams. Everything we needed was within walking distance.

Alone in the crystal-clear pool, we kissed and held each other. I couldn't get enough of her.

"Ahm, are you sure you love me?" I asked. "I mean . . . do you really, really love me?" I just couldn't believe this 23-year-old Asian beauty would fall in love with a 45-year-old American man. She could have had any man she wanted.

Ahm looked up and shook her head slowly, seemingly lost for words. "Mac, I . . . I love you . . . as big as sky," Ahm said so emotionally that her lips trembled. Tears filled her big brown eyes. "I never leave you, Mac. Never."

Ahm displayed a respect for my family in America as well.

"Did you call your daughters?" she would say to me. "Don't forget Ali's birthday coming soon. Buy her something and send it."

What confused me was Ahm's concern for Virginia.

"Don't forget your wife in New York, Mac. She is number one wife."

I patiently explained the pain that I had endured for so many years while being married to Virginia.

Ahm listened carefully and placed her hand alongside my face and said, "Mac, you cannot forget her."

Chapter 23

THE intensity of my business meetings increased as my departure date for Cambodia neared. Haig, J.T., Harley, Captain Chin, and I spent hours at each meeting. The Übel brothers were causing havoc through their constant manipulation of the deal. The brothers wouldn't spend a dime on the operation and now they were demanding that I raise more money to buy a larger load. They even tried to convince me to do a load of heroin, but I quickly rejected that offer. After twenty years of staying away from people who worked in "synthetics," as I called it, I would not start now.

J.T. spoke to Captain Chin about the political and military personnel involved in our operation. Apparently, Captain Chin was highly connected. He informed us that I would be able to cross the border and meet his Cambodian contacts just after the annual Songkran water ceremony held in April.

We would then sit down and plan our operation to move 40,000 pounds of herb from the Cambodian mountains to a point off the coastal waters of Cambodia in the Gulf of Thailand.

After one such meeting, where I had to argue and attempt to reason with the Übel brothers, I returned to the Omni. Ahm greeted me at the door, where I always removed my shoes.

"Darling, you look tired. Lie down. I make tea," she said as she combed my hair with her fingers. "Come on, Superman. Smile. Come on, smile, Superman."

I told Ahm that I had to go away and that I would be back in a couple of days.

"Where you going?" she asked.

"Chiang Mai. I need to look at a property to buy for a hotel I want to build."

"Okay, I go with you. I help you."

"Not this time, Ahm. Stay here with your family. I'll call you every night if I can."

Ahm was silent. She wanted to take care of her man.

We would float weightless in the Omni pool and hug and kiss for hours. Ahm would tell me about her life, her thoughts, and her dreams. She would say in her sweet voice out of the blue, "I love you, darling." I would say, "I love you, too, sweetheart."

At night, we sometimes went out to the clubs down the street. Men would always look at Ahm. She was incredibly sexy. One night, we stood in front of a pub and waited for a sidewalk vendor to prepare some pineapple for us. I went inside the pub to buy a Singha to drink outside. From inside the pub, I could clearly see Ahm through the front window.

Suddenly, a group of foreigners noticed her. They didn't know that I was with her. They all turned and went nuts when they saw this Asian angel. One of them said, "Oh my God! Look at that girl out there!" Another said, "Holy shit! Look at her!" This group of guys already had girlfriends with them, but they were just taken by Ahm's unusual beauty.

I turned to look at them with their mouths open as Ahm and I walked away, hand in hand.

Ahm and I hit the clubs at Nana Plaza. We drank and watched the sexy go-go girls perform. The music was hot and the cognac was smooth.

At the Omni, we made passionate love. We would doze off, wake up, make love again, and then doze off with our bodies intertwined. I loved how we slept with our bodies so close together, with her face and lips near mine. If we weren't in the gym working out or in the pool, we were making love. Ahm and I were turned on 24 hours a day.

The morning of my departure to Cambodia, Ahm made breakfast and even had my toothbrush ready with toothpaste carefully applied to the bristles. She didn't want me to go.

"I promise, sweetheart," I said. "I'll be back in a couple of days. Don't worry. I'm only going to Chiang Mai to look at land." I couldn't bear to tell her that I'd be crossing the border into one of the world's most dangerous countries. I couldn't tell her that I had to meet with angry Khmer military commanders and reorganize a new covert operation with them to move tons of herb from landmine-infested jungles to the Gulf of Thailand and then transport the cargo through pirate-occupied waters to our waiting ship.

Ahm cried as we held each other.

∼∼∼

APRIL 16, 1998

Captain Chin was waiting in front of the Omni to pick me up for our journey into Cambodia. We would drive to Klong Yai, a small fishing village on the border, stay overnight there, and then proceed through the final checkpoint early the following morning.

Captain Chin instructed me to use the name "Joe Harding" while in Cambodia. "If anything happens to you," he explained, "our people in Phnom Penh will know it's you and they'll help us."

The closer we got to Cambodia, the more mountainous and dense the jungle became. It took us nearly five hours to reach our destination.

Just before we reached Klong Yai, Captain Chin pointed out a Red Cross station. "Here is where thousands of refugees died of disease and injury during the war," he said.

I could see a memorial at the entrance.

Early the following morning, Captain Chin received the call from the Cambodian general's assistant.

"We cleared to go now, Joe," he said in his heavy Thai accent. "First, we have meeting on the Thai side of border. Then, if everybody agree, we cross border. You no need passport. We take care of that."

Within walking distance to the border checkpoint was a shantytown market-place. The haphazardly-built booths, where food and old collectibles could be purchased, lined the sloping, narrow, dirt path down to the Gulf of Thailand. Bear paws, tiger skins, ivory, and many other endangered and illegal items were for sale here. I was the only Westerner and, as such, I attracted a lot of attention from the sellers.

Our meeting would be held in a restaurant at the end of the sloping market-place along the Gulf of Thailand. In the corner of the open-air restaurant was a long table where three uniformed men sat. Standing around them were six soldiers who appeared to be bodyguards. As Captain Chin and I approached the group, the standing soldiers saluted us and then the three seated officers stood up and shook our hands. Captain Chin and I took seats opposite them. Seated on the left was the Navy commander, Nun, who was responsible for all Cambodian waters both inland and at sea. He was a middle-aged, heavyset Cambodian with an angry scowl on his rough, pockmarked face. He wore a light tan uniform with many Navy medals placed across the left side of his chest. To the far right was the police commander. He was a thin, dark-eyed, spooky kind of guy who stared at me. His name was Colonel Tu and he wore a dark-blue police uniform. I noticed his empty holster.

In the center sat Colonel Sacor. He was a handsome, friendly-looking man in his mid-forties. He wore an olive-drab army officer's uniform. He also had an empty holster on his hip.

The five of us talked and drank Mekong whisky and Singha while the bodyguards stood nearby, noticeably nervous. Captain Chin spoke Khmer and translated to me. I could tell that Colonel Sacor was a personal friend of Captain Chin. He seemed to enjoy my company. Nun and Tu projected more menacing personas. They sat in relative silence, seemingly trying to determine if I was an American undercover agent or a real American marijuana trader.

Colonel Sacor said through Captain Chin, "You are the first Westerner to cross this border since last year. Before that, it was a journalist many years ago."

Captain Chin went on to explain, "Not even Bob Ratner went where you will be going when he came to Cambodia. Ratner only saw a sample that was brought to the border. You will go into areas that no Westerner has ever gone to meet people that no Westerner has ever met."

I nodded affirmatively and smiled.

"Sacor say you have honest face," Chin said. "He will forget last year's problem."

I handed out Partagas cigars to all the men at the table. Even Nun and Tu smiled at my offer. We toasted each other and drank until Colonel Sacor decided it was time to leave.

"He wants you to come now to Cambodia and meet the Major General," Captain Chin explained.

We all walked to the border crossing where Thai and Cambodian soldiers manned the gate. A Thai army Jeep with a 50-caliber machine gun was parked next to the entrance.

The guards saluted us and we crossed over without showing any identification. Just across the border was a long wooden bench where Nun, Tu, and Sacor stopped to fill their holsters with their firearms. Our newly heavily-armed group of soldiers and I drove in four Jeeps to Colonel Sacor's home, approximately ten miles from the Thai border.

Cambodia was nothing like Thailand. I took close notice of my surroundings as our Jeeps sped over dirt roads. I was fascinated by the rural Khmer life around me – Cambodia was very much an impoverished third-world country.

At Colonel Sacor's lavish home, I was escorted inside and felt impressed at how clean and spacious it was. I was introduced to his wife, who held a one-year-old baby in her arms. There were others whom I assumed were family members. We sat down in the living room on a polished wood floor covered by straw mats. There, we discussed our plans further. Nun and Tu had gone ahead, and only a few guards stood to the side in Sacor's living room as we talked.

Captain Chin interpreted for us as we discussed my plans to invest in the rebuilding of Cambodia and the advancement of its people after the operation. We spoke for over an hour and sipped green tea. Captain Chin interpreted for me.

"Colonel Sacor said that, here in Cambodia, you are worth twelve cents per pound. That's the cost of dog food. If we thought that you lied to us, it would already be too late for you."

"America and Cambodia are very different," I said. "In my country, dogs are man's best friends. Here, man is a dog's best meal."

Colonel Sacor and Captain Chin both laughed at my response.

Colonel Sacor signaled an aide for his radio as his hearty laughter trailed off. Captain Chin explained that we would depart to meet Major General Hopp.

When we stepped outside of Colonel Sacor's home, I was surprised to see that the number of heavily-armed Khmer soldiers had grown. There were at least 25 uniformed soldiers surrounding us as Captain Chin, Colonel Sacor, and I walked a short distance to the Cambodian town of Koh Khong.

It became apparent to me that this was an important day when our squadron of soldiers rendezvoused with another group of armed, uniformed Khmer soldiers on a hill overlooking the town of Koh Khong. Our troops doubled in number, and Colonel Sacor's lieutenant brought the men into a marching formation so that half of the soldiers were behind me while the other half were in front of me.

Captain Chin was to my left and Colonel Sacor was to my right. Someone behind me gave orders in Khmer, and the procession of soldiers moved forward toward the main street of Koh Khong.

People came running out of their homes and businesses to see what was happening. Children looked on with expressions of wonderment as they witnessed their first Westerner, and then ran along with the parade in excitement. It was a strange feeling being so high-profile. I felt uneasy about it. Before me, I could see the end of the main street. There, I saw docks and boats lined up at the base on the half-mile-wide river. Many people gathered around this commercial dock area. The glare from the sun reflected off the water and made it shimmer like diamonds. Unconsciously, I found myself stepping to the cadence of the soldiers around me.

Someone in the squadron gave an order, and soldiers peeled off from the column and manned several waiting, motorized longboats. Captain Chin instructed me to board the colorfully-painted boat before me. Several soldiers boarded with Colonel Sacor, Captain Chin, and I. The other soldiers boarded different boats. The townspeople were excited, and there was a festive energy around us as the boats moved off the docks and into the vast, fast-moving river.

I had to yell to be heard. "What's the name of this river?" I asked Captain Chin as our flotilla motored across the choppy, churning waterway.

"It is called the Kon Kret River," he yelled back.

"What does that mean in English?"

"It roughly translates to 'South of the Thunder' River! We're on our way to an island called Sow Tong to meet the Major General!"

The South of the Thunder River flowed into the Gulf of Thailand, which then led into the South China Sea, and which in turn led into the Pacific Ocean. This part of Cambodia was an important seaport area as it linked poor Cambodia with the rest of the world. I could see many Khmer longboats packed with Cambodians wearing conical hats. It looked like these long, narrow, wooden boats were used to transport cargo as well as people. I also noticed traditional Thai or Southwest Asian fishing boats with their high bows and heavy beam construction.

All around our motorboat were similar boats loaded with Colonel Sacor's soldiers. The blue sky reflected off of the choppy water. I could see thatched huts built on stilts along the water's edge and groups of small homes on the hillsides. Before us was a group of stone buildings with Mansard roofs and large, commercial, Asian-style fishing trawlers docked in front.

Our marine fleet of soldiers disembarked at a concrete landing, where Khmer boys ran to help tie our ropes to the pier.

Colonel Sacor, Captain Chin, and I were swarmed by soldiers as we walked side by side up the inclining shoreline toward the complex of old, stone, commercial buildings, which were located directly on the water's edge.

As we got closer, I saw that we were heading for a restaurant that sat between the buildings. We waited outside for a moment as a half-dozen of our soldiers entered the large banquet room to secure the place for our entry. Colonel Sacor's men signaled that it was safe to proceed.

I noticed a long table in the center of the room set up with glasses, flatware, flowers, and a tablecloth. The table was about 40 feet long. Chairs surrounded it in a neat, evenly-spaced manner.

I was asked to sit at the table next to the head seat. I faced Captain Chin, and Colonel Sacor sat to my right. The head seat was to my left.

A waiter brought a bottle of cognac and poured drinks for Captain Chin, Colonel Sacor, and I.

The table was filled with soldiers. The higher their rank, the closer to us they sat. At the far end of the table were the younger privates, who seemed very happy to be a part of the event.

"Major General Hopp will be here soon," Captain Chin said. "He also speaks English. But speak slowly, like you do with me. He is out of practice."

Suddenly, a rush of air and a whooshing sound attracted my attention. I quickly looked to my far right where the commotion was coming from. There, I saw unfamiliar soldiers entering the room. Behind them walked a distinguished 60-year-old man in an officer's uniform. He was closely guarded by his men. I was swept up into the crowd of soldiers around me as I stood to walk and greet Major General Hopp.

Remembering my Asian manners and customs, I first gave the general a high wai, showing respect for my elder. With my head slightly bowed, I said a Khmer greeting, "June thrip sool."

The soldiers all sighed in relief, while some laughter and clapping could be heard in response to my correctness.

The general responded with a return wai and a Western-style handshake.

I said to him in English, "It is an honor to meet you."

He responded with a Khmer accent. "It is my pleasure to finally meet you."

Together, we walked over to the banquet table. Everyone stood at their places and waited for the general to sit down. Now, there were many soldiers standing on guard around the table and the perimeter of the room. We were under constant protection. Even later, when I went to take a piss, I was escorted by two soldiers carrying AK-47s.

Cambodian food was served, and we all drank plenty of alcohol. Captain Chin, Colonel Sacor, Major General Hopp, and I spoke about the new Cambodia. They hoped that I would be the one to help change the way of life in this war-torn, rural part of the country by supplying jobs through companies that we would start in the poorest areas.

"Now that Hun Sen is Prime Minister, we can prosper," the general said with a confident smile spread across his handsome face. Moments later, General Hopp stood up and held a glass of cognac up in the air before him. He spoke first in Khmer and then in English, saying, "I welcome and give my support to my new American friend."

I then stood up, toasted him, and drank the smooth cognac as the room full of soldiers roared and clapped to our show of friendship and solidarity.

Outside, through a large picture window that lined the walls of the banquet room, a long procession of military vessels could be seen drifting down the river. The general pointed them out to me, clearly proud of this show of military might.

When we'd had our fill of the scene, I handed a gift-wrapped box of XO cognac to the general, and shortly after, he departed with the same beehive activity and seriousness as when he had arrived. After a lot of saluting and hand-shaking, the meeting was complete. We returned to Koh Khong.

Colonel Sacor was delighted with the outcome of our day. Captain Chin interpreted for me as the colonel said, "You have the full support of our military. After you meet Di-Mai – the Khmer warlord and the provincial governor – we can set a date to finalize our operation."

~ ~ ~

I was bushed when I finally returned to the Omni in Bangkok. It was early evening when Ahm's mother, her sister Eng, and the children greeted me with warm and smiling faces. Ahm was quiet and emotional. After I removed my shoes, she hugged me and walked me into the master bedroom.

"Take shower, Mac," she said, removing my clothes and turning on the shower. She quickly removed her own clothes and stepped into the warm shower with me. "Mac, I worry 'bout you. I scared you have accident."

Ahm spoke in a sweet, caring voice as she held me close. After she had washed me, we made love in the shower. Our passion couldn't wait.

Ahm's love and care was powerful medicine. I felt calm now after my tense journey.

She laid out fresh clothes for me on the bed, then buttoned up my shirt and finished dressing me. "I love you, darling," she said in her sweet voice as she carefully combed my hair.

We rejoined her family. Ahm's mom and sister had home-cooked Thai food waiting for us on the table. Everyone treated me like I was family. It touched my heart and I loved them all for what they were doing for me.

Viewing the room, I noticed the freshly-cut orchids in a glass bowl of water that Ahm had set on the table. Next to them was a copy of the Bangkok newspaper. In the corner of the room was a small shrine with a golden Buddha seated in a lotus position, with candles, flowers, and incense all around. By the front door, the rows of shoes were neatly lined up.

The following morning, J.T. and Haig questioned Captain Chin and I in greater detail about who we were aligning ourselves with in Cambodia. I understood why they were asking. I knew that these questions were not just to satisfy their curiosity. Haig and J.T. had ulterior motives. I knew by now that they had CIA connections who would owe them big favors for this information.

This was a very important conversation for J.T. and Haig because Cambodia's most important election in its modern history was only months away. The United States government despised Prime Minister Hun Sen and had openly said so. Reports of political killings were rampant in Cambodia at this time, and the U.S. government wanted to bring Hun Sen to trial for numerous crimes. My only concern was moving this load out of Cambodia.

At one point, Haig said, "Get the Bird over here! We can't wait for him forever."

This was the first time he had asked me to send for the Bird from America, but he made it sound as if he had asked me many times before.

These guys are going crazy, I thought as I made arrangements to bring the Bird over.

Captain Chin informed me that our next trip into Cambodia to meet the provincial governor and the Khmer warlord would be in about a week. I was ready, and the Übel brothers indicated that they were also in position to move.

Ahm and I had developed a kind of telepathic closeness. She could tell when I was feeling troubled or crazed from my meetings. I was now waiting for the Bird to arrive and for Captain Chin to arrange our next journey across the border when, after breakfast, Ahm asked, "Would you like to go with me to the Buddhist temple?"

"Sure," I said, and we headed out of town to a small temple on a hill not far from Bangkok. At the temple, Ahm walked me through the different stages of meditation and prayer in the ornately-decorated rooms. She showed me the different rituals of lighting incense, picking sticks with numbers and characters, and locating small, paper cards with our fortunes and advice printed on them. We meditated before beautiful Buddha statues. Afterwards, we lit fireworks in a special place outside to oust any bad spirits we may have possessed.

My anxiety waned when my fortune said that success was in my near future.

Ahm and I sat close together on a hand-chiseled stone bench. The monk supplied Ahm with special, colorful strings and she slowly weaved them around my wrist and tied a knot.

"There," she said. "This will bring you good luck." She then became still. She placed her delicate hand on the side of my face. "I will love you forever, Mac."

Chapter 24

IT was early April of 1998. The Bird had arrived and was having the greatest time of his life. He stayed in the NaNa Hotel which was located about a hundred feet from the NaNa Plaza and hundreds of beautiful, fun-loving Thai girls. Ahm and I called the Bird "Mickey." His light and happy personality was a pleasure to be around, and Ahm and the children enjoyed him when he came to visit us at the Omni. We would all go out to dinner together and laugh all night.

Mickey, of course, fell in love with a different Thai girl every other day, and Ahm and I tried to help him choose the right girl. This tall, blonde-haired, Key West boatman was not the romantic type. Ahm and I would crack up when, again and again, he would say the most hilarious things to girls he wanted to go out with.

"Why can't I find a girl like Ahm!" the Bird said. "I love her looks and . . . " He stopped and began to blush as he remembered that Ahm and I were really close. When it came to girls, he became soft in the head as I'm sure any guy would be on his first trip to Thailand. I had not been an exception.

Eventually, the green light was given to enter Cambodia again to meet the provincial governor and the Khmer warlord.

The night before my departure, Ahm was very quiet and tearful. She had all the clothes and items I needed ready for me.

"Mac, what you doing?" she asked as she held my face in her hands, trying to read my eyes. "You no go to Chiang Mai. I see you with soldier and I hear you talk to Bob and Mickey. Mac, please let me go with you. I help you. I take care you."

I just couldn't take her with me – not when I was working in Cambodia. Maybe to Klong Yai, the small Thai fishing village on the border, but not this time. This time, I had to go alone.

The journey to Klong Yai took five hours. Chin and I checked into the same hotel we had used on our first visit. I collapsed onto the hard bed and faced the slow-moving, wobbly ceiling fan, as I cursed myself for having a fever again. Captain Chin thought I might have malaria because I became sick so often. Whatever it was, it was bad and wearing me down.

The following morning, we left the hotel in Klong Yai to cross the border by boat. Two soldiers picked us up and took us to meet Colonel Sacor and Colonel Tu at Colonel Sacor's home. From there, we traveled over dusty dirt roads for approximately five miles. En route, it became clear to me why the buffalo was an important animal here. The people who lived in this rural area used these massive animals to pull large wagons, plow fields, and move logs. I didn't see one tractor.

"First we meet Di Mai, the Khmer warlord," Captain Chin explained. "Then we meet general who is provincial governor to make final agreement. If you no like cargo, we no work. We all go home."

Our two green Jeeps slowly pulled into a lightly-wooded area along the South of the Thunder River. Next to the shaded trees where we parked was a small Buddhist temple. A long set of concrete steps cascaded down from the temple to the concrete boat landing with a red-tiled awning.

This landing was about 150 feet away from the small temple on the hill. After we parked in the shade, Sacor, Chin, our three bodyguards, and I slowly walked up to the temple entrance. Everybody removed their guns and their boots before entering the old temple to pray for good luck. One of the soldiers stayed outside to watch the weapons until another soldier replaced him. I took off my own boots and entered behind them.

An old Khmer monk stood on a scaffold, painting the walls and ceilings in this quiet, incense-filled room. The story of the Pol Pot years was being told through his artwork. Colonel Sacor explained through Captain Chin how Khmer children came to this temple to learn the history of the country and to learn how to read and write from the Buddhist monks.

The soldiers and I faced the old Buddha statue sitting before us in a peaceful lotus position. I took this opportunity to ask the gods of the universe to pull the fever from my body and to protect me on this mission. I donated money to the old monk, who motioned for me to leave the baht in a stone bowl near the statue. We then slowly walked out into the bright, hot sun. My companions collected their weapons and we all walked down the long steps to the river. We sat down on wooden benches located under the covered landing as the temple stood above us, overlooking the river valley.

Thirty minutes later, a motorboat arrived with a soldier dressed in army fatigues. Captain Chin informed me that this was a soldier of the warlord's private army. We all boarded the small speedboat and headed northeast for our meeting with the Khmer warlord, Di Mai.

The sun was scorching hot. My back was burning, and with my high fever, I could feel heat blisters forming as the small boat navigated up the river. Along the way, I noticed that Cambodian river life was very primitive. Long, handmade wooden boats and rafts transported cargo and people. Fisherman threw their nets, trying to catch freshwater fish. Along the shoreline were small, wooden homes placed on stilts.

We slowly docked alongside a wooden pier where several of Di Mai's soldiers tied off our boat-lines and helped us onto the sturdy landing. There was a well-built, wooden building next to the dock. A line of clay pots filled with flowers could be seen along the front of the building. Next to the flower pots was a line of AK-47s. *Guns and roses,* I thought, chuckling to myself.

A dark-skinned Cambodian man who stood at about 5'8" and who had a receding hairline stepped out through the front door of the building. Everyone saluted him as he was introduced to me.

"This is Commander Di Mai," Captain Chin said.

Di Mai's smile was slight. His rough appearance reminded me of New York wise guys – street smart, but lacking social etiquette. He spoke briefly to his men and then to Colonel Sacor.

Captain Chin translated to me that Commander Di Mai only wanted me and Captain Chin to accompany him to his jungle community. Di Mai looked at me as the captain spoke.

"He say no white man has ever come to his community. He has heard good things about you though, so he allow you to come."

The tough Khmer warlord and I communicated our enthusiasm with our slight smiles and subtle nods of approval.

Di Mai, Captain Chin, and I boarded a motorboat and continued up the river. The scorching sun attacked my fever-racked body. The blisters on my back stung like wasps. My stomach cramped and my head pounded as we journeyed to Di Mai's clandestine jungle community.

Slowly, we veered off the river into a cove. The calmer water made the boat move more smoothly. Traveling only a short distance, Di Mai turned into a small waterway and shortly turned again into an even smaller tributary. There were so many inlets and offshoots to this complex waterway that there would be no way for me to find my way back without Di Mai's help.

The jungle now surrounded us. The tree canopy was so dense that it looked like dusk, although it was only mid-afternoon. The ancient silk-cotton, mangrove, and banyan trees had huge, spider-shaped roots exposed where the water met the trunks. Long, pale, green moss hung from the wicked branches like dead skin from a creature in a cheap horror film.

Di Mai slowly maneuvered in and out of dark, narrow tributaries over still, murky swamp-water that was infested with fallen trees and rotten stumps. The stillness, thick growth, and steaming vegetation around the giant spider roots became thicker.

The swamp grew too shallow for Di Mai's motorboat so he turned off the engine. He paddled a short distance toward the shore but the twisted roots just below the surface scraped the bottom of our boat, causing us to get stuck in the rotting murk beneath. The jungle was so quiet. Only the sounds of tropical birds and the buzzing of insects could be heard.

Di Mai spoke briefly and Captain Chin informed me that we had to take off our boots and walk the rest of the way to the shore. The thought of walking barefoot through this snake-infested, muddy swamp sent chills through my body that made my aching bones rattle with pain. However, I couldn't complain, so I removed my boots and stepped into the slime-covered swamp. My bare feet sunk into the mud and my toes slipped between the slimy roots below the surface. I felt the roots sliding and gripping all around my feet. As I took my first step and brought my right foot back down, I landed on an awkward spot and felt my little toe snap against a root. I was sure it was broken. Later, the pain would tell me just how right I was.

As I followed Di Mai and Captain Chin toward the shore, I waited for a water-snake to strike my skin with its sharp, venomous fangs. Eventually, we reached solid ground – which was an incredible relief. This, however, was a short-lived illusion because, as we moved through the dense jungle, the hot ground became covered with thorn bushes. My feet were impaled by sharp thorns from which there was no escape.

The pain shooting up from the bottom of my feet joined with the pain coming from my broken toe and aching bones from the strange Asian fever, make this tortuous place in time unbearable. Sharp palm fronds scraped and jabbed me. I climbed barefoot over logs, roots, and vines. Every step was a small battle. I endured and stayed focused while following the captain and Di Mai without falling behind.

Eventually, we made it to an open field. The brown, short grass helped me walk with the thorns still embedded in my feet. My teeth were clenched from the sharp pain.

I asked Captain Chin why the field that we walked through was pocked with craters.

"Oh, they are only detonated landmines. Just walk where we walk," he responded.

Christ, I thought. *Now I'm walking barefoot through a fucking minefield!*

We crossed the field with the moon-like surface and reached a tree line. After we crossed this narrow stand of tropical vegetation, Commander Di Mai's jungle village came into my view. There were several small structures neatly placed near larger wooden buildings. I could see soldiers, along with many women and children. Everyone stopped and stared at me as though I was an alien from another galaxy.

Soldiers appeared with AK-47s, and Di Mai ordered them to leave us alone. I limped to a large wooden warehouse that had a covered deck in front, and sat down on the floorboards to inspect my feet. My toe was mangled and blood poured from the places where thorns were embedded. Di Mai handed me a wet cloth and a wooden bowl. Captain Chin pointed to a barrel of water as Di Mai opened the doors to this well-built warehouse.

After I had wiped down my throbbing feet, I carefully stepped into the warehouse with Di Mai and Chin. Before me stretched about five tons of packaged herb neatly piled into a long row. Di Mai grabbed a kilo-sized package and carried it outside. We all sat down on the wooden landing. The warlord pulled out a long knife to open the well-sealed package.

Because of my fever, I was in a dreamlike state. The bright sun made everything seem vivid and detailed. The sounds around me became sharp. I could clearly hear the sounds of everyday life in Di Mai's secret jungle village. I sat cross-legged as sweat poured off me. My khaki shirt was soaked. Di Mai punctured the wrap with his sharp knife. I could hear the sound of air being sucked in from the pressure-sealed package. Di Mai smiled as he saw that I understood the product was freshly packed and vacuum-sealed.

I moved slowly and rarely spoke in order to conserve my energy. Although I felt sick and weak, I couldn't let the two men know how out of it I really was. I checked the fragrance and nodded in approval at its pungent, Thai-style aroma. I felt the dense buds and broke one in my hand to check its inner fragrance. I pulled a small magnifying glass out of my brown leather shoulder bag and checked the crystals on the buds to examine their structure and stage of development.

I indicated my approval to Di Mai, who sat blank-faced during my thorough inspection. Finally, I rolled a fat joint with the rolling paper that I had tucked into a side pocket of my bag. I lit the perfectly-shaped joint and smoked it.

Soon, my fever and aching body felt the much-appreciated relief that the potent herb offered. I exhaled a plume of smoke and smiled.

Di Mai and Captain Chin had broad smiles on their faces, acting like they had just witnessed a magic show. I drank cool rainwater from the wooden bowl and finished only half the joint.

I softly spoke to Di Mai about his farming methods and told him that I wanted to be there the next season to observe the planting and fertilization techniques he used. I told him that I was impressed with his well-cured fresh herb.

We spoke for about an hour and covered all of our common interests. Soon, the load of herb sitting in the warehouse behind me would be in the possession of our transporters – the Übel brothers.

Di Mai handed me a pair of sandals and we went back on our route to the temple from where we had started.

Colonel Sacor, Captain Chin, Officer Tu, the two soldiers, and I drove in two Jeeps to a two-story hotel in Koh Khong. The Koh Pell Hotel was located in a large field not far from the South of the Thunder River. Here, we would meet General Wa Nat.

Captain Chin explained to me how we would get together with him in the morning. I was pleased to learn this and retired to my room to tend to my thorn-impaled feet and my aching, feverish body. After pulling as many thorns out as I could with a pair of tweezers, I smoked a joint of Di Mai's herb and passed out on the hard bed.

The following morning, after I had showered and dressed in clean clothes, I met General Wa Nat. With him was Lieutenant Hour, the general's assistant and interpreter. The two of them faced me in the hotel restaurant. Captain Chin sat to my right and Lieutenant Hour to his right. Several bodyguards sat and stood all around us.

The general, who also happened to be the provincial governor, was dressed in a dark gray suit with an open-collared white shirt. He was a handsome Asian man in his mid-fifties, and had a full head of dark hair streaked with gray. He appeared to be in remarkable shape.

The general studied me carefully and listened closely to my responses to Lieutenant Hour's interpretations. Lieutenant Hour was also dressed in a suit. His receding hairline made him look older, but he was only in his mid-forties.

Captain Chin sat and observed the conference. Unlike the fanfare we had experienced on Sow Tong Island with the Major General, here we just had coffee and maintained a serious dialogue.

We covered the amount of money that I would allocate for security, and Captain Chin interjected that he had these funds in his possession. I could tell that the general was concerned about if I was a United States agent trying to entrap the CPP just before the big election. Everybody seemed really paranoid about the prospect of Hun Sen getting discredited. To his credit, the general had every reason to be nervous on this particular occasion. The Funcinpec and Sam Rainsy parties would have just loved to expose our little operation and have Hun Sen indicted for conspiracy to export marijuana to America.

The fact that I was paying in cash for this cargo and security seemed to help my credibility in the eyes of General Wa Nat. These men worked closely with the one-legged police commander, Colonel Hing Peo, in Phnom Penh. Since they all shared the security money and reported directly to Hun Sen, cash was always appreciated.

"How do we know that you will return to Cambodia after the mission and help rebuild our country?" the general asked through Hour.

"I've been in the marijuana business for twenty-five years," I said solemnly. "It's time for me to retire and I'd like to spend that retirement helping rebuild Cambodia. I plan to be here for many years, working to create jobs and helping to educate the people so they can better operate in the world marketplace."

General Wa Nat smiled as he shook my hand. Our meeting ended on a positive note, and I was relieved to know that the series of Cambodian meetings was over and that we could now concentrate on completing our mission.

Chapter 25

I T was early May of 1998 when I limped into my apartment at the Omni in Bangkok. I was a mess. The pain from the remaining thorns in my feet, my fucked-up Asian fever, aching body, and sunburned face made me a sight to see.

Ahm looked at me in the doorway. "Darling, what happen you?" She started to remove my shoes and clothes as she reprimanded me. "I tell you let me come wit you! You no listen to me!" Ahm gently bathed me and removed the thorns that I had not been able to reach. She washed me and put medicine over the blisters on my back. "How this happen? Where you go?" she demanded.

"I went to Chiang Mai to buy land," I responded.

"Bullshit! What you doing, Mac?"

I could see the turmoil in her eyes. "Please, Ahm, not now," I said.

"Where you go? Tell me!"

"Sweetheart, soon I'll be finished with my job. Then we can get married and have a good life together."

"Yes, if you no die first! Please, Mac. You are my husband. I come with you so I can take care you!"

"No, Ahm. Please!" *If only I could tell her*, I thought. *She doesn't know that it's for her own good not to know.*

Ahm threw the towel down and ran out of the bedroom.

"Fuck!" I said loudly as I sat on the edge of the bed.

After two days, Ahm's intensive care and a bag of multi-colored pills turned me around. I asked her if she would like to get out of the apartment and go to

Pattaya Beach. She had been upset over my stubborn refusal to tell her what I was doing.

"Really?" she said with a smile.

"Yes," I said. "We can leave today."

Ahm hugged and kissed me like a little girl and then started packing.

~ ~ ~

The Bird returned to Bangkok from his R and R in Pattaya a day after Ahm and I had returned to the Omni. I knew our in-country mission would soon be finalized. J.T. sat in the oversized armchair and maintained his cold stare at Captain Chin as he spoke.

"U.S. DC-10s with AWAC-capabilities are still in our staging area," said J.T. "There are also U.S. destroyers in the region. We can't afford to have a run-in with the U.S. Navy."

Captain Chin responded slowly. "Thai Navy headquarters can alert us of any aircraft in our area. The U.S. destroyers are located near the oil-drilling platforms. We will be out of their operational zone and will be in communication with headquarters for any changes in U.S. military movement. The trouble in Indonesia will keep military attention focused there, not off the Cambodian coast."

We all sat around the nautical chart of the Gulf of Thailand. Captain Chin marked on the chart the location of Thai and U.S. military ships. J.T. marked the location of Haig's ship and ground zero, which was our point to transfer the load.

Captain Chin explained how he had already allocated the funds for our security and that, if we missed the May 15 deadline, we would have to pay for security again. It was now May 12 and Haig had just returned from his meeting with my brother and partners in the U.S.

I was pissed. I had told Haig not to go – that our timetable would be too close. Our chance to be on time with our mission was crushed when he contacted us while we were at the Rembrandt having a meeting. Using the SatCom on board his ship, he explained how the revolution in Indonesia had exploded and how the Indonesian government had closed down the seaport, preventing ships from leaving and entering the country.

"I will attempt to run through the blockade tomorrow night," he said. "If I make it, I'll refuel from bunkers in the South China Sea."

In spite of his efforts, Haig was unable to meet the May 15 deadline.

I contacted my partners in New York and put them on notice to send another $50,000 for security expenses. It was not easy to get. My investors were growing weary of the $1.6 million they had spent since the start of the *Oktedy* operation.

On May 23, the Bird and Captain Chin traveled to Klong Yai and prepared to finally move the cargo out of Cambodia. I remained in Bangkok waiting for a wire transfer of the security funds. The load was ready to be moved over land to the gunboats. Chin, the Bird, and I were ready to cross over into Cambodia to expedite our mission when J.T. notified us that he had a delay. He had a problem getting his trawler and crew out of Thailand. Again, we aborted our mission and, again, we had to offer another security payment of $50,000.

On June 2, J.T. notified me that he was on his way. The election was very close and the opposition parties were looking to expose Hun Sen – which would certainly hamper our mission.

"Captain Chin," I yelled. "I don't have the security funds transferred yet. We have to hold on a little longer."

"We must work now and pay the security money later. We can send the money to Phnom Penh after the transfer is made," Captain Chin explained.

"It's your call, Captain. I'll leave Bangkok with the security funds as soon as they arrive."

Immediately after speaking with Captain Chin, I called Harley.

"Hi, it's me," I said. "I need feedback from Haig or J.T."

"What's up, King?"

"Captain Chin advises me to go forward without another security payment. He says we can pay after the fact. I want everyone to know our status."

"When is your security money arriving at the Hong Kong Bank?"

"Twenty-four to forty-eight hours from now."

"I'll call you right back. I'll speak to Haig on the SatCom."

Twenty minutes later, my cell phone rang.

"Harley here. I spoke to Haig. He says go for it. He added that he likes Captain Chin's style. You know Haig. He enjoys putting one over on the big guy."

"I just wanted to let everyone know what was happening. I'll leave here after the funds arrive."

"Roger, King. Call me later."

After I had hung up, I thought about something Haig had said to me years ago. "I love coups. Just think about it. It's the ultimate human experience."

~ ~ ~

When I returned to the Omni, I intended to tell Ahm that she could come with me this time. I knew that I would not have to go into Cambodia. I would just deliver the security money to Klong Yai and return to Bangkok.

When I entered my apartment, I saw Ahm sitting by the window looking out over the city. A warm afternoon rain poured over the hot buildings and streets causing steam to rise off the hot surfaces like water in a frying pan.

"Ahm, are you all right?" I asked her.

She silently walked over to me to take my shoes off and neatly placed them by the door. Without saying a word, she went into our bedroom and lay face down on the bed. I walked in and lay down next to her. I could hear the rain falling outside.

"Ahm, what's wrong?" I asked.

She turned toward me and hugged me. "You no love me anymore!"

"What? Are you crazy? I can't live without you!" I kissed her and she warmed my heart with her sweetness. "Ahm, pack our bags. We're going on a trip." I watched as she became still and waited for me to finish. "I have to deliver papers to Klong Yai. We can leave tonight."

A heart-warming smile radiated from her face.

"Oh, Mac. Come on, take shower. Then we go!"

The white Mercedes-Benz from the Dusit Thani Hotel picked us up at the Omni. We placed our bags – along with my briefcase that contained the security money – in the trunk. By now, Ahm knew very well that I was not buying land in Chaing Mai. We were traveling west 200 miles to Klong Yai. I told her that I could not talk about what I was doing.

"Darling, Klong Yai near Kampochea?" Ahm said.

"Yes. We will not go into Cambodia, though. We'll stay overnight in Klong Yai and then return to Bangkok."

As we got closer to the border of Cambodia, we approached the first Thai checkpoint. The Dusit Thani Hotel car, with its identification plaque in the windshield, helped pass us through this and every other checkpoint. The Thai soldiers would take a quick look into the back seat of our car and wave us through.

Our sedan cruised toward the Thai-Cambodian border through the heavy monsoon rain.

Ahm spoke briefly to the driver. "He say you look familiar," she told me. "He say you are in shipping business."

I laughed. "Tell him he has a good memory." I knew he was confused.

It was late on June 4 when we arrived in Klong Yai. Ahm and I checked into a hotel outside of town about a mile from where I had stayed before. I called Captain Chin's cell phone.

His aide answered. "Chin and the Bird leave already to Cambodia," he said. "Chin say, wait for him. He will call you after they finish."

My cell phone woke me early on June 5. It was Harley.

"King! Pack your bags and get to Bangkok now!" His voice was quivering with fear.

"What's wrong?" I said, trying to jumpstart my sleeping brain.

"J.T. and his crew have been kidnapped and I've just received a message that J.T.'s got a gun to his head! They want three million baht. Get back here, now!"

"I'm not leaving until I get them back!"

"King, from a security standpoint, we don't know if you're also in danger. We can't afford to lose you and your team. So leave Klong Yai now for Bangkok!"

"Hey! I know you're upset, but keep your head. I'll contact my people in Cambodia and get Bob and his crew back. Alive!"

I hung up and called Captain Chin's cell phone number. His aide answered.

"Get Chin and the Bird back to Klong Yai," I said in broken Thai. "Have him call me as soon as possible."

Three hours later, Captain Chin called. In the meantime, I had spoken to Harley several times while I waited for Chin and the Bird to return. I had received some updated information, and the situation did not look good.

Captain Chin came to my hotel to speak to me in person. He explained how, the night before, they had mechanical problems with their vessel and had to abort.

"The vessel was loaded. We go out short way and then return last night," he said.

"Is the Bird okay?" I asked.

"Yes, he okay. Just tired. He sleep now at hotel."

"Listen, Chin. This is what I know so far. Early this morning, Harley called me. He said that J.T. had called him from his SatCom. He explained to Harley that he was waiting for your vessel when two small powerboats attacked him. The men who boarded J.T.'s boat had guns. They fired some shots and held them at gunpoint. J.T. and his crew were made to give up their guns, clothes, jewelry, everything – even their shoes, socks, and underwear. Harley said the leader of the group demanded to know where the money was hidden on the boat. They're holding him hostage for three million baht, or 75,000 American dollars. They're holding them on land – in a barn with his crew. Harley claims he's never heard J.T. sound so scared."

Captain Chin was silent for a moment and then said, "Pirates. J.T. is being taken by pirates. The area he was in last night was pirate area. We must pay them or they will kill him for sure."

"Listen, Chin. You contact your Cambodian army, navy, and police personnel. You tell them to track J.T. and his crew down and make sure they are all brought back here alive!"

"Okay. I will contact them now. We must pay them for expenses so they can move quickly."

"How much?" I asked.

Captain Chin paused to think. "We will pay 250,000 baht to start. If they need more, I'll let you know."

I gave Captain Chin the money and he left to organize our army, navy, and police contacts.

It was early afternoon and already I felt fatigued in the humid, 100-degree heat. In my hotel room, the Bird and I waited for a call from Captain Chin to tell us the latest news. The Bird had told me what had happened to him the night before.

"This is the operation from hell," I said to the Bird. "I'll be amazed if we get this project back on track."

My cell phone rang and a familiar voice resonated. "Haig here," it said.

"Good to hear your voice," I said.

"King, I don't have to tell you what I'm going through. We've got to get J.T. back. Is there any update yet?"

I filled him in before putting the Bird on the phone to brief Haig about the mechanical problems he'd had the night before. The Bird handed me the cell phone when he had finished.

"Listen, Haig. I'm not going to let this setback stop me from completing my objectives."

"I have too much invested in this operation," he replied. "As soon as J.T. and the crew return, we'll establish a new plan."

"I'll get J.T. back. We're working on it as we speak."

"You gotta get out of the area because that's the Wild West down there, buddy. I don't want the same thing that happened to J.T. to happen to you. Leave a message for Chin to meet you in Bangkok."

"I don't feel right leaving," I said. "I don't want these guys to feel like I'm quitting or abandoning them."

"No, no, no, they're not gonna feel like you're quitting or abandoning them.

I mean . . . it's just that you're . . . you gotta understand . . . we're partners. We've been friends for twenty years and we just underwent a very difficult thing and I need to see you immediately. You've got to understand that you have a loyalty to me as well as to them. I need to see you."

"Okay . . . I'll . . . I'll be there tonight and I'll get Chin there, also," I replied.

After I had hung up with Haig, Captain Chin called me. He informed me that J.T. was not kidnapped by pirates as he first thought. He said Colonel Hing Peo, the one-legged commander in Phnom Penh, was behind the abduction. Colonel Hing Peo was upset because he thought we were going to work without paying him another security payment. Captain Chin explained how Colonel Hing Peo's military police went out to J.T.'s boat to shake him down for money. Chin further explained that J.T. and his crew were transported naked to Hing Peo's base in Phnom Penh.

"J.T. tell Hing Peo that he was United States DEA agent," Captain Chin said. "Hing Peo believe him because J.T. have five Thai policemen with him."

"What?" I said. "J.T. conned them into thinking that he was a U.S. agent?"

"Yes. A powerful general from Thailand verified this to Colonel Hing Peo!"

"That must be Uncle George!" I said. "J.T.'s old Thai general friend. He's retired, but still very influential."

"Yes, I know him. He very powerful."

"When will J.T. and the crew return?"

"J.T. and his crew will return to Bangkok in a couple of days."

"This is crazy," I said. "Listen, meet me in Bangkok tomorrow. I have to talk to you."

"Okay, Joe. See you tomorrow."

⌐⌐⌐

Ahm spent the next morning taking care of me. She brought me a cup of coffee with a joint on the saucer and placed it next to me on the nightstand. The coffee got cold and we smoked the joint much later. We couldn't stop making love.

It was mid-afternoon when we finally got out of bed. I called my partners in America and Southeast Asia. Everyone in America was shocked at the incredible story.

"I wish I was making this all up, but I'm not," I said to Woodstock Willy. Skip, Daniel, and my brother were speechless and amazed that the project was still on.

Captain Chin and I met at the Landmark Hotel to discuss the updated information.

"Colonel Tu have tape recording of J.T. in Phnom Penh," Captain Chin said. "He tell Colonel Hing Peo everything about our mission! Why he do that?"

"I guess to prove that he was a real U.S. agent," I explained. "He was scared and had to convince Hing Peo. Listen, Chin, I have known Sam and Bob Übel for over twenty years. I know they worked in the past with the CIA and the Thai military. But the two of them are not police or DEA."

Later, when talking to Harley, I was a little less reserved.

"Harley, if I hadn't known the brothers for over twenty years," I said, "I'd swear this was a foiled CIA operation to meddle in the Cambodian election. I hear on the VOA how the U.S. hates Hun Sen and wants him to lose the election. J.T. did tell us to bring a Hun Sen emissary with us."

"King, you're over-speculating. We're all burned out. We have to stay focused and finish our mission. J.T. is going to stay out of the picture. He doesn't want to bring any attention to you and our team here in Thailand. Haig's moving *Echo Charley* to the island in Indonesia. Tomorrow, I'll come to your apartment with a new operational plan that Haig is sending us. We'll go from there."

⌐⌐⌐

It was now the rainy season in Southeast Asia, and I sat down by the open window in my living room at the Omni to try to sort out the events that had unfolded. Harley sat on the couch with Haig's new operational plan. The Bird and I sat across from him as he rolled out a nautical chart on the table between us.

"J.T. and his crew are back and safe," Harley said. "They all said 'thank you' for your effort to help. Haig has changed the method of moving our cargo back to the original six-dimension plan. You'll have to acquire a Thai fishing vessel, like we spoke about originally. You'll have to take possession of the cargo in Cambodia and transport the cargo to Haig's island in Indonesia. Here is the route you'll take." Harley drew a line on the nautical chart that went from Koh Khong in Cambodia out to the Gulf of Thailand between the Malaysian coastline and the oil platforms in the Gulf to the Honesberg Lighthouse in the Strait of Malacca.

"We'll meet you here at the Honesberg Lighthouse and pilot you to Sam's island from there," Harley explained.

I looked at the route Harley had outlined. "Isn't this route a little too close to Malaysia?" I asked.

"No, this is the route we always use. It's a proven route. If you have any problems, we can get to you quickly. Haig will be stationed in Indonesia on *Echo Charley*. You can contact us by radio. So stay along this route."

"I'd rather go outside the oil platform area. It may take us longer, but it's not so close to Malaysia."

"Listen, this is the plan. We go this way all the time. Just stick to this route and, soon, the whole mission will be behind you."

"I don't like this route," I repeated. "It's too close to Malaysia."

"King, this isn't an issue. Just follow Haig's plan and this operation will soon be history."

The following morning, Captain Chin called me. He had a Thai fishing vessel that we could rent for 500,000 baht for an eight-week period.

June 25 was our departure from Bangkok. In forty-eight hours, the Bird and I would leave Bangkok to finalize our mission. Ahm was upset that I was not taking her with me.

"Mac, let me come with you. I can take care you."

"Not this time, Ahm," I said as I held her in my arms. "Ahm, I will never stop loving you."

"I scared, Mac. I don't want you to go."

My last days in Bangkok, Ahm and I stayed close at the Omni. For the first time in all of my years of covert activity, I felt out of control. If I had not been in the position I was in, I would have aborted the whole fucking mission. I only knew that I had no choice but to go and attempt to finalize this thing.

My last night with Ahm was as depressing as a gray and cold autumn twilight. As I sat and listened to the steady rain outside our apartment window, I thought about how I would miss this life, our laughter, and our lovemaking.

Ahm quietly entered the dimly-lit room and hugged me. She nuzzled her pretty face next to mine and kissed me. "Mac, why you no tell me what you do in Kampuchea?"

"Sweetheart, if we have a problem, I don't want you to be involved. After I finish my job, I will tell you."

Ahm turned and looked into my eyes as she held my face in her hands. "I love you, my husband. I see you have danger in Kampuchea. Mac, I no like Bob and his brother – Harley, either. I no trust them. I no care you make big money. I only want you. We can have a good life here in Thailand with little money. You smart man. We can start business. I can help you. I love you, my husband."

Ahm broke my heart. I was overcome by her love. This was a new experience for me. In my marriage to Virginia, money always came first. My safety was second.

"I want to show you something, Ahm." I brought her into the bedroom to the safe. She sat on the bed as I removed my real passport. I sat down next to her and showed her my real name. I felt that I no longer needed to worry about compromise. I knew in my heart that Ahm loved me and would never hurt me. Ahm looked at my photo and saw my real name.

"Oh, Mac, I love you name. It have good sound," she said with her Thai accent. Her smile was radiant.

"I love you too, Ahm, my wife."

Ahm did not take my departure well. Even the Bird, who was with me, was taken by her emotional display.

Finally, she surrendered. "Mac . . . I wait . . . you come back, Mac! You come back!" Her pleading voice broke and she wept deeply.

I looked out the rear window of the service car as we pulled away from the front of the Omni. Ahm stood crying, her heartbreaking eyes fixed on mine. I watched her until I could no longer see my Asian angel.

Chapter 26

June 26, 1998: Klong Yai, Thailand

THE rain never seemed to end. The Bird and I walked to the marketplace in the center of this small fishing village on the Thai-Cambodian border to have our fix of spicy seafood and noodle soup. We sat on plastic chairs under a high overhang that covered the large, open marketplace. The smell of wood burning was in the air. Vendors arrived there every morning and stayed until late at night, selling any food item you might want.

Captain Chin and his aides stayed at the hotel only two blocks away and waited for the call from General Wa Nat to let us know when to proceed into Cambodia and finish this phase of the operation. Captain Chin, the Bird, and I had inspected the eighty-foot fishing vessel that we would use to move the cargo out of the perilous waterways near Di Mai's base to the South of the Thunder River. From there, we would follow the Übels' plan and move out to the Gulf of Thailand and head south along the Malaysian coastline to the Strait of Malacca, where we would rendezvous with Haig near the Honesburg Lighthouse off the coast of Singapore.

"I don't like it," I said to the Bird as we walked in the rain through the narrow, wet streets of Klong Yai. It was warm, but the dampness gave me a chill.

"I'll call Harley when we get back to the hotel and request a route change one more time," the Bird said. "I don't like getting close to Malaysia, either. I've heard bad things about that place."

We walked over a small, curved bridge. I enjoyed seeing the small homes with their pink, yellow, and green paint now fading from years of weathering.

Mothers and daughters peeled tiny shrimp in front of their homes. This was the economic staple of the village. That and smuggling.

On June 27, at 22:00 hours, an aide to General Wa Nat arrived with a message for Captain Chin. We were to cross the border the next day at 15:00 hours to meet him at the Ko Pell Hotel. We would move our cargo that same evening.

"That's it," I said. "We're clear to go. We'll take the fishing boat to Haig's island in Indonesia. Captain Chin will stay with General Wa Nat."

That night, as I watched the ceiling fan spin slowly above me, I thought about the bizarre events that were going on around me. My loyalty to the Übel brothers in spite of their coldhearted personalities was undiminished. *Bob and Sam, DEA agents? If they are, it's over. If I return to America right now, it's still over.* Plus, the U.S. government already had enough evidence against me by then to indict me. They didn't need to send me into this dangerous country to make a marijuana conspiracy case, so the thought that the Übel brothers were U.S. agents trying to set me up made no sense. For all I knew, the CIA bailed Bob out of the jam he was in, and this information was being kept secret.

Only Ahm and my three beautiful daughters wanted me to stop and settle down. The trouble was that they didn't know all the circumstances that surrounded me. Everyone else was pushing me to go and finalize the project.

I remembered that, a couple of weeks before, I had called Virginia and expressed my anxiety over how the negotiations that I was having with the Übel brothers were making me ill. I had said to Virginia that I felt like ending the project and returning home to face whatever my future would present.

"No! You've gone this far, finish it!" Virginia had snapped.

I fell asleep with a sick feeling – the same kind of feeling one would have when facing the electric chair or the gas chamber.

Time had stopped for me. I was in perpetual autumn, held in a sunset twilight, a leafless, dead, and cold gray scene. I was in need of something, but I didn't know what.

I suddenly thought of the pain Virginia had caused me and then I thought of Ahm. In my heart, I knew that Ahm was right. I should not trust the Übel brothers. But my honor and my responsibility to my partners and family overrode my common sense. I could not stop the mission now. The momentum was too great.

~~~

JUNE 28, 1998

In the car on the way to the Cambodian border, I thought about Ahm – how I had taken away her desire to protect me and take care of me. Engrained in her culture, the wife was responsible for aiding her man. I had placed Ahm in a powerless position to care for me. Just before I had left, she looked as if she was dying inside.

The Khmer warlord Di Mai had already moved the Thai vessel that we had procured and had loaded its wide hull with the fresh, fragrant herb from the warehouse I had visited in his clandestine base weeks before.

The night before our border crossing, General Wa Nat's aide picked up the money I was holding for security. This operation had drained all our working capital. I knew how volatile the area was. So many spies, splinter groups, and defectors were all looking for hard currency. The powerful Khmer generals and warlords were looking to feed their armies in the mountains. There were no guarantees that I wouldn't be killed or captured during this covert operation. With our cash resources depleted, I was as good as dead if things went wrong.

The sky was a solid cloud. It bulged weightily over Klong Yai and I looked in vain for the sun, which seemed to have been swallowed. Some light sifted down, gray and powdery. My mood was anxious fear.

Later, Captain Chin reminded me as we crossed the border in a Khmer long-boat on the Gulf of Thailand: "Remember, you are Joe Harding. If anything goes wrong, use this name. Our people know you only by this name."

The Bird, Captain Chin, our aides, and I walked up the rocky shoreline to meet Colonel Sacor's men.

We all met General Wa Nat at the Ko Pell Hotel in Koh Khong, Cambodia. Captain Chin interpreted for me.

"The plan changed," he said. "You must stay here with me. The Bird, Sham, and two of Di Mai's people will go." Captain Sham was Chin's man.

The Bird and I didn't have any problems with this new set-up.

The meeting broke up and everybody embraced and left to activate our mission. After the Bird and I hugged, I watched as they all disappeared into the dark monsoon rain as I stood in front of the Ko Pell Hotel. This operation would end my two-decade-long legacy.

From my open window in the hotel, I could smell the steady rain and hear its soothing sounds. Through the darkness, I could see the twinkling of distant amber lights. The wind was picking up, and I thought about the Bird and his crew navigating the South of the Thunder River toward the Gulf. *What a night to be out there*, I thought.

I started to feel restless, so I decided to go downstairs for a drink in the restaurant nightclub. I ordered a Singha and listened to the live Cambodian band playing Santana songs.

I had been in the club for about 45 minutes when I sensed some activity outside the entrance. I started to feel uneasy as I looked for a back way out in case things got ugly. I got up to leave through a rear exit that I had spotted when a group of four Khmer soldiers entered with their weapons drawn. They quickly surrounded me.

In a guttural voice, one soldier said, "You! Come."

They became hostile when I tried to pay my tab. The one soldier pulled the paper from my hand and threw it on the floor. I was ushered out of the club to the sound of Santana as workers and patrons froze in fear.

I was abruptly escorted to the lobby, where we met a dozen more rough-looking armed soldiers. They grabbed me and pulled my arms behind me to handcuff me.

"What's this all about?" I asked the leader of the group.

No response was given.

The hotel clerks behind the check-in counter stood mortified as I was led outside into the pouring rain. There, I saw Captain Chin and his two aides already waiting by the army truck, also handcuffed. My pockets were searched and my money extracted. I saw my leather bag being thrown into the front of the cab of the flatbed truck. The four of us were shoved onto the floor in the rear of the truck and were quickly surrounded by soldiers with guns.

In the dark, we were driven in the storm two or three miles to a field. I saw a barn set back in the rear of the field. The soldiers grabbed us and walked us through the grass that was sluiced with 10-inch-deep water.

The inside of the barn was dimly-lit by lanterns. In the center of the old, decrepit structure was a long table with chairs around it. A large, cloth banner was attached to the wall toward the head of the table. In the dim lighting, I could make out the words: THE CAMBODIAN PEOPLE'S PARTY.

My mind was racing. I felt fear swelling my heart, turning my stomach.

The soldiers roughly herded us inside and lined us up against the long wall that was facing us. Drenched and shivering, I looked for an escape, looked for a familiar face to reason with. These soldiers were not the ones I knew. These were from a different commander's group. One officer in particular was raising hell, screaming and yelling. One by one, they shoved us in front of the CPP banner and photographed us.

Moments later, the Bird, Captain Sham, and two young Cambodian deck-hands were brought in, also soaked from the relentless storm outside. There were six of us now, excluding the two deckhands, who were let go. I knew that, if I could communicate with whoever was in charge, I could work out a solution, a compromise, so that we could get our mission back on track. I didn't want Haig and his crew to have to wait long for our rendezvous. So the sooner I got this occupational setback over with, the better.

Suddenly, Colonel Sacor entered the barn. He spoke to the soldiers who had their guns aimed at us. Slowly, their guns came down. Sacor looked upset as he walked over to Captain Chin and spoke softly. I could see Captain Chin's face as he listened intently to Sacor's words. I felt that, already, our people were starting to unravel the misunderstanding.

Colonel Sacor left. I was not able to speak to Chin because he was too far from me. The soldiers then signaled for us to sit on a row of old desks that they had pushed against the wooden wall.

I felt like I had been sucker-punched in the stomach. In spite of the fear that simmered in my chest, I felt strong. I had faith in my ability to overcome this temporary setback, this show of treachery that I knew I would soon uncover and face eye to eye.

As the malevolent-looking Khmer soldiers aimed their AK-47s at us, others attached old rusty steel chains to our ankles. The heavy chain was wrapped around us and then locked with equally-rusty old padlocks. The six of us leaned against the barn wall in uncomfortable positions, facing the table before us.

The soldiers threw our bags on the table and started to go through them. Piece by piece, I saw the memories of my life taken from my leather bag – photos of my family, my silver joint-holder, personal artifacts, lighters, a cigar trimmer, my old wallet, a leather-bound pocket atlas, items that I had saved for over twenty years – all being stolen by these deranged killers.

One loud, overdramatic officer pulled out a wad of cash from an inside pocket of my leather bag. He held it up in the air and screamed like he had found the evidence that he had been looking for. His anticlimactic show ended as he quietly pushed the cash into his large front pocket.

For at least two hours, the six of us watched the soldiers drink Makong whisky and tear apart our personal belongings. We were shaking from being soaking wet. The roof leaked, and steady drips of rainwater kept us chilled all night.

Through the cracks in the barn's wooden walls and roof, flashes of lightning could be seen. Rolling thunder from the north echoed as I uncomfortably tried to position myself so the heavy, rusty chains would stop digging into my ankles.

In the darkness, I observed our captors. Some were in uniform, while others wore ancient Khmer cloth-wraps with their AK-47s tucked under their arms. Their menacing gun muzzles peered out from under the red and white checkered cloth when they took aim at our shivering bodies.

I watched as our three remaining captors took my cigars and passed them around to one another. They coughed when they inhaled the imported smoke. They drank Mekong whisky and took what looked like meth pills.

Great combination, I thought.

As the night wore on, they became drunker and crazier. They played gun games with us, pointing their weapons at our heads and laughing. I noticed that they had tattoos of wild-looking dragons covering their bodies. These were mountain men with guns – tell them to kill and they will kill, as others like them once did for Pol Pot.

All night, the truculent heavens poured their anger down onto the wooden Khmer structure holding us captive. Water dripped through the worn roof onto our chilled bodies in the musky room. I knew that I would understand, later, what was happening. Right then, I had to focus on the present moment. I hadn't slept all night. We were all chained together. There was dried blood under the rusty chains that bound me.

Slowly, dawn emerged through the cracks in the walls. Shortly after sunrise, a group of soldiers returned. We were led out of the CPP station and into the field. The wind blew onto our wet clothes as we stood in the ten inches of water under a cold, gray sky. We were shivering as an army truck pulled up. Colonel Sacor had arrived again. He spoke quietly to Captain Chin, who didn't speak. Sacor was controlled, but appeared clearly upset about what was happening.

The six of us were still not able to speak to each other much. The rusty chains were removed and our wrists were bound – some by rope, some by steel handcuffs. We sat on the floor of the truck as we were driven to Jachot Dock, five miles away. There was a crowd of people gathered around the main dock as we pulled up.

We were led through the dense crowd to a large transport vessel – the type typically used to move passengers from port to port. The soldiers placed us in the rear seats of this enclosed vessel. It must have been 150 feet long, and had an aisle with three seats on each side. Captain Chin and I sat together. We hardly spoke. Other passengers arrived and were kept from our area in the rear.

Suddenly, a familiar face appeared: Major General Hopp. He stood at the doorway, looking angry. He spotted us, and then leaned forward and whispered into Captain Chin's ear. Then he left.

"Hopp say he will try to help us," Chin said.

For Major General Hopp to be out of the loop meant that a power above him were working to alter our operation. There was only one position above him. Somehow, Hun Sen himself had become compromised.

The transport vessel moved out onto the South of the Thunder River. The water was rough, but not as rough as it had been the previous night. When the Bird and I were finally able to speak to each other, he explained what had happened.

"Sham and I were brought to a dock in the jungle outside Koh Kong," he said. "The fishing boat that we rented was already loaded and running. Di Mai shoved two young Cambodians on board and motioned for us to leave. His men untied the ropes and the next thing I knew, the boat was in the storm heading east on the river."

The Bird described how the big diesel vessel had lumbered along in the blinding storm as he had tried to get a fix on his GPS. He had used his small flashlight to check his chart as Sham navigated the vessel through the storm. There had been little visibility. The fog and rain had made it nearly impossible to see.

"We were told to look for a gunboat – that this would be our escort," the Bird said.

The Bird and Sham had maintained their course as the strong currents swept their vessel toward the Gulf of Thailand.

"The rain kept coming hard. There was thunder and lightning. I kept looking out for the gunboat." Sham and the Bird had noticed red and green lights coming toward them out of the darkness.

The gunboat with the soldiers on board had not been the escort vessel that the Bird had been waiting for. Instead, the gunboat had come alongside the Bird's boat and soldiers had quickly jumped over and pushed everyone onto the deck.

"My first reaction was to jump," the Bird revealed. "But where could I have swam to? I was the only blonde-haired guy in the country. Plus, I probably would have drowned in that crazy river!"

Now, as the transport vessel plowed through the Gulf of Thailand, Captain Chin and I sat next to each other and quietly discussed our options.

Two hours later, we docked in Kompong Som. I was tired and seasick, and my hands were cut from the rough rope. We were led from the boat through a huge crowd of people around the dock area to a line of waiting trucks. We were separated as they put three of us in each truck. There were army trucks in front of us and behind us. I was placed in the back of one open truck with Chin's two aides.

Out of the crowd, I spotted General Wa Nat's aide, Lieutenant Hour, approaching me.

"Joe, are you all right?" Hour asked when he got up next to the truck.

"Yes," I said. "Do we still have control of the load?"

Lieutenant Hour slowly nodded.

"Stay on top of it," I said. "Make sure we don't lose it. We must finish our mission. We must get our load back and finish!"

The lieutenant stared into my eyes. "Okay, Joe," he said. "You go to Phnom Penh now. I see you there!"

The trucks' diesel engines whistled as they changed gears and slowly moved through the large crowd of Cambodians surrounding us. I watched as Lieutenant Hour stood facing me as we pulled away from the chaotic scene.

I was surrounded by six armed soldiers. The heat and blazing hot sun baked me on the steel flatbed of the truck. The people of every village we passed ran out to the roadside to see the long caravan of military trucks. We stopped for nothing. Cars, trucks – everything got out of our way as we bullied our way through.

The distance to Phnom Penh was approximately 125 miles. Our column of trucks roared through Bakor, Kompong Trach, Takeo, and Kompong Speu. Cambodians with apocalyptic stares lined the road as we pushed our way to the capital city of Cambodia.

Approximately five hours had passed. I was functioning on pure adrenaline.

I had no food, no water, and the intense sun beat against my bruised body that was covered in dried blood. After five hours of being banged against the hot steel truck-bed, I looked like a wild animal. As the army trucks slowly entered the dense traffic of Phnom Penh, I was pushed to my knees, and my arms were tied behind my back with hemp rope.

Cambodians had been tortured and killed here. Others were captured and imprisoned in work camps in the north, where millions had died at the hands of the vicious Khmer Rouge. This show of military power ignited painful memories that I saw reflected in the onlookers' faces.

I was paraded through the main streets of this impoverished city, but was forced to kneel so that I could be easily seen as if I was a trophy from the hunt. It was an oddity for the people to see a Westerner tied up and surrounded by Khmer soldiers the way I was. Cambodians looked terrified as I passed them. I felt doomed to die a painful death.

As we moved deeper into the city, the traffic became chaotic. There were no signal lights, no signs, just mass traffic. Eventually, we entered a complex through gates guarded by soldiers. The old, French-style buildings with their pale-yellow stucco finishes were poorly maintained. I quickly scanned the place. It was a military base of some kind – a walled-in Khmer fortress in the forbidden city of Phnom Penh.

Captain Chin, the Bird, Sham, Chin's two aides, and I were quickly separated into rooms that lined a dimly-lit hallway. The interior of this place resembled an old public school that I had once attended when I was a child. The heavy doors and buffed floors inlaid with stone made the sound of our abrupt movements echo off the high ceilings and masonry walls. I was led into one of the rooms of this mysterious hallway.

The soldiers sat me down on a wooden chair before a small desk. There were only a few papers scattered on the top of it. A window with steel bars was situated to my right, and I could see the late afternoon sun casting long, purple shadows over the cluster of ancient Khmer buildings in the distance. There were only two other chairs in this sparse 15-by-15 foot room.

Suddenly, three Asian men wearing plain clothes entered the room. One of the men had dark eyes and was slight in build. He sat on the edge of the desk before me. The other two men stood side by side next to me and had dangerous faces. Their dark eyes were void of any kindness. I sat rigid in silence, prepared for the worst.

The man on the desk offered me a cigarette. I reached out and pulled one from his pack. "Thank you," I said.

"You are American, I see!"

"Yes," I said as he lit my Cambodian smoke.

"Good. I speak enough English, so we can communicate. Now, tell me why you are here?"

"I don't know why. I was sitting in a restaurant in the Ko Pell Hotel when Khmer soldiers abducted me and brought me here."

"What is your name?"

"My name is Joe Harding."

"Joe, what were you doing in Koh Khong?"

"I'm a businessman. I'm here in Cambodia to do business."

"What kind of business, Joe?"

"I'm trying to build an ice factory and prawn farm in Koh Khong."

He looked calmly at me as he repeated what I was saying in Khmer to the other two men as they wrote down what he was saying.

"Tell me why you were with a Royal Thai Navy intelligence officer if you are trying to do business in the private sector? Or are you involved in the American military or intelligence business?"

"No, I am not involved in the military or intelligence community. I am trying to start a business here to benefit the Cambodian people."

"We have information that is not consistent with what you are saying. How do you explain this?"

"You have heard lies," I said.

After he had repeated this in Khmer, the other men in the room laughed. Then they all left and three other Asian men, similar in dress, entered the room. Again, two men stood taking notes as one man stood leaning against the desk before me. This man before me was larger in stature and older than the first. The two men he had arrived with were serious and quiet and also stood beside me.

The man before me asked, "What is your mother's name?"

"Rose Harding," I answered – a lie, of course.

"What is your father's name? Your brother's? Your sister's? Where do they live? How old are they? What do they do for a living? Did they go to school? What are your children's names? What is your wife's name? Does she work?" he questioned.

I lied in response to every question.

"What is your minor wife's name?"

I knew then that they had knowledge of Ahm. They must have reviewed the photos in my leather bag. I gave them a phony name and address for her, as I had done for all of my family members.

He interrogated me for over an hour. Up until then, his questions seemed completely out of color under the circumstances.

"What do you know about three young foreign men who were killed here?" he asked me.

I was familiar with the incident he was talking about. "I know their nationalities and that they were kidnapped by a Khmer Rouge general. They were killed when their ransom money didn't arrive."

"What do you think about that?"

"It was a terrible incident. I think it could have been prevented and that it is bad publicity for your country."

"Who are your contacts here in Cambodia?"

"I have none. I was hoping to develop contacts during my stay here."

"What do you know about the fifth of July coup?"

"Only what I read in the papers and saw on the news." I didn't go into my knowledge about the funding of the coup or share any other details that I had learned about it since then.

"What is your interest in the election?"

"May the best man win," I said.

"What do you know about an American CIA operative named Bob?"

The expression on my face must have reflected something because, when I answered that I had never heard of him, the interrogator's demeanor changed for the worst.

In an angry voice, he said, "We don't care about ganja. It is hardly a crime here. We want to know why you are really here, Mr. Joe Harding, and if you do not tell us, you will be very sorry."

I could sense the anger in these men and was relieved when they left the room. The first interrogator returned with the same two men as before. I was feeling run down and just wanted to close my eyes and sleep. The dark-eyed man offered me another cigarette and I accepted.

"Your girlfriend in Bangkok . . . do you love her?" he asked.

I was surprised by the question.

"Yes," I said.

"Is she beautiful? Is that why you love her?"

I wondered why such questions were being asked. Were they trying to break my concentration? Was Ahm under arrest in Bangkok? I became very worried. I tried to hide my concern. "Beauty is in the eye of the beholder," I answered. "I love her for reasons far more complex than her beauty."

He smiled at me. Suddenly, I heard screams from one of my comrades down the hall. I couldn't detect who, but it sounded bad. Someone was being beaten.

It had been dark outside for some time and the cold, bare light dangling from the ceiling gave the baby blue-colored room an ominous presence. This was the kind of room the Khmer Rouge had used during their torture and killing sprees.

The second interrogator returned with his two men. Now, all six men surrounded me. The second man brought in a beautiful, well-dressed Khmer girl who looked to be about 23 years old. They sat her to my right, facing me.

"Do you think she is beautiful?" the second interrogator asked.

"Yes, she is," I said.

He then said something in Khmer to the calm, pretty girl and she looked me over from head to toe as though she was going to purchase me.

"Would you like to go out with her?" the second interrogator asked me.

"No, she is married," I said.

"Why do you think she is married?" he asked in an irritated voice.

"I can see she's wearing a wedding ring on her finger."

"She is not married!" He was visibly angry.

I remained focused and maintained a strong, unwavering appearance in spite of my exhausted condition. *I can't believe they are trying to break my concentration with this Khmer girl.*

The sexy girl was led out of the room, but not before she had given me another hard looking-over.

The first interrogator sat down in front of me again. "Your friends are all talking and we know the facts," he said in a calm voice.

"Then you don't need me anymore," I said.

Suddenly, the dark-eyed man got in my face. "Are you ready to confess your crimes against the Royal Kingdom of Cambodia?" he screamed. "Are you ready to tell us the truth? Do you know what happens to people who do not cooperate?"

I looked into his dark eyes and said, "Yes. You kill them."

Silence. One by one, everyone left the pale blue room. Under the harsh light,

I sat alone in the smoke-filled space, further away from home than ever. I could see outside the window. It was late. I was tired, hungry, and confused. I knew that no one had talked in spite of the fact that my interrogators told me that everyone had cooperated.

Two guards returned with the second interrogator. He said in a low, confident voice, "I can make your life easier if you cooperate and tell me the truth."

"I told the truth."

"What religion are you?" he asked.

"Catholic."

"Do you go to church?"

"When I can."

"Do you know that lying is a sin?"

"Stealing a man's personal belongings is a sin. Your men stole my money, my Rolex watch – everything. What about that?"

"We have no record of you having any money or personal belongings. If you don't tell us the truth, you will be very sorry."

He looked at me hard, and then walked out of the room. The remaining men escorted me out into the dark hallway. As we walked toward the other end of the hall, I saw, to my right, Mr. Chi sitting in an interrogation room similar to mine. He was a frail, 50-year-old Thai man who had been serving as Chin's aide.

I instinctively turned into the room without asking and walked right up to him. I put my arm around his shoulder. His eyes were bulging, his face was red, and I could see blood from his nose and lip drying on his bruised skin. There were some rough-looking guys standing around him. One grabbed my forearm and squeezed.

"Hmm. Strong, ah!" he grunted.

"Yes, strong," I said. Luckily, I was twice the size of everyone else in the room. I slowly lifted Mr. Chi off his chair.

"Come on, Mr. Chi," I said, and carefully brought him out of the dark room.

We were both taken to a concrete cell. The steel door slammed shut behind us. One by one, all six members of our team were shoved into this small, concrete box. There was not enough room for everyone to lie down. We took turns standing, sitting, and lying down in order to catch some sleep.

That night, one by one, we were pulled out to be interrogated even further.

Captain Chin, the Bird, Sham, Mr. Chi – we all held up and took the abuse. Only the Bird and I were not beaten.

Although we were all exhausted and our minds begged for sleep, we discussed what was happening. Captain Chin and I spoke at length. He believed that the U.S. government was behind this event. The fact that Bob's name was mentioned in context with the CIA meant that, when he was abducted on the fifth of June, something happened that we were not aware of. An agreement must have been struck between Hun Sen and the U.S. government. Captain Chin's theory was that Hun Sen and his people were caught up in our mission and, in order to prevent exposure and to salvage the election, he had used us as sacrificial lambs. Hun Sen would then look good to the observing world, which was accusing him of corruption. The U.S. could benefit by manipulating Hun Sen into a position in which he had to obey U.S. demands.

"We will soon learn the truth," Captain Chin said as we tried to stay awake long enough to finish our thoughts. "Our people will help us, Joe. Be patient."

"Chin," I said, looking over at the captain, "I hope that we can overcome this situation soon. Lieutenant Hour said that the load is still safe. If our people can control the cargo and release us, we can finish the project. Haig will wait for us. As soon as we're out, I'll contact them and set up a new ETA."

"Yes, Joe. I will try to help you. But first, we must wait for our people to come take us out."

The heat in the four-foot by eight-foot airless, humid concrete box was claustrophobic. The bright fluorescent light stayed on 24 hours a day. The loud buzzing sound that it made was annoying. We were subjected to the constant attack of crawling and flying insects. Our toilet was a hole in the floor.

Despite these conditions, we remained strong. By the third day, we were in bad shape. Our sweating bodies, hunger, and extreme exhaustion were all unbearable. Mr. Chi gave his gold ring to a guard for food and water. The guard's wife brought us rice, water, and small pieces of chicken. We all used our hands and shared the food until every grain of rice was gone.

On the fourth day, General Wa Nat and Lieutenant Hour arrived. They closed the door to the office that was in front of our cell. They brought apples and water. They didn't want any of the personnel in the building to know that they were speaking to us. The general explained using Lieutenant Hour as his translator.

"This base is controlled by the Minister of the Interior," he said. "The U.S.

government somehow became involved in our project and blackmailed Hun Sen into taking this action to abduct you. The media is paying for information because the election is very close and any corruption on Hun Sen's part would make election-altering news. This is creating a tense environment." He also explained how U.S. foreign aid was being used as leverage to control Hun Sen. "How the U.S. government found out about our project and who we were working with remains a mystery."

"I must complete my mission," I said to General Wa Nat as we stood face to face through the small bars in the 15-inch space in the solid steel door.

"There are spies everywhere. We must move slowly and find a way to release you. Be careful. Trust no one – even in your Embassy. Kenneth Quinn, the U.S. Ambassador, is very friendly with Hun Sen. He will be instrumental in communicating with Hun Sen about this potentially disastrous situation. So don't discuss anything with him. He will come soon to see you."

General Wa Nat and Lieutenant Hour left after they had spoken at length with Captain Chin.

Throughout that night and into the next day, interrogators took turns questioning us. No one knew who would be next or when they would come for us. There was little air and the heat was stifling. We made fans from old newspaper that we had slept and sat on. The empty plastic bottles were used as pillows when one of our turns came to rest. I felt sick to my stomach. The stench was overwhelming.

～～～

July 3, 1998

The guard pulled the Bird and I out of the box. "You see American Embassy now," he grunted.

Across the hall in a small room was a pleasant-looking American man.

"Hi! I'm Bruce Howard," he said, shaking our hands. He looked like he was 40 years old. He had wavy, short blonde hair and wore wire-rimmed glasses. I later learned that he had grown up in Maine and joined the Peace Corps in Thailand. After college, he had married a Thai girl and ended up working for the U.S. government at the Embassy in Phnom Penh after a short teaching career. He

let the Bird and I know that he was not interested in why we were there and said
that he did not involve himself with the CIA, DEA, or with Embassy politics.

"My only concern is your well-being. I will try to come and visit you and
communicate with your families."

The Bird and I looked at him in silence. I then asked him how long he
thought we would be detained.

"It's hard to say. If they send you to T.3 prison, you'll be the first Americans
to be imprisoned there. Anything is possible here." He paused and spoke softly.
"Some foreigners end up in prison here for a long time. Some just disappear." He
looked up at the ceiling and waved his arm. "First, you'll both have to complete
these forms."

The Bird and I were wary about this, but filled them out anyway when he
said that he could give us phone access when we had completed them. I wrote
down my name as Joe Harding, following the instructions to use this alias in
Cambodia. After we had filled out the short form, the Bird called his family and
asked them to send money through the Embassy.

Because I didn't want Bruce to know my real name, I decided not to call
Virginia. Instead, I asked Bruce if I could call my girl in Bangkok.

"Sure," he said and handed me his cell phone.

I dialed Ahm's number and she answered after one ring.

"Ahm!"

"Mac! Where are you?"

"I'm in Cambodia, sweetheart. Are you all right?" I was worried that she may
have been detained in Bangkok.

"No, Mac. I worry 'bout you. I cry every day, Mac. When you coming
home?" Ahm started crying. Her voice made my heart ache.

"Please, Ahm. I will be home soon. I have to take care of something here.
Then I can return to Bangkok. Listen, Ahm. Don't let anyone have what's in my
safe. Take everything and hide it."

Bruce tried to pretend that he didn't care, but I could tell that he didn't like
what I'd said.

Ahm's trembling voice said, "Oh, darling, I sorry. J.T. and Harley come here
already. They say you have problem in Cambodia and they want me to open safe
so they can hold you papers. I open for them, darling. I sorry!" Ahm was crying
hard now.

Damn, I thought. I knew how persuasive J.T. and Harley were – especially to a Thai girl. I stayed calm.

"That's okay, sweetheart. I wish I could have called you sooner."

"When you come back, Mac?"

"I will let you know as soon as I can. If I'm not back home by July seventh, move our things to your mother's house. My lease is up at the Omni that day."

"Okay, Mac. I do. Please come home, Mac. I love you!"

"I love you too, Ahm," I said, choked up. "I will call you again soon. Be careful. Don't worry. I'll be back. I love you."

"I love you too, Mac!"

I handed the phone back to Bruce. My throat was tight. I could hardly talk now – just hearing Ahm's voice upset me.

"Listen," Bruce said. "Take my advice – don't delay getting out of Phnom Penh. This election is really heating up and T.3 prison will not be a safe place to be. So do whatever you have to do to get out of this situation you're in. Here are the names and numbers of some lawyers that the U.S. Embassy has on file. I don't know them, but at least it's a start."

At that point, the second interrogator entered the small room.

"Mr. Chea, hello," Bruce said.

Now I know his name, I thought.

Mr. Chea said in a flat, matter-of-fact voice, "These two men will be going to T.3 prison in the morning. That is where you can find them if you need to see them again. Of course, you will need permission from the prison commander, Koon Boon Sorn. I'm sure your office can arrange this."

"Excuse me," I said. "Have you located my personal belongings or my money yet?"

"I told you we have no record of this."

I could see that he was angry that I had brought this up in front of Bruce.

"Well," I said, "let me know when you plan on visiting New York. I'll see to it that you receive the same hospitality that you've given me."

"Goodbye, Mr. Harding. I hope that you enjoy your stay in T.3," he said before walking out angrily.

"That Chea fellow is an important guy around here," Bruce said. "He and Colonel Hing Peo run this base. He's a bit of a gangster so be careful what you say or do with him."

"Thanks, Bruce. I really appreciate your help."

"Let's try to meet once a week. I'll pick up or drop off your mail. I'll bring my cell phone so that you can call your lawyers. You'll also need money, so I'll hand you magazines with cash inside. Without money, you'll have a hard time in T.3. Just inform your families to send the money to the Embassy."

We shook hands and I returned to my sardine can. Ahm's voice lingered in my head.

Chapter 27

T.3 Prison

A sudden blow startled and awoke me. All six of us stood up as the steel door flung open. There were a half-dozen Khmer men standing in the office in front of our small cell.

One soldier pulled Captain Sham out first. One by one, they photographed and fingerprinted us. I knew that if our people didn't get us released soon, the Cambodians would soon learn my real name by running my fingerprints through Interpol. Then the U.S. Embassy would be alerted and the DEA would learn what was happening.

We were all filthy, tired, and hungry. We had spent over six days in this 4-foot-by-8-foot box and, although we were told that T.3 was a living hell, it couldn't possibly get any worse than this.

I was wrong. Very wrong.

~~~

July 4, 1998

An entourage of Cambodian military trucks and personnel moved our weak, disheveled bodies from Colonel Hing Peo's dungeon out onto the busy Phnom Penh streets. Strangely, the glaring sun and intense heat were a welcome diversion from the suffocating hell we had just come from. This time, all six of us were handcuffed and seated on the bare floor of a flatbed military truck. No one spoke. We were surrounded by soldiers, so escape was impossible. Again, the bystanders froze in their tracks and leered at the Westerners on display.

In a plume of dust, we arrived at Asia's most dreaded prison. The crumbling, brick exterior loomed above us as we were all pulled onto the ground before ancient, rust-covered doors that were about fifteen feet wide and had a curved top. Within the large doors was a small steel door, which slowly opened with a foreboding creaking sound. This notorious prison was apparently in the middle of Phnom Penh. Old, toothless Cambodian women, rag-clad children, chickens, and families with pots and boxes of food, all waited outside this door looking for a prison official to bribe so they could give items to their loved ones inside.

Captain Chin, Sham, Mr. Chi, the Bird, Tong Lap, and I stepped through the small opening into another world.

"Holy shit!" I said to the Bird, who stood next to me just inside the doors.

A dark-skinned soldier with an AK-47 started screaming and motioning for us to walk. We were in a courtyard. A Cambodian flag hung motionlessly on a 30-foot-tall pole before us. Rocks the size of bowling balls formed a circle around its base. The guard marched us over the dusty surface. The courtyard was about 100 feet by 100 feet and was surrounded by high brick walls that were badly decayed. A two-story structure that was French in design stood to our left and in front of us.

The French-style windows and shutters on the second floor of the building to my left were encased in masonry walls that were cracked and weathered. The building was finished in a multi-colored stucco and exposed worn bricks that gave it an ancient appearance: mustard yellow over pale orange and off-white stucco peeling off the pitted, red-brown brick walls. In front of us, across the courtyard, was another set of rusty steel doors. Just before these doors were open rooms with light-blue steel bars that faced the courtyard.

There were inmates – though they could more appropriately be called the walking dead. Their thick, baggy blue Chinese uniforms hung on them like pajamas. Their thin faces and anguished eyes were haunting. They moved slowly like apparitions. There was no life left in their steps.

We were separated. The Bird and I were shoved into the room on the left.

The roof was rotted and the sky could be seen through the holes. Before us was a battered wooden desk where an expressionless officer sat. He didn't speak, but just pointed to a closet-sized space. The guard pushed the Bird and I into this area. We could see the wretched life in the compound out of the steel bars. Sweat rolled off our faces in the oven-hot heat.

Mentally, I was prepared for the worst. I planned to fight to the death if I found myself in a position to be tortured. My heart pounded. The Bird looked the same. We saw Chin and the others walk past, all wearing the blue pajama-like long-sleeved shirts and pants.

A psychotic-looking soldier grunted Khmer words to the Bird and I and motioned for us to move forward. Out of the closet and into the sun-baked compound, we followed this hard-looking Cambodian soldier to the front wall. We then walked to our left, and found ourselves between an old brick building and the outside wall. A stone wall about twelve feet high stood before us. In it, we saw a door made of steel bars.

The Khmer soldier unlocked the old padlock and pushed the rusty bars forward. Before us was a depressing enclosed compound. There was a long, white masonry building with a weathered, orange-tiled roof surrounded by a high wall made of brick.

Across the dirt area, between the building and us, was sparse vegetation and a cracked, concrete pad that connected the building to us. I could see faces looking out of the small openings in the building. There were eight openings with rusty bars. All eyes were fixed on the Bird and I while the guard relocked the door.

I scanned the area, looking for a way out. The yellow haze of the sun made the scene dreamlike – the heat was thick and oppressive. Through the white-washed wall of this building, I could see Khmer writing in black letters that faintly pushed through the white paint like ghostly words from another time – words that may have described how the new revolution would change the lives of these good people. I smelled Pol Pot and the blood that he must have spilled on this ancient ground. We now walked toward this Khmer tomb before us.

The Bird and I stood next to the T.3 guard as he unlocked the padlocks to the steel doors located on the right end of the one-story building. The stench and humid air hit me when he opened the door. We walked down a dark corridor that felt damp and airless. The floor was concrete, pitted, and slimy with sticky sweat. On either side of us were small steel doors with tiny barred openings framing the faces of the curious Cambodians locked in their cells. We stopped at door eleven. The guard with army fatigues unlocked the padlock and pulled the small door open. He grunted and motioned me inside.

After I squeezed in, I was startled by the smell of sewage and reluctantly inhaled to hold off from fainting. My legs weakened and I quickly sat down on a two-foot high concrete ledge before me. There were four Khmer men in the room. One had a deformed head that looked like it had been beaten with a heavy club. I couldn't move. The prisoners stared at me with their black, terrified eyes as I sat in shock in the small, hot, airless dungeon.

I felt faint as I glared around the cell. The stained mustard-colored concrete walls and ceiling were covered in cobwebs and were thick with dead insects. The size of the rough concrete floor was six feet by ten feet. We had a concrete water trough that wasn't much longer than three feet. Next to that was the hole where we pissed and shit like dogs.

I sat on the ledge. My feet were on the damp floor next to the door. I already was dealing with a lack of sleep, the stress from the interrogations, and my shattered heart resulting from the separation between me and my loved ones, and now I had to deal with this. I needed to gather my thoughts. This was going to be tough. I needed energy to draw from. Right now, there just wasn't any. I tried to stabilize myself. I'd only been in this concrete box for three minutes, but it felt like an eternity.

One of the inmates stood up and walked over to me. He held out his hand, saying, "Hello. I speak little English. My name is Mista T."

I slowly reached out to him and said, "Hello. My name is Joe." I tried to get my equilibrium and stood up. The other three inmates made room on the floor and gave me a spot in the left corner. Each of us had just enough space to lie down straight. The perimeter wall outside the cell was only eight feet from our building and prevented a breeze from coming through. Insects, birds, bats, and anything else could enter through this opening that was too high to look out of.

I looked around the cell. It was filthy. The walls bore decades of stains that were brownish-yellow. The smell was indescribable. I stepped up to the upper space and everyone pointed at my loafers. I removed them and left them by the door. I sat down on my space in the corner. I thought it was a good spot, being the furthest from the shit hole. Sweat poured off me like I had just run a marathon.

Mr. T's broken English was a great help. Slowly, we communicated. He explained how, because I was a foreigner, I could get out into the yard twice a day at 7:30 AM and at 2:00 PM. I remembered Bruce Howard telling me that if they didn't let me out for air twice per day, a human rights violation charge would be brought against them and their foreign aid would then be reconsidered.

"Most of us Cambodians can't go outside," Mr. T said.

"Why?" I asked.

"We cannot afford to."

I had to get used to being stared at. Cambodian country people, even uneducated city dwellers, had a habit of staring at foreigners. So there I sat with all eyes focused on me. One of the young Khmer men was fascinated with my skin. He would look closely at every inch of me and point out every insect bite or scratch that I had.

"If you get hot," Mr. T said, "take a bucket and dip into water and pour over yourself, over there." He pointed to the sewer hole by the water trough.

I noticed that their bodies had bites everywhere. This place was infested with insects, just like Hing Peo's dungeon had been.

I was tired, and when I laid down on the hard floor, Mr. T handed me a plastic water bottle to use as a pillow.

My body was racked with misery. My thoughts floated from my daughters in America and how I needed to take care of them to wondering when our Cambodian contacts would get us released to Ahm to how she filled the void in my heart.

I looked up at the cobwebbed ceiling. It looked like a room in a horror film. In the center of the room some wires dangled, and they were attached to a single, naked light bulb.

I must be strong, I thought as the song that Ahm and I had used to listen to played in my head: "Somebody tell me why / one dark morning / when this life is over / I'll see your face . . . "

My body lay motionless, shutting itself down to regain strength. It was in a state of suspension.

My four cellmates rearranged themselves in a circle and squatted, Asian-style. They handed out metal plates and spoons. I could hear sounds coming from the hall outside the small steel door.

This must be dinnertime, I thought.

I heard the sound of the padlock being undone and the old, rusty hatch cranking open. A Khmer inmate passed two dented, metal pots onto the floor inside our cell. One contained rice that looked like shit, while the other was full of soup. The water looked black and carried dark-green leaves garnished with small stones. It smelled as horrible as it looked. I was handed a battered plate, but I declined. I was hungry, but the smell turned my stomach. I returned to my space instead of consuming the foul food.

I dozed off, dreaming of my days in the sun with my family at our home in Milford. The video in my mind played a scene of my daughters swimming in our pool. I saw the majestic views through the vista beyond, smelled the sweet scent of the pine forest, and heard the cheerful laughter of my children.

~~~

DAY ONE: T.3 PRISON JULY 5, 1998

The following morning I heard a clanging sound, like metal on metal. Then a strange song played over a crackly loudspeaker. All the doors opened. I got up and noticed a puddle of sweat beneath where I had slept. I met the Bird in the hall.

"Hey, you all right man?" he asked.

"Yeah. You?"

Breathless, the Bird spoke. "We gotta get out of here."

"I agree."

We walked out into the glaring sunlight. I couldn't shake the sick feeling I had. In the 100 degree heat, we assembled in the compound. A Khmer soldier stood in front of the eighty or so inmates. I could now see that the Bird and I were the only Westerners in our section. Everyone stood in four straight lines of twenty. The Bird and I stood in the rear line as the soldier in front, dressed in army fatigues, read a long Khmer speech from a white sheet of paper. Bird and I didn't understand a word that he said.

After the speech, everyone had to do calisthenics. When everyone got down and did push-ups, most of the inmates quit at five or ten. The Bird stopped at thirty. As sweat poured off me, I did sixty good ones. Everyone turned and watched. When I got up, I could see the smiles of the inmates around me. This released the anger that I had pent up inside.

The Bird and I walked the perimeter of the compound, looking for a weakness in the structure.

"I wonder where Chin and the rest of the guys are," the Bird said.

"I don't know," I said. "I need an interpreter so that I can deal with these guards. Then maybe we can see the others."

They never gave Bird and I the blue prison garb. I assumed that we were too big for it. I still was wearing my tan shorts and short-sleeved, button-down shirt. I could see that my shorts were getting loose from the lack of food, so I tied a shoelace between the two belt loops on my right side to help hold them up.

Bird said that he felt lightheaded and went to his cell to lie down. I continued to walk around the compound, making mental notes of it.

No one spoke to me. Most of the inmates had returned to their cells. About twenty of the inmates remained outside. After several trips around the perimeter, I found our way out! I would show the Bird this escape route. Only a man over six feet tall could attempt this, which is why it had never been done.

There were two large water troughs by the steel-barred exit door. These were our sources of drinking and washing water. I felt weak, so I held my hands under a stream of water leading into the concrete trough from a pipe.

As I cupped my hands to catch the flowing water, I looked up and noticed that, in the corner by the door to the tomb-like building where our cells were, an inmate was kneeling with his hands cuffed behind him. Standing over him was a dark-skinned guard with slicked-back hair. He was beating the small young man with a black club. The guard violently swung the club, seemingly as hard as he could. He hit the young man in the head, back, face, everywhere. The inmate cried out and stole glances up at his abuser in pleading astonishment. I felt helpless. I knew that it wasn't my place to intervene. It just went on for so long. When the guard kicked him, he rolled over. I noticed that he was one of my roommates.

Another guard called everyone inside. All we got was about an hour of air and light and then we had to go back into the dungeons. My roommate that had been beaten senseless was in bad shape. He still had his handcuffs on as he lay on the concrete floor, bruised and bleeding.

Mr. T explained how this beaten man and a group of other inmates were working near the front gates when they all saw an opportunity to escape. They made it halfway to the final fence before the guards captured them at gunpoint. We cleaned his wounds as best as we could.

The following day, the attempted escapees had their hair shaved off, except for two clumps on the tops of their heads which resembled mouse ears. This would make them stand out for awhile.

They would also have to wear the steel cuffs twenty-four hours a day, for sixty days. They now couldn't leave the cell for fresh air or sun for an undetermined period of time.

I got to know the 23-year-old beaten man and found out that he was serving a 20-year sentence for political reasons. That was all that I could get translated. I liked him and tried to help him in any way that I could.

At 2:00 PM, Bird and I and about twenty paying inmates were let out for air. I carefully showed the section of the exterior perimeter wall to Bird. We were behind the tomb building that contained our cells. Here, we were out of view from the manned tower. The decaying condition of the old wall created cavities in the brick-work, leaving a climbable pattern and, because we were over six feet tall and not the standard five-foot-tall Cambodian man, we could stretch and get a hold of key spots on the twelve-foot-high wall.

My plan was to carry a woven mat – which were plentiful in the compound – to the top and hammer down the shards of sharp glass that were stuck in the mortar on top of the wall by using a rock. I then would lay the mat over the barbed wire that was on the outside of the wall and jump to the other side. If I held onto the wall on the outside, it would only be a six-foot drop to the ground.

One problem with this plan was that we could only do this in the daylight when we were out of our cells. The other was that, if we did reach the other side, where would we go? We would certainly stand out in Phnom Penh.

"We need outside help," I said to Bird. "A waiting car to take us away might be necessary."

"What about the brothers or Harley? Get in touch with them to help us!"

"I agree. When Bruce Howard comes from the Embassy, I'll call a lawyer using his cell phone. As of now, we don't even know what we're being charged with. Then we'll use the lawyer's phone to call the Übel brothers."

Bird and I stood in the alley between the tomb and the perimeter wall, sweating and trying to grasp the situation.

"Listen," I said, "if our people can get us out of here and recover our load, I say we complete our end of the operation. If not, we have to get out one way or another. This place is fucked up. The water is bad to drink. The food is worse. If we get sick, we're dead. We're either living or we're staying."

"I'm with ya, boss," Bird said.

"Bird," I said, "we have to stay in shape. We may have to run to the Embassy from here. Every morning before the day gets too hot, we'll run in the alleyway and do both push-ups and sit-ups."

We looked at this place between the wall and the building. It looked to be about nine feet wide and ninety feet long. We started walking back and forth down one side. Then we did an about-face at the end, and returned back. Back and forth we walked while we discussed our plan. At one point, we stopped at the far end of the alley to look at something that had an ominous feel about it.

There, embedded in the concrete wall that was perpendicular to the other perimeter wall, and parallel to the end of the tomb building, were two rusty steel rings. All around these two steel rings were bullet holes in the concrete. Facing the wall to the left was a narrow alleyway about three feet wide between the end of the tomb and the wall. Under our feet was a drain in the concrete surface. It was later explained to us what this area was used for.

The unfortunate one was handcuffed to this ring, shot from the opposite end of the alley, and then dragged away in the three foot alley to the left. The blood-stained drain below us had an obvious purpose.

From that day on, Bird and I met every morning – when we weren't too ill – and ran from one end to the other for forty-five minutes. This got our heart rates up and made us sweat like dogs. We stayed in shape by using the area we came to call "execution alley."

The head guard would signal us inside after only one hour. We would be locked in our small, airless cells for twenty-two hours each day.

From my hot box, I could hear Buddhist monks chanting from the other side of the wall. "Nan wu guan shi yin pusa – Nan wu guan shi yin pusa." The chanting and occasional gong sound went on for hours as I lay on the rough concrete floor in my filthy, mustard yellow-stained dungeon. Mealtime had the same horrible food as before: bad rice and smelly black watery soup. I was starving, so I accepted a battered tin plate and spoon and joined my cellmates.

I remained on my small spot on the floor. Even after sunset, the stifling heat kept my skin dripping with sweat. At night, the naked light bulb above our heads attracted insects through the opening in the exterior wall. My right arm never stopped fanning my overheated body. I used a piece of torn plastic from an old water bottle. When I dozed off, the fan remained poised and ready, so when I returned from my dream state, I could resume my relentless fanning.

Most evenings, the men in the Section C tomb where Bird and I were housed would sing old Khmer songs. Their voices echoed from their small door openings in the dark hallway. I would lie on my back and listen to the beautiful sounds. Sometimes, one man would take the lead and sing a verse of spoken Khmer words, and then a chorus of voices would respond to his words with heartfelt singing. In the midst of such suffering and hopelessness, creative expression and beauty emerged.

The light of the dawn filtering through the rebar opening meant that I must have let the whole night slip past my consciousness as though in a trance in the thick, stifling heat. I learned from Mr. T that the sound I was hearing every morning was a guard banging a hanging steel truck tire rim with a metal bar. The old song that I heard over the old public address system was the Cambodian national anthem. At 7:00 every morning, I awoke to the clamor of the steel-on-steel banging and the screeching, crackling sound of the national anthem, which sounded like an old Chinese black and white propaganda movie from the Mao-era.

Soon after the anthem, the drone of Buddhist monks chanting over the loudspeaker outside the wall set the pace for the sweltering day before me. I grew to enjoy the morning national anthem. I hummed it as it played each morning. It was a slow, tragic song – beautiful, but sad.

After my morning workout, I was usually thoroughly drenched in sweat, so I would stand next to the outdoor water trough and bathe. I would pour cold water over my head using a battered rice pot. Every morning, I washed with soap and water as 45 to 50 Cambodian prisoners watched me. These were the prisoners that were left out in the morning to carry water. Their intense stares were sometimes comical. If I missed a small lather of soap from under my arm, 30 or more men would simultaneously point and notify me of the missed lather. I would thank them and pour a rice pot full of water over the place of interest.

One day, I stood next to the water trough to bathe. The steel-barred door behind me was open and many prisoners were saying farewell to a popular inmate who was leaving. The departing inmate was the former Minister of Finance. The young Cambodian politician had gotten caught up in a pre-election power struggle that landed him here in T.3 prison. I could see his white Toyota four-door sedan poised in the outer courtyard facing the large, rusty, steel exit doors.

Inmates from Section C, where the Minister of Finance had been living, surrounded his car and cheered. Seconds after the dark, steel exit doors swung open, gunshots rang out from the outside and a return salvo of gunfire erupted from the T.3 guards. A mass of prisoners in their blue Chinese-style uniforms ran toward me, screaming as the white Toyota raced out.

Soldiers from the Minister's opposing party fired into the prison. The T.3 guards fired back from the towers and walls at the attacking soldiers. A T.3 guard ran in front of the massive swarm of yelling prisoners. The excited guard pointed at me and screamed something in Khmer as bullets ricocheted off the walls.

My wet body was covered with soap as I dove to the ground behind the water trough. Like a stampede of crazed cattle, the inmates raced by me, kicking up dust in their wake. The Minister of Finance literally had to shoot his way out of T.3 prison on that sweltering-hot day in July.

I jumped up and poured water over myself and rushed inside to find the Bird. He was ill and was in his cell trying to rest his feverish body. I was short of breath when I described what had happened.

The Bird was delirious but had still heard the commotion. His fever had risen since I had seen him earlier. My roommate Mr. T gave me some bottled water and some aspirin.

"There is no medicine here," Mr. T explained. "If you get very sick, a Buddhist monk comes to extract the evil spirits from you. My wife gave me this water and aspirin. You take to your American friend. I will tell my wife to bring more."

The Bird was in bad shape. His high fever, spinning head, and aching bones and muscles were not going to go away soon. I had to do something.

I noticed a quiet Cambodian inmate who had a small herb garden growing in the yard. He had a kind face, short hair, and wore round, steel-rimmed glasses. He was slight in build and soft-spoken. I noticed that the guards and other inmates treated him with respect. I asked Mr. T about him and learned that he spoke English very well and that he was highly connected.

I returned to the yard. I hoped that, through this Cambodian man, I could learn how to get things done around here. I spotted him sitting next to his herb garden. I walked up to him slowly and gave him a wai, saying, "Hello, my name is Joe Harding."

He returned my wai and motioned for me to sit down next to him. He carefully placed his freshly-picked herb leaves into a wooden bowl.

"I flavor my fish and vegetables with my garden herbs. It really does make a big difference in the taste," he said. After he had completed his work, he extended his small, smooth hand. "My name is Ganson Brower."

"You speak English very well," I said.

Ganson smiled. "Fortunately, I have lived in America for many years." Ganson slowly explained how he had worked in the Ministry of Industry and had joined several committees. "I was kidnapped and brought here to T.3. I'm negotiating my ransom. It's a slow process."

"How long have you been here?" I asked.

"Six months. So far, I've worked them down to my paying $400,000 to get out of here. My family is prepared to pay, but I insist that they hold off and wait for me to reduce the amount. In these situations, you must practice patience. I have been observing you since your arrival here, Joe, and you really must calm down and move slower. Remember where you are."

His well-spoken voice mesmerized me. He almost had me convinced to lay back and dig in. However, decades of struggling, overcoming obstacles, and relentlessly pushing myself overrode his convincing advice.

"Ganson, I hear what you're saying and appreciate your kind advice, but I've got other plans, and dying here in T.3 is not one of them."

When Bruce Howard arrived from the U.S. Embassy, he smuggled in a *Time* magazine with cash inside from our families. My brother had sent money and Ahm had spoken to the Übel brothers to let them know that I would be calling them. As a result of my fingerprints being taken, my true identity was relayed to the U.S. Embassy. Bruce Howard treated this revelation all in stride. After all, this was Southeast Asia – the land of illusion.

"Intelligence and DEA agents are trying to enter T.3 prison to speak to you," Bruce told me. "But the commander here is refusing to allow them in. But there's a two party system here at T.3 and when Koon Boon Sorn, the prison commander, is away, the second in command here can allow these agents in – for a price, of course. So be prepared to be questioned by U.S. agents at some point."

Bird and I were weak. Our health had deteriorated since our capture on the June 28. It was now mid-July. Bird had a fever, I had dysentery – our skin was raw from insect bites and heat rash.

Bruce set up a phone link with our families through the Embassy. On his cell phone, he could call his office from T.3 and they would call the States and patch us in from there.

When Virginia's voice hit me, I felt crushed. My family seemed farther away than ever. Her voice struck a chord that forgave all the pain that she had ever caused me. It didn't matter – it was Virginia on the other end of the phone and that was home, that was my family. It was an emotional conversation. When Arli spoke to me, it was hard to hold it in.

"Dad, are you all right?" she asked.

"Yes, sweetheart. I . . . miss . . . you." I couldn't speak any longer.

Bruce suggested that I contact a lawyer while I still had the cell phone. I called one of the lawyers on the Embassy list and made arrangements to meet him the following day. Seeing and speaking to Bruce Howard was comforting. He was a Western face – an outside contact.

"Any further calls that you would like to make?" he asked.

"Yes," I replied. "I need my sneakers and some clothes sent from Bangkok. Can I call Ahm?"

"No problem. You can call anyone that you need to."

Ahm answered her cell phone.

"Mac, where are you?"

"I'm still in Cambodia, sweetheart."

"Oh, Mac, I worry 'bout you. Please let me come. I can take care you!"

"Ahm, I'm in prison here. You can't come here. Listen, can you send me my sneakers and some underwear, t-shirts, and shorts?"

"All right, darling, I do for you. Mac, I move from Omni to my mother's. Mac . . . Aleaf and Na miss you . . . I miss you. When you come home, Mac?"

"I'm trying hard to get out of here."

"You are my only love, Mac. Only you."

"I'm sorry, Ahm. I'll get out of here soon." My heart was aching.

"Be strong, Mac. Don't worry 'bout me. I can do for myself. I be here when you get out. Now I want to come see you!"

"Not now, Ahm. It's too dangerous here. The election is soon and it's not safe for you to come."

～～～

The following day, the Embassy-approved lawyer never arrived. Ganson explained how these Embassy-approved lawyers were not very dependable and lacked resources.

"I can introduce you to the chan wan – in English, the prison commander – Koon Boon Sorn," Ganson said. "I can interpret for you, also."

I thought about it and agreed with him. "Set up a meeting."

At night, I bore the endless attacks from flying and crawling insects, and the pain and stiffness in my joints caused from lying in one position on the sweat-soaked concrete – no cots, no beds, nothing. Also, the waves of stomach cramps from my dysentery. But these were minor torments compared to the torment that existed in my heart.

Now I gazed around the ancient Cambodian prison cell. The glare from the dangling bare light bulb irritated my eyes. The queer light that it cast caused the smudges and stains on the filthy walls to form images – mostly faces. One biblical-looking face – one that Michelangelo might have drawn – sternly leered out from the corner above the sewer hole. The Moses look-alike face with a long beard and fiery eyes was surrounded by other faces. Some looked like gargoyles that I remember staring down at me through my Mercedes' sunroof when I drove over New York avenues on cool fall days now a world away.

I was delusional, dehydrated, and slowly baking in a filthy concrete box.

Next to me, Mr. T carefully relieved the pressure from boils located on another prisoner's head by lancing them with a razor. The oozing fluid mixed with the man's blood trickled down the poor man's back, as tears welled up in his eyes from the pain.

I would soon experience this same primitive surgery when my skull became the host for boils the size of golf balls cut in half. It was time to lance them when it became too painful to rest my boil-covered head on the plastic water bottle pillows.

Outside, over the perimeter wall, I could hear the cluk, cluk, cluk, of the noodle vendor. I was told that each traveling vendor had a distinct code that was played out by hitting hollow wooden blocks with wooden sticks. This signaled customers in advance that he or she was coming. My stomach ached and cramped. I realized that I never pissed. I drank as much water as I could and never urinated. I sweated all the water out through my raw, insect-bitten skin.

~ ~ ~

"Look, the indictment was dated June 24, 1998," Bird said, sitting near me in the courtyard. "We were in Bangkok then. We didn't come into Cambodia until June 28. The Feds could have busted us in Thailand! The indictment is for the *Oktedy*, six months ago!"

We both thought in silence.

"Why did they allow us to enter Cambodia?" I asked. "They must have been watching us. It makes no sense to let us enter Cambodia during such a dangerous time."

Bird rolled his eyes and threw down his sandal that he was trying to repair. "Looks like we can forget finishing our project, even if we can get out of here soon and recover our load."

"We'll see. I'll speak to the brothers and find out what they want to do. If they abort the operation and we have to live over here and wait out the *Oktedy* case, we'll need a way to earn money. Plus, we can't live in Thailand. The DEA is strong there and Thailand has an extradition treaty with the U.S. Cambodia doesn't. I'm going to see the chan wan. I'll let him know that we want out and are going to work and live in Cambodia. I'll even make him a partner! Ganson told me that there're many foreigners living here who have legal problems elsewhere. The owner of the Intercontinental Hotel, Moo Muan, is wanted by the U.S. and he's untouchable here. He's buddies with Hun Sen!"

"Don't forget to tell the brothers that we need our fucking passports. I don't know why we handed them over to them in the first place!"

Ganson walked over and announced that we had to leave for our meeting with Koon Boon Sorn.

I rehearsed my Cambodian courtesies in my mind before entering the chan wan's office. The commander's personal aide opened the office door and escorted us to two chairs near a large wooden table. The commander of T.3 prison stood up as I greeted him.

"Jun thrip sool," I said as I gave him a deep wai to show my respect.

He responded in kind. We then sat down. Ganson was to my right at the end of the table. The chan wan sat across from me, slightly to my left.

The wooden table was partially covered with papers. There were two phones and a black briefcase. The walls and furniture were filled with memorabilia, files, and plaques. Koon Boon Sorn looked 60 years old, was slight in build with thinning hair combed back, and had a hardened face. His eyes were just slits. His military uniform was clean and crisp, and he carried himself like an important man should. I sat at attention with my hands folded before me.

The chan wan looked me over as Ganson spoke Khmer to him. Then Ganson listened as the chan wan spoke.

"He wants to know if you're a boxer."

I smiled and said, "No, I just work out."

He looked at my folded hands and smiled as I said this.

Ganson and Koon Boon Sorn spoke at length. When they had completed their conversation, Ganson interpreted it.

"The chan wan informs me that he is well aware of what is happening to you. He says he is close to people who you are working with. He has already been informed that they are trying to obtain your release. However, there are others who are not part of your group who are trying to use you for political purposes and want to keep you here.

"The chan wan is trying to keep the DEA and CIA out of T.3. He says not to trust anyone. There are spies even here in T.3 – inmates and guards alike."

I asked Ganson to ask the chan wan if there was any way that I could use the prison phone system, as I needed to have communication abilities.

Ganson interpreted and the commander sat and silently thought. He then looked up, and with his eyes opened wider than before, he spoke. Ganson translated.

"He said that he can give you a cell phone to use. However, you must try to hide it from the guards that search the cells. You're not supposed to have a device like this here and you must be careful."

Ganson interpreted the chan wan's plan to release the Bird, Captain Chin, his aides, Sham, and me.

"First, you must hire a special lawyer. The chan wan can call him from here. He is a close friend of his. The lawyer will handle your release. You will be sent to see His Excellency, Judge Om Sadithd. Because it is only a marijuana case, and because there seems to be political reasons for your abduction to begin with, he feels confident the charges will never be brought against you as long as the right people are paid. Timing is important. Much depends on the circumstances surrounding the election. Joe, he says there is still something going on with your situation that he does not understand. It has to do with the U.S. government. He says to be very careful."

The chan wan dialed the lawyer's number. After a brief conversation, a meeting was set for that afternoon. The chan wan stood up and opened his desk drawer and handed me a carton of 555 cigarettes. I stood and wai-ed him as I accepted his gracious gift. This was an expensive, imported brand and was worth a half-month's salary for a Cambodian school teacher.

I returned to my cell feeling energized – like there was still hope to complete the mission.

Ganson had said that the maximum penalty in Cambodia for marijuana was

30 days in jail, no matter how much weed we had. Plus, there were no conspiracy laws in Cambodia. As far as Ganson knew, this was the first marijuana case that he had ever heard of in Cambodia.

"No one gets arrested for marijuana here," he'd said. "It's sold in the marketplace. Little old ladies use it to spice their soups. Even the pizza place in Phnom Penh sprinkles marijuana on their pizzas – it's called 'happy pizza.'"

~ ~ ~

Te Poe, the Cambodian lawyer that the chan wan had called, met Bird and I in an office located off the main courtyard. He was about 5'8" with thick black hair combed back and a smooth, friendly face. I figured that he was 45 years old. He spoke English fairly well. We all sat casually in the office under a slowly rotating ceiling fan. The open window with steel bars overlooked the courtyard. Moments after we had arrived, a guard entered with a brown paper bag.

"This is for you both to enjoy," Te Poe said.

"Holy shit!" Bird said as he pulled two cold beers out of the bag and a whole roasted chicken with French bread. Bird and I ate like wolves while Te Poe spoke.

He explained his fee: $70,000 for Bird and I and $30,000 for the three Thais and Sham. He then explained how he had to pay important people. His uncle, "His Most Excellent Excellency," was one.

"You tell His Most Excellent Excellency to keep sending the food and we'll make a deal," I said.

The Bird laughed. I asked Te Poe if I could see Captain Chin so I could discuss the financial arrangements.

"Yes, let me know. I can do this for you," he said.

"I also need to speak to my partners in Bangkok. Can I use your cell phone?"

"Yes." He handed me his pocket-size cell phone.

I dialed J.T. After one ring, he answered.

"Hey, it's me!" I said excitedly.

"Yes, King. How are you, buddy?"

J.T. sounded so calm, like nothing was wrong – unlike his frantic calls for help when he was in Cambodia at the hands of Hing Peo only a month earlier when he had pleaded for money and help. I now briefed him on what our status was in Cambodia.

"Don't worry. We'll take care of everything. Send your lawyer to Bangkok so we can speak to him. We'll try to cut a better deal."

"Listen, don't worry about a better deal. We can still recover our cargo and complete our project. Is Haig still in a position to work?"

"Yes. In fact, we are working on sending our share of the load to your people in America as we speak. I would rather pay your lawyer with the profits from the operation. I'm sure you understand our position."

I understand, I thought. *When he was kidnapped, the money was made available. I even spent a large amount of my own cash trying to help him. Now we need help and it's not a big concern to him.*

"Why don't you allocate the funds and reimburse yourself after the project is complete?" I asked.

J.T. stuttered. "I really don't want to discuss this any further over an open phone line. Just send your lawyer. We'll discuss this with him."

J.T. was skirting the issue. I could hear music in the background and ice cubes clinking around in his drink. I could hear him periodically take sips of the beverage.

"Where are you?" I asked.

"I'm in the Crown Royal."

"Is Ahm there?"

"Yes. Would you like to speak to her?"

"Yes, put her on."

I could hear Bob speak to Ahm. I heard the cell phone move outside. Then Ahm spoke.

"Mac, where are you?"

"I'm still in Cambodia, sweetheart!"

"I walk outside, Mac, so I can talk to you. Mac, J.T. he no good. He act bad to me. He look like he happy you hurt, Mac! He try to touch me." Ahm was crying now. "Please, Mac, let me come see you. Let me take care you!"

"Ahm, it's too dangerous here. Wait. Soon, I will be released. Then you can come here. Maybe you can live here with me for a while. Would you be willing to live here with me?"

I knew that I couldn't return to America and Thailand was also too hot for me.

"Mac, I live with you anywhere in world. I just want to be with you, darling – I don't care where we go to live."

"Soon we will be together. Then we will start a new life. Sweetheart, I want you to stay away from J.T. He's a bad man."

"I know, darling. He . . . he so ugly to me."

"Soon I will have a cell phone. I'll call you. Please, Ahm, just a little longer!"

"Okay, darling, I wait for you. I love you, darling."

"I love you too, Ahm."

Fucking Bob Übel, I thought. *What a lowlife.* I remembered one night when Harley had invited Ahm and me out for drinks to a new restaurant in a luxury hotel. As we entered the lobby, Ahm and I had noticed that Harley's girlfriend and her sister had been sitting with him, having drinks. Ahm knew both girls well, and when Ahm and I walked toward them, Harley's girlfriend's sister – whom I knew to be not only beautiful, but a good-hearted person as well – had jumped up and ran right past us with an expression of fear on her face. I noticed at the same time that she hadn't even sipped her fancy cocktail with a pink umbrella on top. She had just blown by us. She hadn't even said hello.

I asked Harley why she had left like that and Harley responded, "Oh, she just learned that Bob was coming in a little while."

Now Ahm was upset because of his selfish, disrespectful perversions.

Now he's telling me to relax and enjoy Asia's most dreaded prison after he had cried like a baby when he had been in my shoes on June 5.

Over the next few weeks, I had several phone conversations with Bob Übel from T.3 prison. While I was suffering from illness in the heat and unthinkable conditions, he was at least 95 percent of the time at the Crown Royal, enjoying the air-conditioning, alcohol, and pretty girls. Since my abduction, he had made this place where Ahm worked his second home. He had never spent this kind of time there before.

I kept control over my emotions. As it turned out, Bob had stalled any attempt to help us. No money was sent. He cancelled his meeting with my lawyer and continued to hang out at the Crown Royal.

Every time I would call Ahm, he was there partying. Te Poe and Bird watched me sit in silence after my latest phone call.

I returned the cell phone to Te Poe. I had a bittersweet feeling about the conversation with J.T. *The operation is still on! Incredible!* I explained to Te Poe that I needed to see him again so we could make arrangements to send him a retainer.

"Tomorrow, Joe, I will come here to see you," he said.

The Bird and I returned to Section C.

After the chan wan had equipped me with my own cell phone, I contacted my brother, who was in close touch with the Übel brothers and all the partners involved in the project. Everyone was relieved that the brothers were coming in with a load. The 6,000 pounds they were bringing in would generate enough profit to make our original plan workable.

I would need these funds to take care of my family while I was living in Southeast Asia. I would return to deal with the *Oktedy* case when the time was right. My brother informed me that August 21 was the brothers' ETA. Skip, Woodstock Willy, and all of their people were getting ready to accept the much-needed load of Thai herb.

When I spoke to my brother, he said, "Sit tight. Sometime in October, we'll get you out!"

Amazing, I thought, *now the Übel brothers and my partners in America are all in agreement to let us rot.*

I decided to find our own way out of T.3 prison while the operation was underway.

~~~

It was early August. I was now visibly worn from my fever and dysentery. I had lost many pounds and I moved a little slower.

I sat upright at a wooden table across from Judge Om Sadithd. Te Poe and two court clerks were also present in the cluttered judge's office. I knew that my actions didn't match my appearance. I tried to project a strong, confident front, but my longish hair, red and sickly eyes, and gaunt face were telling another story.

The judge's interpreter asked me a series of questions about why I was in Koh Kong. I described my business interests: the ice factory, the prawn farm. After a half hour of relatively easy questions, I was asked how many ships my partner Captain Chin had in the Gulf of Thailand for smuggling contraband.

I strongly denied that he had any such ships, and I insisted that he was a good man. After more questions about my view on U.S.-Cambodian politics, I was asked to sign the statement. I asked the interpreter to reread the document before I signed. The judge was friendly toward me and offered me a bottle of cold water to drink, which I was happy to accept.

The part about Captain Chin was all wrong, and I would not sign the paper until it was corrected. It seemed strange but the judge was trying to make Captain Chin the fall guy. I would not let this happen. The document was reworded to my satisfaction, portraying Chin as a legitimate businessman, before I signed off.

The Bird went into the office next and had a similar experience.

On our way back to T.3, Bird and I discussed our options. The Übel brothers had refused to help us. Because of the U.S. indictment, it looked like we had to stay in Cambodia. The chan wan said that he could supply security for us in Cambodia and help us get a license to start a business.

Thailand was out, even after the cargo was sold and money was available. The DEA would be waiting for us to return to Bangkok. Bob informed me that he and Harley had both been confronted by the DEA, so the writing was on the wall. We could live in Cambodia or return to America and fight the dark side.

Virginia agreed that I should stay in Asia. After the mission was complete, my brother and my partners would give her a large part of my profits. She would then be able to support our three daughters, sending them to the best colleges and living a normal life. My family and I would arrange to meet in Europe.

Weeks before the election, Bruce Howard sent us a message. He explained that it was too dangerous for him to come visit us – the area around T.3 prison was a political hotbed and there was too much gunfire.

At night, the inmates in our cell played a game they called "Guess the Guns." Enthusiastic discussions would erupt whenever a larger boom was heard. They jumped up and debated what heavier ordinance was fired, like a 37mm or a 57mm round or mortar shell. Most of the inmates were soldiers or policemen, and most were there for political reasons or for kidnapping. In Cambodia, kidnapping was rampant. There had been one situation where a Japanese businessman was kidnapped by the police. A $300,000 ransom was paid from his Tokyo corporation and the man was released.

Officers in the Cambodian army found out about this successful kidnapping and quickly kidnapped the policemen who were responsible for the original kidnapping and held them for $300,000 ransom.

With Ganson's help, we were living better. I changed rooms. I was now in room 16. I had better roommates, too – they were mostly educated students from Phnom Penh. Bird and I would buy whatever was needed through the guards.

Unfortunately, everything I ate my body expelled because of the dysentery. On and off, the Bird and I suffered from fever and strange illnesses.

If it weren't for Ganson's help, I don't know what would have happened. Bruce Howard was not able to see us because of the danger around T.3 prison. No matter how much food we bought, we always ended up with just enough to live on. If I bought a bunch of bananas, they weren't my bananas, they were just a bunch of bananas and any of the poor and starving prisoners would help themselves. The communist way of thinking still lingered in the minds of many Cambodians. I could have brought two chickens, but in the end, I would have been left with a small leg and a wing.

I had several meetings with Te Poe and Captain Chin. I even arranged a meeting with all six of our team members. We met in an old shack in Section A of T.3. A sign had been nailed above its weathered wooden door that was childishly hand-painted in red. It read, *Khmer Rouge Re-Education Center*. The place looked like a bomb had hit it.

When I finally saw Captain Sham and the Thais, their ordeal was etched on their haunted, stubbly faces. Their eyes were red-rimmed and their bodies bone-thin. Little did I realize that I looked the same to them.

Bird and I were resigned to the fact that we might have to wait for the mission to be completed before we could get everyone released.

~~~

It was mid-August. Hun Sen had won the election by a hair, and Prince Norodom Ranarithd and his Funsinpec Party and Sam Rainsy and his party protested the outcome. Stories leaked into the media about election fraud. Before a new cabinet could be formed, the Royal Cambodian government was in a peculiar state of non-existence. Until the formalities were completed, there was no Cambodian government. Hun Sen held his power through his army.

Several weeks after the election, all the government ministers, party chiefs, and other officials traveled to a beautiful government estate in the countryside. Hun Sen would now be sworn in as the first Prime Minister of Cambodia.

On the way to the assembly, Hun Sen's car was attacked by an anti-tank rocket. The deadly explosive missed his car by a matter of feet and blew up a home across the street, killing four innocent people. The attackers were never caught.

After Hun Sen was sworn in, a photograph was taken of all the members of the government, all dressed in white. It showed Hun Sen looking to his left, over to the other end of the group at his suspected enemies Sam Rainsy and Prince Norodom Ranarithd. I will never forget the angry, dangerous look I saw upon his face when I was shown the photograph.

Bird and I had made arrangements to have money sent to Koon Boon Sorn and our lawyer, Te Poe. Mike's family, Virginia, and my brother sent money. Captain Chin promised to transfer his portion of the legal fees to Te Poe's bank account. However, in Bangkok, Captain Chin's wife Nok explained to us how her bank account had been frozen by the Thai police when the U.S. DEA notified them of our attempt to transfer funds to her.

The Bangkok and Phnom Penh newspapers were running articles about us. One article stated that we were attempting to bribe the Cambodian government with five million U.S. dollars. This misinformation caused major problems in our efforts to finalize our negotiations to be released.

Colonel Hing Peo showboated the situation by holding a public burning of 7,000 pounds of marijuana. The marijuana was piled up and burned in Phnom Penh so the world media could witness how Cambodia had turned itself around and become a law-abiding nation that had joined the world in its fight against drugs. Again, our names were mentioned during this high-profile maneuver to gain acceptance from the world.

The timing was perfect for Colonel Hing Peo, as an international convention was about to begin in Europe where Cambodia stood to gain a position to receive millions of dollars in foreign aid for the war on drugs. Colonel Hing Peo's show of police commitment was all staged in order to receive aid that would eventually be skimmed by corrupt Cambodian officials and then deposited in secret bank accounts in Europe and the Caribbean.

Our lawyer, Te Poe, met with the Bird and me, and he was lost for words over how difficult it had become. He said that the U.S. government was all over our attempt to be released from T.3 prison. All the Cambodian government authorities involved in our effort to be released were being watched for any corruption or favoritism. Meanwhile, no charges were brought against us.

~ ~ ~

7:30 AM: AUGUST 21, 1998

My cell phone rang. I was alone in my cell, but I answered quickly anyway.

"Hi, Art. It's me, Virginia," my wife said. "I'm calling to tell you that your brother called. He's under arrest. He said to tell you that the Übel brothers were behind the *Oktedy* seizure and your capture in Cambodia. This last mission was also a setup! He said that he saw the brothers through his hotel window in Seattle just before the Feds busted him. The brothers were leaning against their white Cadillac, laughing! It's over, Art. All your friends have been arrested!"

I tried to take it all in. It filled my senses beyond assimilation.

"What do I do about money now?" Virginia asked.

"Don't worry. I'll work it all out." I spoke without thinking. I was just reacting to her crazy question. "Try to speak to his lawyer. I'll call you again tomorrow at the same time. Try to find out more information."

"Okay, Art. Sorry I had to tell you this."

"Thanks for telling me. I'll speak to you tomorrow."

I felt faint. I tried to comprehend what I'd just heard. I slowly walked down to Bird's cell.

"We're alone, Bird," I said as I walked into his cell. "My brother, Skip, Willy, Greg – everybody's dead. They were all arrested in Seattle. And to make matters worse, the Übel brothers were behind the whole thing. Even the *Oktedy* seizure."

Bird was shocked. I could have told him that it was the end of the world and he would have reacted the same way.

"I'll continue to negotiate a better price with Te Poe," I said. "We'll get out of here one way or another. Ganson has a private island off the coast in the Gulf of Thailand. We can go there to live until we sort everything out." It was all I could say to him.

Bird shook his head and cursed. "Those lowlife fuckers! I always hated those stuck-up pieces of shit! Those fucking rats set us up! For what? Why? They weren't under arrest – or in trouble! Why would they do such a fucked up thing?"

"I'm too sick over this to think straight. Soon, we'll find out the details."

Bird was still ill. "I don't know how long you and I can take this place," he said. "You're sick. I'm sick. You gotta get us out of here."

"I'll call Te Poe and arrange another meeting," I said. "I gotta lay down. I'm dizzy."

In a state of shock, I returned to my cell. It was lockdown time again. My new and only roommate, Sett, was already there, preparing something for us to eat.

Sett was an intelligent 25-year-old Cambodian who had attended college in Phnom Penh. He was studying to be an architect. The chan wan saw to it that I had this good roommate who could speak some English.

I lay down on the floor and tried to sort out what had happened and how this would affect our lives. I drifted in and out of consciousness. The hum of mosquitoes and other flying, biting insects hovered over my body, searching for fresh flesh to devour, but there was hardly any uneaten skin left on my aching body. I was so upset, the shock was wearing off and the pain of reality was settling in.

There was a hateful wrongness about the world beyond the mere mechanical cruelty of it. Deception, deceit, lies, conspiracies. *How . . . how could Sam and Bob . . . after all these years? Twenty years! I have always been loyal to them. How could they stab me, my brother, and everyone in the back?* If only I could have seen, sensed, or perceived the magnitude of deceit that surrounded me.

My honor is my life. I must take care of my family, my loved ones, and my friends. I must find a way.

The sweltering Cambodian days and nights droned on. The Bird and I would walk back and forth from one end of "Execution Alley" to the other while we tried to reason out the unreasonable. Sure, there had been signs. We saw them all so clearly now. But at the time, they were overlooked – written off as people's idiosyncrasies or our paranoia that we blamed on our stressful situation.

I filled the Bird in on the information that my brother and his lawyer relayed to me through Virginia. Apparently, the Übel brothers had recorded our meetings on video. Of course, now Bob Übel's strange reactions to my questions regarding the money I gave him to clear the register at the Bay Shore Hotel or the $30,000 we gave to Sam in New York City all made sense. Bob had sat in the oversized armchair in the Rembrandt Hotel so that the left side of his profile had faced the camera. Bob had nodded and signaled for me not to speak when the dialogue about the cash we gave him or his brother came up. Back then, I had thought that Bob was just being his usual weird self. I know now where the video camera was. Whenever I had gone near the computer on the table ten feet away from me, Harley had directed me away from it. These hypocrites had been stealing money from the operation and I found out now that they had never told their government partners.

Two weeks had passed since the stateside bust. I would lie in my cell at night in the relentless heat and under the glare of the dangling light bulb. I would piece together all the disturbing signs.

All the time, I would question why, Bob, Sam, and Harley would give such an out-of-place or manipulative statement. Of course, there was the granddaddy con-job of them all – the arrest of Bob Übel by Hing Peo's Marine Police on June 5.

How naïve could I have been? I thought. *My loyalty, my eagerness to believe the Übel mystique, my blind faith.*

Sure, Bob Übel was released when he said that he was a DEA agent, but that was because he and his crew really were DEA agents. This was the turning point when our contact, Colonel Hing Peo, had changed sides. This was when the U.S. caught Hing Peo, a CPP member, red-handed, working on our operation to move tons of marijuana out of Cambodia. This was when Hun Sen and his CPP were blackmailed.

Of course, it was just before the election. There was no way that Hun Sen would put himself in a position to lose the biggest single most important event in his political life. It was all becoming clear to me now. The political conversations on and off camera about Hun Sen . . . the time when Bob Übel insisted that we bring a Hun Sen emissary out to the loading point where he would give gold Rolex watches to Hun Sen's man and Captain Chin.

The U.S. government was trying to ensnare Hun Sen into our operation. The Übel brothers knew that Hun Sen's people had loaded the *Oktedy*. They conned my partners and I back into Southeast Asia to do another operation. How clever they were. They used Minh to lure me into a dialogue with Ratner's people, who were connected to Hun Sen without Minh's knowledge.

When I found out from my brother that Ratner had been also working for the DEA ever since the *Oktedy* had sunk near Seattle, it all came together. Yes, it was real. Poor Minh was being threatened by the *Oktedy* suppliers. The fact that the U.S. government placed me in known danger when they manipulated me into sitting down with these people who were threatening to kill Minh, and the fact that the Übel brothers' instructions had me offer them a way to earn money by working again this year in the six-dimension plan was now clear.

It was perfect how I'd been manipulated into Cambodia, and how I was used as a pawn to discredit Hun Sen. The chan wan had said at our meeting that he wasn't sure himself how the U.S. government was involved politically. It was me all along. Without knowing, I was the pawn being used to alter Hun Sen's position.

Now it made sense to me why Hun Sen denounced us in the news media interviews and why he openly rallied behind the U.S. drug war. I also knew that, once Hun Sen had the power firmly in his control, and when he had extracted enough cash from the foreign aid and drug war funding he was promised, he would go back to his old ways. He had to go back to his old tactics because his supporters in the countryside, his loyal backers outside of Phnom Penh, needed to earn money, too. It was just a matter of time until this front – this farce – would pass. Hing Peo and a dozen other Cambodian officials would line their pockets with U.S. cash and then return to the only way a poor nation like Cambodia could survive.

The only losers would be the American taxpayers, who would not only be losing money, but who would be lied to, conned, and manipulated into thinking that the war on drugs was a necessary war that the U.S. government must never give up on.

~~~

Next to T.3 prison was a crematorium. The Buddhist monks who ran the old mortuary temple had to use tires for fuel to burn the sixty bodies that had died that week. For days, flakes of ash floated around us like a blizzard. The smell of burning tires and human flesh, mixed together with the dust in our throats, tasted acrid on my tongue.

The droning sound of the Buddhist monks chanting, "Nan wu guan shi yin pusa – Nan wu guan shi yin pusa," and the sound of the metal gong they hit during the ash storm that had slowly covered everything with the remains of the Khmer people – all appeared like an omen. I would have to find a way out of T.3 or we would die there.

The Bird and I spent money on bribes for food, yard time, having fewer prisoners in our rooms, and medicine. We had approximately $50,000 left. Te Poe and the chan wan claimed that this amount was not enough.

We had been at T.3 for over four months. It was now the end of October. Bruce Howard said that he would give us new passports. We signed the papers while inside T.3 and all we had to do was drop off photos of ourselves and we could get the new passports. Bird and I both knew that it was important to have our passports when we finally got out of T.3. The Übel brothers planned ahead when they took our passports from us with the excuse that they would handle stamping our visas.

I began to apply pressure on Te Poe and the chan wan. I let them know that, if they didn't find a way to release us, we would have them send the money we had given to them back to America, and we would find another avenue to end this long, torturous ordeal.

The pressure was on. I began demanding that they transfer the money back to America or release us. Te Poe and the chan wan both explained how they were on our side, how they wanted to do business with us, and that they looked forward to a long-term relationship with us in Cambodia. They promised to protect us in Cambodia and even help us to become citizens.

One problem was the media. The Übel brothers knew that we were trying to pay our way out. Through their DEA contacts, they would insert editorials about us in the Thai and Cambodian newspapers, explaining how we were trying to buy our release. Information published like this only created havoc on our end. The judge, Minister of the Interior, prison officials, all had to stop their effort to release us when the newspapers exposed our fight for freedom.

Te Poe would say, "How can we move you out when, every time we try, the world knows our intentions!"

It was early November and we were still in T.3. Often, the dysentery would strike and an uncontrollable rush of stomach cramps mixed with anguish would grip my body. I would gasp and wither under the pain. Then the brutality of an existence filled with agony and despair prompted desires to escape at any cost. The dullness of exhausted emotion enveloped me.

Virginia was informing me that, if I didn't do something quickly, we would lose our beautiful home in the pine forest to the bank. She would call me on my cell phone, screaming at me, telling me that I should be in Milford helping her to cope with Ali, our youngest daughter.

"Here, you talk to her," she screamed. "I can't deal with her!"

Ali, sobbing, got on the phone. "Hi, Dad. Mom is driving me crazy. When are you coming home?"

"I'm trying, sweetheart," I said. "Please listen to your mother."

It was all I could say. I was dying a slow death, surrounded by misery, in a Cambodian prison and Virginia was calling me to deal with her domestic problems.

The concrete walls and floors held the heat of the vanishing sun. At night, I lay in my cell and sweat, thinking that I had been pushing Te Poe and the chan wan hard. They had informed me that soon we could start getting our team out.

"We can't let you all out at once," Te Poe said. "There is a list that the prison authorities receive with the names of the prisoners who have been released. They will place your names on this list one at a time. We will wait for some of these officials to be out of town when we actually release you." Te Poe then explained to me that I must go first, then Bird, and then the others.

After months of hammering them, they had finally accepted my lesser offer and we were now waiting for the proper time when they would release us.

Bird agreed. "No problem if you go first," he said. "They said they would release me one week after you. Then I'll be clear to go. You'll be out to make sure they do the right thing. We gotta start somewhere."

T.3 was getting old. The Bird and I were taken by the violence that occurred practically every day. Every new man that entered our section was pulled to the rear of our tomb to Execution Alley. There, the scared and confused prisoners had the shit kicked out of them by sadistic prisoners that worked for the guards.

This was how they let all the newcomers know that they had to stay in line and not cause any problems. For small infractions, prisoners were made to kneel on a hot concrete slab in the sun, next to a smelly pile of rotting rice. The prisoners knelt while holding two heavy rocks over their heads. When they lowered their arms due to the developing pain, the soldier standing behind them would club them in the back.

It was all getting to me and I was sure that it was also getting to the Bird.

Since the chan wan gave me a cell phone to use, Ahm called me every night and kept me updated on what was going on in Thailand. It didn't surprise me to hear that Bob Übel and Harley disappeared from the Crown Royal just before the arrest of all our friends on August 21. The rats had left Thailand a few days before the bust so they could have meetings in Seattle with my brother and my partners. They again videotaped those meetings. The rats had not been seen since. I also learned that Bob and Harley had bugged my apartment at the Omni.

Those lowlifes recorded Ahm and I for their own perverted pleasure, I thought.

By the time the smoke cleared, the Übel brothers, Ratner, and Pill, with the backing of the U.S. government, had violated laws more detrimental to liberty, life, and our American values than any law I may have violated.

The fact that in the eleventh hour, the plan was changed and the Bird and I were instructed to go through Malaysian waters in order to reach Sam's island was nothing short of attempted murder. Malaysia punishes those in the possession of marijuana with the death penalty by beheading. We found out later that our Thai fishing boat would have definitely been stopped by Malaysian army patrols in Malaysian waters. The discovery of the marijuana on our vessel would have meant the last thing we would have heard before our heads were cut off would have been, "Allah is great!" If by chance, we had made it through Malaysian waters, they would have been waiting for us in Singapore, where they offer death by hanging. The six-dimension plan was a plan to have us killed.

We were lucky that we had never made it out of the South of the Thunder River on that stormy night on June 28.

Every night, Ahm sent my heart through light-years of pleasure and pain during our one-hour cell phone calls. Every night she said that she was coming to T.3 prison to see me. She explained to me that she could stay in a hotel nearby and come see me as often as she could and bring us food.

"Mac, I can take care of you all day. Maybe we can make love!"

Several times, Ahm had purchased airline tickets to come see me with her sister. She was afraid to come alone. I had convinced her every time to wait for my release before she came over.

Finally, on November 11, 1998, Ahm refused to listen to me. She said that she was coming to Phnom Penh to see me. I could not convince her to wait any longer. She had tickets and her sister Eng would accompany her.

Knowing that I could not change her mind, I made arrangements with my roommate's mother to pick her up at the airport. Sett's mother would bring Ahm and Eng to a hotel nearby and then she would bring Ahm to T.3 to see me. Everything was set and I would soon see my love – my lifeline to reality.

On Tuesday, November 12, at 10:30 AM, Ahm's flight would arrive in Phnom Penh. That morning, I bathed and put on fresh clothes that I had washed the day before. I even borrowed an aftershave lotion from one of the guards so that I smelled good. There was no mirror at T.3, so I used a puddle of water to catch my reflection. I could see clouds suspended behind my head and upper torso. I really didn't know what I looked like. I just knew that I had lost a lot of weight, and that because I exercised daily, my body was tight and defined.

That day, at 7:15 AM, just after the Cambodian National anthem played over the loudspeakers, my cell phone rang. It was Te Poe.

"Joe," he said, "I must see you at nine o'clock. You be ready. I see the chan wan and you today."

"All right, Te Poe. I'll be ready. I have a visitor today. Ahm is coming to see me from Thailand."

"Okay, Joe. No problem. I see you at nine o'clock."

Bird and I were excited. Ahm was coming and we knew that as long as she was nearby, we would be eating good food. Ganson had left in October, and since his departure, there hadn't been the same quality of food coming in. I told Bird about my meeting at nine o'clock.

"Squeeze him, man. We've got to get out of here!"

"Don't worry. I always do."

I was still worried about Ahm coming.

Chapter 28

AT 9:00 AM, the chan wan's aide escorted me to the yard in Section A that was surrounded by ancient buildings that were too destroyed to be occupied by anybody. This was where I often met Te Poe. As I approached him, he was on his cell phone. He stood by an old brick staircase that led into a burned-out, 200-year-old structure. I stood by him and waited for him to finish his conversation.

Te Poe ended his call and placed the phone in his pocket. "Joe," he said, "today you must go out. You cannot go back to your section. You must leave from here!"

"What? What about the Bird?"

"He go out in one week. First, you must go – like we talk before. There are spies in your unit and you must leave from here."

I was caught completely off-guard. I could not believe that I was getting out! I wanted to get Bird and the rest out before something out of control happened.

"Te Poe, I need your phone," I said.

I dialed my roommate's mother and explained to her what was going on. I told her to pick me up at T.3 before she went to the airport to pick up Ahm. Sett's older brother Boldero translated over the phone for me.

My adrenaline was pumping. I was getting out and I would see Ahm that day at the airport. This was all too much for me to take after this long ordeal.

Sett had my cell phone in our cell. I called Sett so that I could speak to the Bird, but the doors were locked and Sett could not get to him. I explained to him how I called his mother and brother to reroute them.

"I will tell Bird everything, Joe," he said. "Good luck. You come to see me at my home when I come out."

"Thank you for everything, Sett. I'll do whatever I can to help you!"

Te Poe brought me to a room where three Cambodian officials spoke to me and signed me out.

Before I left, I gave them two hundred U.S. dollars each and they were happy.

One of them said, "Be careful, Joe. Do not trust anyone. We know about your problem. We are happy to see you get out now."

It was now 9:45 AM and I was escorted to the front gate. Before the steel door opened, I turned and took one last look at T.3. Then the gate opened, and suddenly, I was standing outside. The busy street before me took me by surprise. I was not used to how the outside world moved. I was holding a bag that a guard had handed me on my way out. The bag had some of my clothes inside.

I had stood outside of the gate for only a moment when a white Toyota pulled up. Sett's brother, Boldero, was driving and Sett's mother, Mrs. Eaht, and his aunt stepped out of the car and waved to me. I couldn't believe the timing. I had only stepped outside for a second and there they were, pulling up to take me away to my new life.

I threw my bag into the open trunk and jumped into the back seat of their car. I had heard so much about them from Sett. They were a wonderful, upper-middle-class Cambodian family. Sett's father was an important government official in the rubber industry. His whole family were educated and a pleasure to be with.

I first told Sett's mother how much I thought of her son and that I hoped he also could be released soon. I had learned that Sett's family had to pay $20,000 for his release.

We pulled into the airport and parked in front of the arrival area. There was a crowd of people gathered in front of the exit door. I was euphoric about seeing Ahm again.

The U.S. could not touch me here. I would start an import-export business. The money I would earn would pay for the college educations of my daughters in America. And, as I knew, extraordinary things could happen in life. My charges could be dropped. I could win at trial. Anything was possible. As long as I had my freedom, I was able to make things happen. My family in America could always come here or to Europe and we could spend time together.

I was so excited that I couldn't stand still. A jubilant crowd of people waited around the exit door. I nervously stood next to a plate-glass window by the door and looked inside at the arrival section of the terminal. People were all around me. I had asked Boldero to wait by the car, which was parked only twenty feet from the crowd.

I kept looking. *Where are they?* I thought.

I turned around and saw Boldero, his mother, and his aunt standing near the white Toyota. I turned back and finally spotted Ahm and Eng walking toward me. They were holding each other close with their arms locked together. They looked scared. I waved my arms, but they didn't recognize me. They walked up to the exit door and disappeared into the crowd. I quickly ran to the edge of the cluster of people where Ahm and Eng eventually had to come out. I knew that Ahm would be looking for a middle-aged woman holding a sign with Ahm's name on it. She was obviously not looking for me.

I stepped in front of the frightened little pair as they moved onto the open sidewalk. Eng held her mouth with both hands. Her eyes reflected her shock when she recognized me.

Ahm stopped for a second and then cried out, "Mac!" She dropped her bag and surrounded me with her arms. I melted as I finally got to hold my love close to me.

I closed my eyes. Peace had entered my heart at last. I could feel the pain fade away. It was all over. I had risen from hell and ascended into heaven.

In that blissful moment in time, under the Cambodian sun, I could feel that my inner war was over.

Ahm looked up at me as she held my face in her hands. "Mac, you lose many kilo!" she said. She then looked at my tan shorts that were tied with shoelaces between two belt loops and said, "Oh Mac, you no eat!"

Eng was still dazed. She also had tears in her eyes.

I said to them, "Come on, let's go."

I introduced Ahm and Eng to everyone, and Boldero interpreted for his mother and aunt. We then squeezed into their car. Ahm sat on my lap. Boldero drove us to a hotel where we could spend the night. On the following day, we would look for an apartment to rent.

I held onto Ahm. It was hard to believe that she was there. She was in shock to see me. She wasn't ready for this. She was a little scared, and I didn't blame her. She was in a strange country with unknown people except for me, and even I was looking very different.

"Mac," she said, "you lose too many kilo. I take care you now." She was sitting sideways on my lap, combing my longish hair with her fingers as she spoke.

We arrived at the Princess Hotel in Phnom Penh. It was a four-star hotel that Boldero had picked out. After checking in, we nearly ran to our rooms. Eng had her own room across from ours. Mrs. Eaht smiled and motioned that they would be leaving us alone now. Boldero said that he would be back on the next day to take us apartment-shopping. They were beautiful people with good hearts. I love them to this day.

Finally, Ahm and I were alone.

"Come on," she said. "We take shower and I shave you."

We undressed.

Ahm left the room to prep the shower and I turned to look into the full-length mirror. "Holy shit!" I said. My body had radically changed. My face had changed.

Ahm was in the bathroom when she heard my surprise. "What's wrong, darling?"

"I just looked at myself. I can't believe how much I've changed!"

Ahm came to me. She looked at our reflection in the mirror. Our naked bodies pressed together as we locked into a deep kiss.

"Not now. First, I take care you," she said and she pulled my arm toward the shower. She slowly shaved off my beard and trimmed my hair. "Tomorrow, we go have your hair cut, darling."

After Ahm washed and dried me, she added some Tiger Balm to my damaged skin. The air conditioning, the soft carpet, the king-size bed, Ahm's sweet care, her warm and soft body against mine – it was all more than I could handle. It was only a few hours earlier that I had suffered in a rat-infested, filthy dungeon. There was not a drug invented that could have made me feel better than I did at this moment in time.

Ahm explored my new body. We couldn't stop kissing.

"You remember how to make love?" Ahm asked in her sweet voice.

"I don't know. Maybe I forgot!" I joked.

"Come on, darling, I show you," she whispered. "Mac, go easy. It long time for me, too."

The following morning, when Eng knocked on the door, Ahm and I were still locked together in each other's arms and legs. We made love all night, only taking catnaps when we had gotten too tired to continue.

"Come back next week!" I yelled to Ahm's sister.

"Come on, Boldero is coming soon," Eng yelled back to me.

I was a free man. The love of my life and I were connected.

"Darling, you can't let you friends wait. Come on, we go now," she said.

An hour later, we met Boldero and his mother in the hotel lobby. Their smiling faces were a welcome sight. I suggested that we first have breakfast. My new friends were polite and accepted my offer. We moved to an adjoining dining area next to the lobby. Boldero, Mrs. Eaht, Eng, Ahm, and I sat down at a round table with a tablecloth, flower centerpiece, and cushioned chairs.

It had been just yesterday that I had been eating on a filthy concrete floor in a foul-smelling dungeon. Ahm and I had, only thirty minutes prior, stepped out of a warm shower. Compared to pouring cold water from a rice pot over my head, this felt like Disney World to me.

I spoke to Boldero and Mrs. Eaht. The ordeal their family was going through over their son Sett was a heart-shattering experience for them. I could see that this was a close, conservative family. Sett's 16-year-old sister wasn't even allowed out of the house after 9:00 PM. I could see that Mrs. Eaht was an intelligent and thoughtful person. Boldero was a handsome young architect and Sett was following in his footsteps. Later, Ahm and Eng asked if Boldero was married or had a girlfriend because Eng really liked him.

That sunny, hot morning, Boldero drove us to three different apartments that Mrs. Eaht thought we might like. One was too small, one was too big, and one looked like it was in a rough neighborhood.

During our search for an apartment, I was able to see many areas of Phnom Penh. It was a sprawling city that looked like it had remained since the 1940s. The streets were in bad shape, the power lines overhead were antiquated, and the buildings had an old French-style with verandas and pale pastel-colored window shutters. The French had withdrawn decades ago, but had left their mark.

I had seen videos of Phnom Penh when it had been cleared out by Pol Pot's Khmer Rouge. During that time, this city of a million people was evacuated except for 15,000 Khmer Rouge soldiers. Now it was crowded again and jammed with traffic. The "ching, ching, ching" sound of bicycle chains and handlebar bells was everywhere. The city looked like it needed healing and rebuilding.

I asked Boldero if we could go to the area near the Royal Palace and

Cambodiana Hotel, which was a famous five-star hotel. I had been told by Sett that this was an upcoming area with cafés and shops on a park-like boulevard along the Mekong and Tonsap rivers. I asked everybody if they were ready for lunch and suggested that we should find a place to eat. Mrs. Eaht laughed when Boldero interpreted my desire to eat again. She knew that I was still like a kid in a candy store.

We dined in an open-air, French-style café. As I gazed at the slow-moving Mekong River across from the boulevard where we were having lunch, I thought that my family in America would like this place. I longed for them to be sitting there with me. My heart began to feel heavy.

After we had finished lunch, I said, "It's getting late and I don't want to tie you up all day." I asked if we could return to our hotel. "I'll hire a car tomorrow to take us around to look for an apartment."

"No," Boldero said. "I'll be by tomorrow to take you. We'll find a place for you together."

On our way back to the hotel, Eng spotted a sign on a second-story veranda above a line of outdoor cafés. The sign read, "Apartment for Rent."

We stopped and Boldero spoke to a couple of people in front of the old French-style building that faced the meeting of the Mekong and Tonsap rivers.

I was soon introduced to Mr. Chet, the owner of the building. He was a happy, easygoing, middle-aged man who spoke a little English. I found out through our short conversation that he was in the construction business. He was happy to learn that I also had a construction business back in America.

The apartment was perfect. There was a bedroom, kitchen, bathroom, large living room, and a veranda overlooking the Mekong River. The place was furnished and Mr. Chet said that he would buy a new television set for us if we took the place. The rent was $200 per month, so I paid Mr. Chet a month in advance, shaking his hand to symbolize the consummation of our deal.

Ahm, Eng, and Mrs. Eaht looked the place over.

I asked Ahm if she liked our new home.

"Yes, darling," she said. "I can clean and make apartment good for us."

I noticed that Ahm's voice carried a certain sadness. There was a worried look in her eyes.

"Let's go," Boldero said. "I'll take you to Lucky Market, where you can buy everything you need."

We all went to Lucky Market – a place that, as it turned out, carried everything from food to hardware. We bought dishes, bedding, towels, cleaning supplies, food – anything and everything that would make our apartment feel more like our home. When we'd finished, we moved all of our new items in and Mr. Chet installed a new TV set.

After Boldero and Mrs. Eaht had left, Ahm began to hand-wash my clothes that she had brought from Bangkok. My pants would have to wait, however, because they were still at the tailor. Getting them altered would be necessary because I had lost so much weight and they were constantly falling down.

After Ahm had finished the laundry, she mopped the floors and cleaned the bathroom. In the meantime, Eng put away all the new kitchen utensils, pots, pans, dishes, and food. Then we all hung new curtains and rearranged the furniture.

After checking out the river-view from the veranda, I returned to the living room. There, I saw Ahm sitting on a teak, Asian-style platform. This platform would be used to sleep and sit upon. Ahm sat, still and silent, with her sister Eng next to her.

I sat down in a small wooden chair next to her. "What's wrong?" I asked.

She didn't reply.

"Ahm, what's wrong? Ahm!" I moved from my chair to sit close to her and face her. "What's wrong, Ahm? Eng, what's wrong with Ahm?"

Eng didn't answer, either, so I looked into Ahm's mournful eyes. Tears had formed, and I could see that she was deeply troubled.

I held her in my arms and whispered into her ear, "Sweetheart, please tell me what's wrong." I held her close. "Ahm, I love you. I just left T.3. I know this is hard for you. Just give it a chance."

Ahm drew back from my embrace and looked into my eyes, saying, "I no leave you, Mac. I love you. I just scared."

For Ahm, I imagined, had drifted into a realm that, in the act of loving me, she hadn't anticipated. This seemed to be where the fear was coming from. Since I had just spent so much time in prison, how could she be sure that I wouldn't leave her again?

We held each other and calmed ourselves down. I knew that, at some point, I would have to let her return to Bangkok to deal with her children and family.

Emotionally drained, I said, "Come on, let's go out."

Ahm, Eng, and I found a small Thai restaurant about two doors down from our apartment. The girl who worked there was from Thailand and Ahm seemed happy to find a Thai girl so close to our place.

This was the rainy season and the sound of the rain coming down mesmerized me. I held Ahm's hand on the small table in the open-front restaurant.

"Ahm," I said. "Just give me a few days to get organized. Then you can go back to Bangkok. After I set up the business, you can return."

"No, Mac. I stay with you. I help you. Eng will help my mother with Aleaf and Na for now."

"Ahm, I can't return to Thailand because they have an extradition treaty with the United States government. I can't go home to America, either. But as long as I keep the right people paid, we can start a business and live our lives here. I also need to support my family in America, so I'll build a profitable import-export business."

Ahm looked troubled.

"My marriage with Virginia is over," I told her, looking deeply into her eyes. "I'll be responsible and support Virginia and our daughters, of course.

"I didn't tell you this earlier, but while I was in prison, Virginia told me over the phone that she was going to start dating. I said I wanted a divorce and she agreed. So it's over with her, Ahm. I would very much like to marry you."

Eng was sitting next to Ahm. She turned and held her older sister close as Ahm held my hand tight.

Ahm looked deeply into my eyes and said, "You are my husband. I am your wife . . . forever, Mac."

～～～

The following day, I met Te Poe and the chan wan at the famous Cambodiana Hotel. I wanted to make sure that they were on schedule to release the Bird and the rest of the team. They both assured me that it was going to be done, asking me to be patient.

"It's only been three days since your release," Te Poe said.

I asked him about a new I.D. for the Bird and myself.

"No problem," he said. "You only need money. Then we issue you a new Cambodian passport."

I didn't have money at the moment, but I knew that it would be forthcoming. In hopes of getting a business loan, I needed to get a message to Daniel. He had always said that if I could supply him with rubber surgical gloves from

Asia, he would buy them from me for his hospital supply company. In short, I could make a decent living supplying thousands of pairs of gloves to him every month.

After the meeting, I used the Cambodiana Hotel phone system to call my family in America. I had tried several times to call them since my release, but there was no answer. It was 9:00 AM, meaning that it was 9:00 PM in Milford.

Ali answered the phone.

"Ali!" I said. "It's Dad! I'm out! I'm not in T.3 anymore!"

"Oh, dad, that's great! You okay?"

"Yeah. I miss you, though, sweetheart."

"I miss you too, Dad! Mom's not here. She's at the gym. I'm home alone."

"Ali, I'm trying to work out a way for us to be together. I can't tell you how much I love you."

"I love you too, Dad."

"Tell everyone I'm out. And tell your mom to check the fax machine."

I faxed a letter to Virginia with instructions to go see Daniel for funds. I had left a bank account number in Phnom Penh so he could transfer the money.

"After I get my new business going," I said, "you can all come here or meet me in Europe."

"Great! What kind of business?"

"It'll be an import-export business. I'll start off by sending surgical gloves to my friend Daniel."

"What's your company's name?"

"I'm going to call it South of the Thunder Imports-Exports."

"Good name! I miss you so much. I can't wait to come there."

"I miss you too, Ali. I have to go now though. Tell your mom about my message. I'll call back after the money is transferred here."

"Okay, Dad. I love you!"

Chapter 29

AHM had already set up her Buddha shrine on the bedroom dresser. She surrounded it with photos of Virginia, my daughters, her mother, and Aleaf and Na. In front of the shrine sat sticks of incense and small flowers floating in a small glass bowl. Every day, Ahm carried out a beautiful, respectful custom. She would kneel and fold her hands in a wai position and pray for the safety and good health of all our loved ones. She'd light the incense and fill the apartment with its sweet, hypnotic fragrance.

A block away from our apartment was the Foreign Correspondents Club. Ahm and I enjoyed the Casablanca-style atmosphere in this place, and at night, we would splurge and buy a couple of cognacs and softly talk about our plans to build a new life in Cambodia. I told her about my conversation with my daughter Ali, and how soon there would be funds sent to our new bank account in Phnom Penh from my friend Daniel in America.

Ahm thought it would be a good idea to start a new Thai restaurant with the money. Her mother could cook and Eng could help run the place, she claimed.

"Mac, it would be good for mom, my sister, Aleaf, and Na to live here, especially if we have business to run. We can do it, Mac! The election is over. It safe now."

I believed her, of course. Her mom's cooking was the greatest, and I knew her family would succeed.

"We'll work on doing that. It's just a matter of time and money," I said as we sat close to each other and held hands.

When I thought of the hundreds of thousands of dollars the Übel brothers had caused me to waste on their self-serving U.S. government scheme to discredit

Hun Sen, I felt sick. The deliberate delays that had cost me $50,000 a pop had drained the last of our funds. Now, my partners and I were almost tapped out. We couldn't even hire good lawyers, which had to be something that the Übels relished – because if we had any money left for lawyers, we had a good chance to win our case on entrapment or gross government misconduct issues. But without money, we didn't stand a chance to fight the government.

Luckily for me and my business aspirations, Daniel was never indicted. In total, nineteen people had been busted, but he'd escaped the axe.

I received faxes explaining the problems that my brother and all of my friends were having. I called back and told them to do what Sam Übel had instructed me to tell them so long ago.

"When the indictments come down," he had said, "tell your people to cooperate with the U.S. Attorney against you. This will lessen their sentences and ultimately won't affect you, anyway. You'll be living in Southeast Asia. This will also help prompt them to invest in my six-dimension plan."

Ahm and I slowly drank our cognac. I was still an emotional wreck, and the stress was making my lifelong bipolar condition swing from hyper to depressed. If not for Ahm's love, I don't know what I would have done.

"I have to hit the head," I said.

I walked into the FCC's restroom. In the foyer, I noticed two posters on the wall. One was a colorful illustration of a Cambodian girl in army fatigues, holding an AK-47 and wearing a military backpack. The next poster had the same girl in school clothes with a backpack for books. Beneath the posters read the words, *The old Cambodian girl* and *The new Cambodian girl.*

Ahm and I walked hand in hand back to our apartment. We had taken Eng to the airport earlier so she could return to Bangkok, help her mother take care of Aleaf and Na, and relay to them what was going on.

During these trying times in Phnom Penh, Ahm and I would lie side by side, facing each other in a dream-like state under the slow-moving ceiling fan.

On one such occasion, Ahm kissed me softly all around my face and whispered, "Mac, you show me love like I never have before – you my husband forever, Mac. When our life become good, I want you and I to have baby together. A son for you, Mac."

Ahm spoke these words in such a heartfelt voice as we drifted into blissful sleep, leaving the turmoil of life behind us.

The following afternoon, I called Mrs. Algers at the U.S. Embassy. She had, for mysterious reasons, replaced Bruce Howard. The Bird and I disliked her because we had caught her lying to us several times. I told her that I would drop off my photos so I could receive a new passport. She was surprised that I was free and asked where I was staying. I told her that I was moving from hotel to hotel and that she could send my passport to T.3. I would pick it up there.

That afternoon, Ahm and I went to a photo shop and had my passport photos taken. Later, we dropped them off at the Embassy.

That night, she and I stayed in. We lit a candle and drank cognac. Our love-making was deep and powerful.

After we had fallen asleep, my nightmares came. I was still fucked up by my T.3 experience. I would wake up and think I was still there. I would look at the bedroom walls and see the ghostly, grotesque faces that had been permanently stained on the walls of my cell.

My startling behavior caused Ahm to hold me tighter. "Easy, Mac," she said. "You with me now. You okay now."

There were no rats here trying to bite my legs, no centipedes trying to crawl under me and sting me, and nothing to crawl in my ear and lay eggs or cause infection. I was safe now.

The following morning, after we showered, I left to use an outdoor phone booth to call Algers at the U.S. Embassy. I stopped at the FCC first to see if any faxes had arrived. One from Virginia was there. She had received my message and said that she had been unable to reach Daniel as he was out of town. She was sorry – she couldn't send any money.

I wasn't angry when I read her words. I felt bad that I wasn't there to bring money home like I used to. I was the family provider and now I was fucked. I could only hope that she could reach Daniel and communicate my need to do business.

My phone call to Algers was annoying. It was a turnoff for me to speak to someone dishonest. I listened to her bullshit as she explained how she couldn't find Bruce Howard's papers that the Bird and I had signed, that she would prepare new ones, and that I could sign them in her presence. I was fucking pissed. This asshole kept rambling on about nonsense until I finally cut her off to tell her that I'd meet her on the street in front of the Embassy.

I returned to Ahm and asked her if she wanted to come with me to the Embassy so I could sign some papers for my passport.

"Darling," she said, "I stay here and make something to eat. We have when you come back."

"Okay, sweetheart," I said. "After I get this passport, I'll start my business. Then everything will be all right."

"I know, my husband. Then we make son for you. We can make good life here!"

As I descended the narrow stairway, I could hear Khmer music coming from radios in other apartments. I thought about going back to the apartment and retrieving the court paper that I had been given by Te Poe the day I was released. I had asked Boldero to read the court document later that night, as it was written in Khmer. Upon finishing the letter, he had said that I must carry it with me and never lose it. It was a very important document from the judge Om Sadhath. Ahm had covered it in plastic to preserve it.

I stood in front of our apartment building and paused for a moment. The gray sky reflected a silver glow on the Mekong River before me. Sampans slowly drifted north and south, granting me a peaceful feeling. It had stopped raining and the smell of humid air, like a Turkish bath, filled my lungs. Already, the water was evaporating off the sidewalks and streets.

I started to feel nervous about going to the Embassy. I walked toward the FCC, where many motorbike touts hung out in front. I picked out the one who spoke the best English and hopped onto the back of his red Honda.

"Where to?" the Khmer boy asked.

"The U.S. Embassy," I said – and off we went.

As we weaved in and out between street vendors and potholes, I looked at my watch. Almost twelve o'clock. *I'll be a little early*, I thought.

We came to the barricade that blocked the end of the street that the Embassy was on. It was manned by Cambodian soldiers hired by the U.S.

The bike boy said that he would wait for me, but that he wasn't allowed beyond the barricade.

I felt tense as I walked up to the Plexiglas booth and announced that I had an appointment to meet Mrs. Anita Algers, extension 973. They called her from their phone and I was told to wait – she'd be right down to see me.

I stepped off the sidewalk and stood in the empty street, facing the authoritative-looking building. I noticed that there were no signs of life other than in the information booth. There could have been scores of people watching me, but I couldn't tell. All the windows were tinted and impossible to see through.

The quiet was unnerving. I stood in the center of the street about twelve feet from the Embassy turnstile gate and waited.

A middle-aged American man in casual clothes exited the Embassy and walked past me, then turned around and returned to the gate. I said hello to him and he said hello back with a queer smile on his face.

Approximately five minutes after he had disappeared back into the building, another middle-aged American man exited the gate wearing the same kind of clothes that the first man had been wearing. This individual was heavyset with a narrow, weasel-like face with white and gray hair. He walked past me and entered a cyclone-fence door behind me. There appeared to be a parking lot behind me.

I became nervous and decided to leave. As I did so, I noticed that the weasel-faced man was standing on the opposite side of the fence behind a screen that hid him except for a small hole – through which I could see part of his hair and face. I didn't like the feeling that I was having and turned to my left to leave toward the barricade that I had entered from.

My heart dropped to my stomach when I saw three Cambodian soldiers, two holding AK-47s and the other holding a pistol, walking toward me. I pretended not to care and gazed to my right in preparation to bolt in that direction. Quickly approaching were three more soldiers, armed as the others were. Now, both groups of soldiers were within ten feet of me. I started to move forward toward the Embassy front gate – my mind was reeling.

They can't be here for me! They can't be here for me!

Instinctively, I spun around and pushed when I felt their strong hands gripping my arms and shoulders. I turned and shoved with my open palms as forcefully as I could and became entangled in their arms and legs. Breaking their holds and pushing toward the gate, I half dragged, half fell forward, hitting the sidewalk. No one spoke a word. All I could hear were my grunts and their exasperated growls.

I crawled the last two feet and grabbed the turnstile's horizontal pipe with my right hand. A heavy boot stomped on my wrist. I held fast to the gate, thinking that as long as part of me was inside, maybe they would leave me alone. Too many hands, too many bodies to fight off.

Steel handcuffs were tightly fastened over my right wrist as they roughly pulled my left arm behind me. A .45 automatic pistol was held to my temple as I was lifted up so that the cuffs could be attached to my other wrist.

I was nauseous and angry. I turned to the white-haired weasel still hiding behind the screen and could see his beady eyes.

"What's this about?" I yelled to him. "I'm a free man. I was released by the court!"

The six soldiers held me tight and dragged me to the barricade. Then they threw me into the back of a military truck that was surrounded by soldiers and drove off.

All I could think about was Ahm. She'd be upset when I didn't return.

Only ten minutes later, we pulled up to Colonel Hing Peo's base.

This fucking place again! I thought.

I jumped out of the truck with my arms still behind my back. I strode up the ancient masonry steps, fucking pissed, looking for a fight. The grunts shoved me into an office near the cell that I had spent time in before. My original interrogator – the one with the dark eyes – sat behind a desk.

"Are you prepared to confess your crimes against the people of the Royal Kingdom of Cambodia?"

I remembered his voice clearly.

I was pushed into a chair before his desk. We looked at each other for a moment.

"What is your name?" he asked.

His familiar voice struck a chord and made me furious to be back here. I answered him. "You don't remember me?"

"No," he said in a tense voice.

"You don't remember me? I'm Joe. Joe Harding!"

His dark eyes lit up and he smiled. "Oh, Joe. You lose many kilos! I did not recognize you!"

"Yeah, I lose many kilos in T.3! Call the chan wan, Koon Boon Sorn. Call Judge Om Sadhath."

As I was yelling, he signaled to have my steel cuffs removed. Blood was everywhere – the abduction had left me scraped, torn, and cut. I was steaming.

"You have no legal right to do this! Om Sadhath gave me my freedom. I have papers I can show you! Get Koon Boon Sorn over here!"

"Wait, Joe. I'll be right back."

Ten minutes later, he returned.

"Joe, you are not under arrest. We know you have broken no laws here. We have brought you here on behalf of the U.S. government."

"What? There's no fucking extradition treaty between the U.S. and Cambodia! What you're doing is illegal, and you know it!"

"I'm sorry, Joe. My chief has given me instructions . . . "

I cut him off. "Your chief? I want to see Hing Peo right now!"

"I'm sorry, Joe. He has left for the day."

"Yeah, I bet he has. He's probably at the Embassy right now, counting his fucking money!"

A couple of English-speaking men in the crowded room laughed at my statement.

"If the U.S. wants me, tell them to come to my apartment. I'll be happy to speak to them. It's a violation of international and Cambodian law, not to mention a human rights violation, to kidnap me!"

"I'm sorry, Joe. I can't let you go."

"Bullshit! Let me stay at my apartment! I'll even pay for the guard to guard me!"

He stood up and said, "Wait here."

I could see through a small window outside the door that it was dark now. *Ahm's probably sick with worry*, I thought.

The dark-eyed interrogator returned. "I'm sorry, Joe," he said. "I know this is wrong, but it is not my decision. I must keep you here. The U.S. Embassy is responsible for you. Maybe tomorrow, they will come. You can talk to them then. Maybe you can go, Joe. This I would like to see."

"What's your name?" I asked.

"My name is Tarot."

"Tarot, this is wrong and you know it."

"I know, Joe, but I cannot do anything to help you. You must stay here tonight. Tomorrow, we will see."

I pulled a business card from my pocket and handed it to Tarot. "This is my landlord's address. My girl lives there. Can you bring her here tonight? She's alone and must be very upset."

"I will do this for you, Joe."

Tarot left the room. About fifteen minutes later, I was taken to the same cell in which I had started this Phnom Penh journey.

I lost control when the soldier slammed and locked the door to the four-by-eight foot cell. The memory of the six of us crammed into this space caused an explosion in me. I turned and kicked the door several times, verbally blasting the soldier who had locked me in.

"You're fucking wrong!" I screamed. "This is a crime you're committing!"

The guard stood and pointed at me as if to say, "Stop and watch your step or you'll be sorry!"

"Fuck you!" I screamed as I continued to kick the steel door. "You're a bunch of fucking puppets! You're in the Embassy's pocket. You're all a bunch of fucking corrupt pieces of shit!

"I want to see a foreign press correspondent! I'll make sure the whole fucking world knows how corrupt the American government is. It's all about money and power, and I'm going to expose the whole fucking thing! Yeah, you! You fucking corrupt piece of dog shit. Hing Peo!"

I was beside myself with anger when suddenly the crowd in the hallway separated and in walked Ahm.

"Mac!"

Ahm ran to my door. I stuck my arm out through the small hole to touch her. She was hysterical. I looked at Tarot standing behind her.

"Tarot, open this door! Let me hold her! Tarot!"

He signaled the soldier and the door was opened. Ahm cried so deeply that, as I held her in my arms and tried to calm her down, her heartbreaking hysteria caused even more people to gather around the office door in the hallway.

Tarot sat in a chair next to us. He said in a loud voice, "If she does not stop, I will remove her!"

I shot a look at him and growled, "Leave her alone! Can't you see she's upset!"

Ahm pulled her tear-covered face away from my chest and quickly held my mouth with her tender hands. "No, Mac, please!" she said.

I was furious. I started to curse at Tarot and his coworkers.

Ahm tried to silence me. "Please, Mac, no!"

I stopped and focused on her. "Ahm, I'm sorry," I said in a low voice.

Her cries were muffled in my chest. The crowd in the hall was clearly moved. Some even had tears in their eyes. Everyone knew that I was being held wrongfully. These people watching us knew that governments couldn't be trusted. These survivors of Pol Pot knew the treachery that lives in the hearts of powerful, greedy people. I could see it in their eyes and the expressions on their faces.

Ahm wiped her tears and turned to Tarot. In a voice shattered with emotion, she said, "Can I . . . can I please stay here tonight with him?" She was barely able to speak as she cried and tried to catch her breath.

"You cannot. You must leave now. Come back tomorrow morning. Bring Joe's clothes and some food for him."

Ahm reburied her tear-streaked face into my chest and continued to cry.

I took a deep breath and said, "Ahm, please. I'll fix this problem. Go home and sleep. I'll see you in the morning."

Tarot stood up. The crowd moved aside to allow Ahm to be escorted out.

"Please, Mac, let me stay with you," she said, holding tightly onto my hand as Tarot attempted to escort her out.

"Ahm, please . . . " I said.

I could hear her cry all the way down the hall as I was locked into the filthy, depressing cell.

CHAPTER 30

11:00 PM: November 18, 1998

AFTER Ahm had left and the outer door had been locked, the deafening silence entered to join my solitude. I rinsed the bloodstains from my arms and legs. The rough, pitted concrete floor that I had to sleep on like a dog hadn't changed. The insects, the smells, the ancient water spigot – nothing had changed. I sat on the floor with my back against the filthy wall.

The night was still. The humid air hung heavy as I gazed up at the cobwebs and stained walls.

Only six days. Only six days of freedom. It wasn't enough.

No, I thought. *No. I'm not going to let those murderers, those thieves, those sanctimonious hypocrites win. Those mentally-warped Übels, Ratner, Pill, the U.S. government – they're all tyrants.*

I wasn't really angry at the Cambodians – only Hing Peo, that one-legged pirate and the biggest gangster in Phnom Penh. When he had been caught red-handed working in our operation, he had switched sides to the U.S. government. There were benefits, of course – foreign aid to fight this corrupt farce called the "war on drugs."

As long as there are laws governing what consensual adults willingly eat, drink, or smoke, there will be people in governments standing by to profit on the lies and propaganda. How ignorant can the people in a society be to allow our leaders to manipulate us so? If the government spent the billions that is now wasted on DEA agents, prisons, false propaganda, and foreign aid and invested it in education, the world would be a sane place.

I recalled that rat Bob Übel telling me while he sat in the Rembrandt in Bangkok, "If you ever go to prison, just sit, relax, and do your time."

I remember saying to myself, "Yeah, sure . . . just like you did."

I sat in my cell thinking how the Übel brothers and Ratner were the perfect DEA informants. They were habitual liars, manipulators, and jealous sociopaths.

Then, suddenly and without reason, I managed to clear my head entirely. I pictured my children playing in the sun by our swimming pool in Milford. I could see the mountain views and the towering white pine trees.

"I will not let you down, kids," I said to myself. "I will *not* let you down."

Chapter 31

NOVEMBER 19, 1998

I was curled up in a fetal position on the concrete floor when I heard the familiar sounds of morning life emerge in Hing Peo's base. I looked out of the barred opening in the exterior wall, but couldn't tell what time it was. The sky was still dark. The fluorescent light continued to buzz. My skin – the same skin that had been making a comeback from my T.3 experience – was now raw from the previous night's attack on the part of every kind of insect imaginable.

Hearing the outer office door being unlocked, I stood up and looked out of the small opening in my steel door. The flimsy, wooden office door swung open. Ahm walked in, carrying brown paper bags filled with items from our apartment. She quickly set them down on the desk and ran over to me.

Tarot stood in the doorway and said something in Khmer to the soldier. The soldier unlocked my cell door and Ahm and I embraced.

She wept and kissed me. "Oh, Mac," she said. "I no sleep last night. I worry 'bout you all night. I cook for you at five. Come on, eat now. I make what you like." She took me by the hand to the desk and started to unpack the bags.

While Ahm organized what she had brought, the soldier checked the items to make sure there were no weapons hidden in the clothes, towels, or food.

I asked Tarot if he could give me some paper and a pen. He reached into the desk drawer and pulled out what I had asked for.

"Can you deliver a message to Koon Boon Sorn, the chan wan of T.3, and Om Sadathd, the Phnom Penh high court judge?" I asked.

"Yes," he said. "I can do this for you today."

"Tarot, you know I am not under arrest – that I have not violated any Cambodian laws – so can you write this down and place it on my door? I want everyone to know the truth."

Tarot nodded. "You write what you want it to say. I will translate it into Khmer."

Later, the white paper sign was taped to my door. It read, *This man has broken no Cambodian laws. He is not under arrest. He is being held here on behalf of the U.S. government.*

I handed Tarot two letters, one for the chan wan and one for the judge.

"I will also go to the U.S. Embassy and ask them when they will come to see you," he said.

"Thank you, Tarot."

"Your girl must leave now. She can return at five o'clock tonight to visit you."

Ahm had cleaned my cell and placed my belongings in a neat arrangement on the floor. She had left the food that she had cooked in plastic containers on the concrete half-wall that separated the sleeping space from the sewer hole.

Ahm spoke softly as she wept. "Darling, I bring you blanket tonight. Please, Mac, see if I can stay with you."

I looked at Tarot. He shook his head.

"Sweetheart, here," I said. "Take this to the FCC and fax it to Virginia."

I handed Ahm the letter that I had written asking Virginia to contact my New York lawyer and a NATO colonel whom I'd been told knew Hun Sen's son from West Point. My plan was to appeal to Hun Sen from both sides.

Tarot intercepted the letter and began to read the contents.

"I must read everything that comes in or out of this cell."

"Ever hear of privacy?" I snapped.

"These are my chief's instructions."

"Tell your chief I want to speak to him."

"I will, Joe."

Tarot handed the paper back to Ahm and smiled at what he had read.

I held Ahm in my arms.

"Please, Ahm, we must be strong now!"

"I will, Mac. I will do whatever you want me to do for you."

Ahm was led away, and I was relocked into my box.

I sat on the bare floor and watched armies of busy ants move in columns, seemingly with great purpose. After a few more minutes of watching aimlessly, I forced myself to think clearly – to focus on what was real and important.

I had to assume that the U.S. government was leaning heavily on the Cambodians to release me so American agents could come and take me to the States. If it was easy, I'd have been on a plane already.

There must be a political glitch, I thought.

The fact that I had been used by the U.S. government as a pawn to discredit Hun Sen and ultimately blackmail him into finally crossing the line and working with the U.S. government didn't matter. The fact that the U.S. government had placed me in known danger by sending me into Southeast Asia to meet with Ratner's people, who were threatening Minh's life, only then to manipulate me into Cambodia to meet Ratner's people was all wrong. And directing our team into Malaysian waters was attempted murder!

The Übel brothers had stolen money from the sting operation. Ratner had stolen money from us before he became a Federal informant, too. So in the eyes of the law, there was nothing illegal about Ratner stealing hundreds of thousands of dollars from us. In the real world, he would have been arrested for misappropriation of funds.

The U.S. government could have arrested us before we had gone into Cambodia and before we had been abducted on June 28 in Koh Kong. It was wrong to prolong our stay in T.3 prison. At that point, it had become a human rights violation and a habeas corpus issue.

Unfortunately, without money, my compatriots and I would have no chance to expose the crimes that the U.S. government had violated. My conspiring with the Übel brothers to move herb from here to there would land me in captivity for ten years. The Übel brothers would be rewarded.

It all seemed like crime promotion, not crime prevention.

~ ~ ~

The food that Ahm prepared for me was good. I thought about T.3 and how sick I had always been. I recalled that having money did not solve all my problems in there, remembering the time that I had bought a bag of dates from a guard. I would carry a small plastic bag of them in my pocket. I would eat them little by little throughout the sweltering days. The sweet, chewy fruit had kept up my energy. After a couple of weeks of eating these, I was told by a

Nigerian prisoner to check the inside my dates – sometimes, he had told me, they contained maggots. I quickly pulled the baggie out of my pocket and opened up one of the dates. Sure enough, there inside was a nest of white, wiggly maggots. The sickening scene turned in my stomach and prompted another dysentery attack of stomach cramps.

Suddenly, the sound of keys and the padlock being removed startled me from my disgusted reverie. I stood up and focused on the outer door.

My heart leapt when Ahm entered the room. The soldier unlocked my door as Tarot stood in the doorway. Ahm looked tired. She was holding our blue blanket under her arm.

"Darling," she said, "I make something for you to eat. Have now while still hot."

"I will, sweetheart. Later, when you leave, it will give me something to do."

Ahm looked tired and worried.

"Did you sleep?" I asked.

"No, Mac."

"You look tired. You have to rest and eat or you'll get sick."

"I can't, Mac." Her voice broke and her tears rolled down her beautiful face. I held her close to me. I felt her hide a paper in my pants while Tarot wasn't looking.In her soft voice, she explained how she had gone to the FCC and had sent out my messages. As we held each other, I spoke to Tarot, who was now sitting by the desk.

"Tarot," I said, "did you see Om Sadhath and the chan wan?"

"Yes, Max," he replied. "They said they will try to help you. There is much pressure coming from the U.S. to keep you here. The Americans want to take you to the U.S."

Ahm heard this and became more upset.

"Tarot," I said. "I want to give Hun Sen a message. I want him to know that if he allows the Americans to take me away illegally, he is putting everyone, even himself, in danger of being illegally extracted from this country. I have heard the Voice of America radio broadcasts. I have heard the U.S. politicians demanding that Hun Sen be taken to America to be tried for war crimes and human rights violations. If he allows me to go, what's to stop him from being kidnapped like they're kidnapping me? What's to stop them from taking him like they did Noriega in Panama?"

Tarot sat and listened carefully. "I understand what you're saying. But I cannot transfer this message for you."

When the soldier who didn't speak English arrived, Tarot left the office as if he had something important to do. This gave me a chance to speak to Ahm.

"Sweetheart, listen," I said. "I wrote a letter. Hide it in your pants. When you leave, go to the FCC and copy it three times. Talk to the office staff there. Tell them that you have a message to give to the foreign press, the local press, and also to the local human rights groups. I wrote all this down for you. Find these people and ask them to read my letter. Can you do this?"

"Yes, darling, I can," she said.

"Be careful. You could have trouble if they catch you leaving here with this letter."

"I be careful, Mac."

I slipped the letters into her jeans when the guard wasn't looking.

Tarot returned and told Ahm that she had to leave now. We held each other and I whispered in her ear to be careful.

"I love you, Mac," she said.

"I love you too, Ahm."

CHAPTER 32

NOVEMBER 20, 1998

I heard the sound of keys and the padlock being undone. I stood up and watched as the outer door opened. In stepped Ahm, and I could see that she was losing weight. She was wearing my olive-drab, short-sleeved shirt and her black jeans. She was starting to look like the FCC poster of the Cambodian soldier girl.

Ahm carried a paper bag that the guard had started going through on the desk.

She explained how she had taken care of my letters. Apparently, the office people at the FCC were very sympathetic to her request for help and they introduced several foreign and local press correspondents to her. She had also met a local college professor who taught journalism. He had said that he would try to help.

"Oh, Ahm," I said. "You did such a good job!" I hugged her and kissed her beautiful face. "Ahm, are you eating?" I asked skeptically.

"A little bit, darling," she said. "I see Thai girl at restaurant. She say many foreigners live in Cambodia with no passport. Many here because they cannot return to their own countries."

"I know, sweetheart. My problem is not the same. Soon, we will know if I can come out."

"I buy two books for you to read from FCC. I hope you like them."

I looked in the bag. Inside was *The Tenth Justice* and *Into Thin Air*.

"Great," I said. "Thank you!"

"I cook last of food we have. I use up money for motorbike, fax, copies, and books."

"Here, sweetheart, use this twenty for food for us." I stuck the bill into her jeans.

"Okay, darling. I bring food to you tonight."

The guard tapped his watch and stood by the door.

"I go now," Ahm said. "I see you tonight."

When she left, I pulled out the paper that Ahm had slipped into my pocket. It was from Virginia.

Art, have you been kidnapped by the U.S. government?

What has happened to you? I have contacted your lawyer in New York. He said that he will try to help you. I also contacted the U.S. NATO Colonel and he said that he would also try to help you. Your family is all behind you. We all love you. I'm sorry that I can't send money. What happened to Bruce Howard? I called the Embassy and he's not there anymore. They said they are looking into your problem. Be strong, Art. We love you.

The pain in my heart was overwhelming. *I can't leave my family destitute*, I thought. *If I can't overcome this problem and make money in Cambodia, I'll go back to my original plan.*

After a long day of intermittent sleep, Tarot entered my cell.

"My chief tell me journalist come to see you," he said. "But journalist was turned away. Guards felt you would not want to be bothered by them. I told my chief you desire to speak to Hun Sen. He say you will be sent to America very soon. Tomorrow, the U.S. Embassy come here to see you."

"Thanks, Tarot," I said. "It sounds like Hing Peo is a U.S. puppet who's scheming big money from them."

Tarot didn't respond.

～～～

NOVEMBER 21, 1998

While we waited for the Embassy personnel to arrive, Ahm and I quietly discussed what we should do.

"Ahm, can you go to T.3 and see Mike?" I asked. She knew that I was referring to the Bird. "Tell him everything that has happened and take this letter to him."

Ahm hid the letter in the crotch of her pants and slowly nodded. I could see that she was afraid. "I see you tonight, Mac."

We passionately kissed each other before the guard escorted her out.

I waited all day. No one from the Embassy arrived.

Ahm returned at 5:00 PM. She briefed me on her visit with the Bird. She said he was upset that I hadn't left Phnom Penh. I had explained in my letter to him that I needed to stay on top of Te Poe and the chan wan in order to get the rest of the team out. Plus, I didn't have enough money to leave the city.

"Thank you, sweetheart," I said. I held her and let her know how important she was to me. I knew how dangerous Phnom Penh still was and how frightening it must have been for her to be alone in this rough city.

Tarot walked into the room, the dim light making his eyes look darker.

"I see the U.S. Embassy did not come. Perhaps tomorrow they come. I am sure they just want to talk to you. Our government has not released you. Maybe you can stay."

Ahm looked at me as if she was expecting a positive response.

I deliberately smiled for her and gave her a hopeful look. Then I turned to Tarot and said, "Maybe Hun Sen is intervening. You know, Tarot, I heard on the VOA that a U.S. senator says that if Hun Sen turns his guns on the demonstrators, the U.S. will intervene and take control of the situation by whatever means necessary. I find this ironic because I remember when Nixon turned his guns on Kent State University students in a demonstration. I didn't hear other countries say they would intervene and come take control of the situation. Did other countries try to bring Nixon to an international court for his crimes like the U.S. is trying to do to Hun Sen? I'm sure that if Hun Sen was aware of this, he'd find it interesting."

Tarot nodded affirmatively and smiled.

Little did I know that the U.S. government was changing gears as we spoke and was now easing up on their attack on Hun Sen. They were now making deals with him. He could be heard on CNN denouncing my team and stating how he was cooperating with the U.S. and helping them return us to America. He would show the world that he was not the warlord that the U.S. had previously portrayed him to be –instead, he was cleaning up his act.

~~~

NOVEMBER 22, 1998

Tarot entered the room five minutes after Ahm and I had reunited.

"The Embassy people are here to see you, Joe," he said. "Your girl must go now. She can return tonight."

Ahm hugged me with desperate intensity. "You come back. You hear me, Mac?" she said in a frightened voice.

"I will, sweetheart," I said. "Be careful."

Tarot and I walked into an office down the hall. The room must have had a dozen Khmer military police in plain clothes and a couple of uniformed soldiers standing around the weasel-faced man who had hidden behind the fence when I was captured. He was accompanied by the same young Khmer boy who had been an aide to Bruce Howard. The boy now carried a disturbed look on his face – a look that I'd never seen before when he'd been with Bruce.

There were three chairs in the center of the room. The boy and the weasel occupied two of them. I was motioned to sit in the third.

The weasel began the meeting as if nothing had happened – like this was a routine visit with a lost tourist. "Hello, mister . . . uh . . . I've brought some forms here for you to fill out," he said.

I responded flatly that I'd seen these papers. They were standard forms that the Embassy handed out to Americans who came into contact with them for any reason. "I completed these forms over six months ago with Bruce Howard," I said.

While he was returning this paperwork to his folder, I decided to lay into him, though I kept calculated control of my anger.

"What right do you have to abduct me in a foreign country?" I asked. "And wasn't that you I saw hiding behind the fence, watching me that day I was kidnapped?"

He mumbled something about being around that day and rapidly blinked his eyes – a nervous reaction, I assumed. He never responded clearly to my question. I asked him what his position was at the Embassy and whether he had taken Bruce Howard's place.

"No, I'm a political analyst," he said.

His aide looked down with a sick expression on his face. He clearly knew that I knew that there was more going on here than was being said.

Great, I thought. *A political analyst. Nothing but a CIA spook who doesn't know how to tell the truth.*

Weasel-face then handed me a State Department memo explaining that my U.S. passport had been revoked. "There will be special arrangements made to send you back to America," he said.

"The Übel brothers, who work for the U.S. government, stole my passport. Now you want to revoke it?"

"Look, I only came here to give you these papers and to see if you are all right."

"Really? Boy, that's nice of you. First you and your other political analyst friends set me up in a pot deal. Then you used me as a pawn to influence the Cambodian election and manipulate a foreign leader. Now you endanger my life by having me kidnapped and held illegally. And you want to know if I'm all right? Look, man, if it hadn't been for outside help, I would not have had anything to eat.

"The U.S. Embassy has been neglecting its duty, sir. This isn't a prison. They do not have cooking facilities here. I'm their only prisoner! This is a military base. I'm in a *holding cell* and these people are not responsible for me. The U.S. Embassy – you know, the ones who put me in here – *they* are responsible!"

The weasel's face flushed. He cleared his throat and said, "I'll see to it that you have food sent in and receive medicine for your insect bites."

"Forget my insect bites! I'm being held here illegally! You're breaking the law! I should be able to live in my apartment. I'm not a fugitive. I have not been to court. I have not been formally charged. You and your cronies have violated more laws than I have."

"I'm sorry," he squeaked. "I cannot let you stay in your apartment. You will be returned to America very soon – a couple of days, at the most."

I stood up to leave. "I love my country, but our government has major problems. Because of people like the Übel brothers and you, our nation has become an embarrassment."

I walked away, leaving him sitting there like a fool. The Cambodian personnel in the room – the ones that could understand English anyway – gave me smiles of approval.

Later, I was startled by the sound of hammering against the old wooden door in the outer office in front of my holding cell. It lasted for about five minutes, and then stopped.

Over an hour later, Tarot walked in and opened my cell door. "I'm going to let you use this office area from now on," he said. "It will be better for you."

"Thanks, Tarot," I said. "Any word yet?"

"No. I have not heard anything from your people yet. I will let you know if I do."

After he had left, I heard the padlock being locked on the outside of the door. I immediately walked over to the door to check its integrity. I carefully inspected every inch of this barrier between me and freedom.

During the Vietnam War, it had been the duty of the POWs to try to escape. Considering that I was a prisoner in this declared war on drugs, like the Vietnam POWs, I decided that I would be acting within this code of conduct. I noticed that the door was made from pieces of wood that had been nailed together with small finishing nails. The two inside panels were approximately eleven by thirty inches in size. The thickness of the material was maybe a quarter-inch of flimsy plywood.

I slowly applied pressure to one of the panels, realizing that I could easily push the panel out of the hardwood frame with little effort. I had separated the panel from the frame by a fraction of an inch before I decided not to cause any further damage. Apparently, the hammering that I had heard had been an effort to reinforce the padlock only.

I walked back to the chair and sat by the desk and thought over my plans. The slowly rotating ceiling fan turned above my head as I reviewed my options. These options, it seemed, now included escape.

Why would they allow me to occupy this room from which I could escape? I thought. *They have to know that I am capable of going through the door at night when there is no one around. Are they baiting me? Are they placing me in a position to entice me to escape so that they can justify shooting me in the back and ending their worries?*

Then I remembered Ahm.

If I escape while she's here, I thought, *they'll hold her as a hostage in an effort to force me back. I've got to get Ahm over the border before I make my move – and I might have to move soon.*

Chapter 33

November 23, 1998

AHM arrived looking tired and scared. We went directly into each other's arms as she entered the room.

"Ahm, listen to me," I said. Even though we were alone, I spoke softly. "You must cross over the border as soon as possible. I have a way to escape, but if you are here in Phnom Penh, they will kidnap you and use you to bring me back. You have to go, Ahm. I'll make my way back to you. I promise."

"No, Mac," Ahm whispered. "I no leave you. I go with you."

"Ahm, please. We're out of money. The escape will be dangerous, anyway. Please Ahm, Aleaf and Na need you. I can't put you in a position to be hurt more than you are now. You have to cross over before I escape."

Ahm wept a deep, soulful cry. "No, Mac . . . please. How you eat, Mac? How you do when I go?"

"The Embassy promised to send me food and medicine . . . " I couldn't speak anymore. I stopped and joined Ahm in her tears. "I love you, Ahm," I said. "More than you'll ever know. I will never stop loving you, but you must pack your things today and get ready to leave."

"No, Mac . . . please let me stay," she whispered.

I grew silent. All at once, it hit me. I had finally found what I had been searching for all those years. Here, holding Ahm in the most pleasantly painful moment of my life, I realized that my search was over – that I'd found what it was – what I was so desperately in need of. I found love. My Ahm had shown me that which no one had – her unselfish, caring heart, her complete desire to take care of me, to place herself in known danger. And now I would be taken away. I would not be given a chance to show my love for her, to take care of her, or to keep my promise.

"Ahm," I said. "I promised to marry you. Before you return to Thailand, I would like to marry you . . . right here."

Ahm lit up. She smiled that incredible smile that I hadn't seen for so long.

"Really, Mac?" she cooed.

"Yes," I said. "I'll talk to Tarot and work it out." Then I took her hand in mine and said, "Ahm, will you marry me?"

"Oh, Mac!" She pulled me to her and hugged me tightly before looking into my eyes and answering in a sweet, clear voice, "Yes, I will marry you, Art."

We held each other in bliss.

Here in Cambodia – the land of ghostly stone temples and barbarous guerilla armies – Ahm and I would become husband and wife.

~~~

NOVEMBER 24, 1998

Gathered together in the heat of this Cambodian night, under the slow drone of an old ceiling fan, three Khmer government officials stood in a straight line, at ease in the semi-dark room next to my tiny cell.

It was late. Tarot said that he was in charge this night and that we could hold our wedding ceremony. He said that he could supply two of his friends that he worked with to be witnesses at our wedding to sign our marriage agreement.

What a strange land, I thought. *These men used to hate me.*

We could hear the sound of the steady rainfall and the run-off hitting the ground outside through the opening in my cell next to us.

Ahm looked so beautiful. She wore an orchid in her long, dark hair. Calm and demure, she seemed completely aware of the importance of this moment in time. She beamed with happiness.

My bride and I faced each other in the dimly-lit room. We stood close and held our hands together between us.

I spoke slowly and softly as the three Khmer men stood next to us in silence and without expression.

"Ahm, there is only one God . . . " I said. "Many religions, but only one

God. Tonight, we will marry under the eyes of God. We do not need to choose a religion. Do you agree?"

"Yes, darling. I understand," she said.

Ahm looked into my eyes with such love. Her breathing was deep, and I could see her chest rise and fall with each breath. I asked Ahm to repeat or answer our vows in any way she liked. She nodded and smiled.

"Do you, Ahm Suma, take me, Arthur, to be your husband," I said, "through sickness and health, for richer for poorer, till death do us part?"

Ahm moved closer to me. She spoke clearly and slowly as she looked into my eyes. "Yes, my darling. I will be your wife forever and ever. I will love you and take care you. I will never stop loving you, my husband." Ahm's last word was choked off by her emotions.

"Under the eyes of God and witnessed by these three Cambodian officials, I pronounce us husband and wife."

We held each other and kissed. Our hearts were now grafted together – our love was complete. The feeling that I had was so unexpected. I felt as if there was a holy presence in that ancient room, like something sacred had occurred.

I glanced over to Tarot and the other two men. Even they seemed to be moved by what was happening.

"Mac, my husband, you make me so happy!" Ahm said through tearful laughter.

"Ahm, I cannot believe how I feel right now," I said.

"Yes, me too, darling."

Ahm and I handed out small bananas to our three guests. We drank bottled water and thanked them for their help.

"Tomorrow, we can sign your marriage agreement," Tarot said. "You can write your words then. Tonight, I am in charge here, so I will let your wife stay with you."

Ahm and I could not have received a better wedding gift. She was so happy. I was moved by his kindness.

"Good night," Tarot said. "We leave you now." He locked the door behind him as he left.

Ahm and I were finally alone. She fixed up our blue blanket bed. It didn't seem to matter where we were. We were together as husband and wife. We would spend our honeymoon in this Khmer dungeon.

That night, Ahm and I made passionate love. We hardly slept. Our naked bodies remained connected on our blue blanket in the stillness. She moved my hands to her cheeks. Slowly opening her eyes, she stared at me, with her lips slightly parted."Mac, you make me so happy," she said. "You my husband. I belong to you. I no leave you."

"Ahm, please. I've never loved like this either, but I can't put you in more danger. Somehow, I will leave this place. Somehow, we will unite forever."

Suddenly, we heard a knock at the door. It was our signal to get dressed, and our signal to end our night of bliss.

Disconnecting myself from her was painful – it felt unnatural, like the separation of Siamese twins. Slowly, Ahm and I came undone.

Chapter 34

November 25, 1998

ALONE, under the slow drone of the ceiling fan, I wrote Ahm's and my marriage agreement. Ahm and I and our witness would sign it. This was something tangible – something Ahm could bring home to her family. A document that would prove our union was real – something to prove that this American loved her enough to marry her.

I knew that what I had done was right, and no matter what happened to me, now Ahm would know that she was loved.

That afternoon, Tarot sat at the desk in the outer office and listened as Ahm and I spoke.

"I go to fax machine at FCC every day," she said. "But no faxes, darling."

"U.S. agents may be intercepting them," Tarot interjected. "I spoke to my people and they tell me that the U.S. government is in close communication with Hun Sen and other high-ranking Cambodian government officials. I'm not sure, though, Joe. Something is going on here. The information I received is surprising. No one ever gets this kind of attention. The U.S. Ambassador Quinn, Prime Minister Hun Sen, and other powerful U.S. and Cambodian leaders are involved in dialogue over your situation."

Ahm squeezed my hand harder and smiled, taking what Tarot was saying as a positive sign.

Without letting Tarot know my plans, I reminded Ahm that she had to return to Thailand soon.

Tarot mentioned that there was an 11:00 AM flight to Bangkok the next day. "I can see that your wife makes it to the airport safely," he said.

Ahm stood up and moved onto my lap and hugged me. Her silky hair lightly brushed my face and arms. This had a calming effect on me. I closed my eyes and savored the feel of Ahm's body against mine.

~ ~ ~

NOVEMBER 26, 1998

When Ahm arrived, it wasn't the same. We were devastated. There was no news to prompt a change in her departure. She would leave me – possibly forever – unless something extraordinary happened to reverse this insufferable action that seemed to be unfolding uncontrollably.

"I bring you peanut butter and jelly, darling," she said. "I buy at farang store. It last. I bring bread, too, but it no last too long. Why Embassy no come back? Why they no bring food? They promise!"

"Sweetheart, don't worry," I said. "They'll come back. They won't let me starve."

Ahm folded her arms firmly and tried to take a stand. "I go after Embassy come back with food for you. Maybe they forget!"

"Ahm, you're not eating and sleeping. You're going to get sick. Please let me do what I have to do. I don't want you to leave either, but you know why you must."

Ahm reluctantly surrendered and buried her face in my chest.

Tarot came to the open door and said that he would be back to take Ahm to the airport and that he would lock the outer door for us in the meantime. I felt like I was on death row and the executioner was letting me know that my time was near. Instead of a last meal, I was receiving a chance to be alone with Ahm.

Ahm looked up at me. "Mac," she said, "what happen if Americans come back and take you away?"

"I'll fight my case, and when it's over, I'll return to you."

"How long that take?"

"I don't know, sweetheart. I only know that I can't live without you."

Ahm raised her soft hands to my face and looked warmly into my eyes. "You my husband. I wait for you." She then pulled me into the cell and we lay down on the blue blanket. "Mac, please make love to me now." She pulled off my shirt.

We made love slowly. Our lips communicated our urgency – our passion for each other.

"Don't move, Mac. Hold me!"

I spoke in a desperate voice. "They cannot take me away from you. I'll be back."

The pain . . . the thought of being separated from her was unbearable.

We stayed in a state of passion and oneness. I was aware of every cell, every molecule our bodies possessed. We shared everything.

I looked at her as if it would be for the last time. I studied the palms of her hands, her beautiful eyes, her hair, her cute little nose, her smooth, tan skin. I wanted to take with me a mental picture of her – to absorb her for the future.

Ahm instinctively understood what I was doing and pulled me to her. She held my face in her hands and kissed me. "Don't worry, Mac," she said. "I am yours forever."

It was time. We had bathed each other and dressed and were now sitting face to face, holding hands under the old ceiling fan while we waited for Tarot to return. I couldn't help feeling guilty about what I had put Ahm through, especially if I was not able to escape or win in court. The thought of making her live ten or more years as a single woman in her culture didn't seem right. She would be shunned. I knew that it wasn't right for me to do this to Ahm, but I reluctantly expressed this disturbing thought to her.

I moved closer and held her hands on my knees. "Ahm, listen to me," I said. You know how much I love you . . . I don't want to hurt you. Ahm, if something happens to me . . . you must go on."

"No . . . No," she cried as she covered her ears with her hands and shook her head. She refused to acknowledge what I was trying to say.

"Ahm, listen to me . . . if I can't come back . . . or if I die . . . please make sure that you find a new husband with a kind heart." It killed me to say this.

Ahm kept her ears covered and shook her head. "No," she cried, her face in anguish.

I could see the pain in her eyes.

"You my husband! I wait for you."

I pulled her hands away from her ears. "Ahm, listen to me!"

"No!" Ahm exploded. She stood and leaned toward me with her fist clenched against her chest. The vain in her neck swelled, and her eyes became expressions of her will as she cried out, "I Ahm! I Thai girl! I strong! I no need farang to take care me! I can do for myself!" Tears rolled down her cheeks.

I grabbed her, holding her to my chest as she cried. "Okay . . . okay," I said, speaking softly as I held her with compassion. "It's all right, sweetheart. It's all right. I'll be back."

Ahm wept in my arms. Eventually, she raised her head to look at me. "You come back, Mac," she said. "You come back!"

At that moment, I heard several voices outside in the hallway. I could see shadows moving under the door. Then it happened – the sound I had hoped would not come.

The guard undid the padlock. The sight of the door opening and the crowd of soldiers and onlookers took my breath away.

Ahm and I held on to each other as the room quickly filled with soldiers in olive-drab uniforms. It wasn't *what* happened, so much as *how* it happened that would create an image in my mind that would last a lifetime.

Ahm looked at me as the soldiers surrounded us. "No, Mac! Please, I stay!" she said. Tears fell from her eyes. Her bottom lip trembled as she spoke.

The scene was chaotic.

What the fuck are they doing? I thought. I didn't see Tarot – only the heartless, determined soldiers all around us.

If I live to be a hundred years old, I will still never feel the depth of pain and anguish that I saw in my wife's eyes in that moment ever again.

The soldiers grunted something in Khmer and tried to pull us apart. We held on. One soldier roughly separated Ahm's arms from me. I quickly moved to protect her. It was madness. The other soldiers pushed between us. Ahm was screaming. "Please, Mac! No! I stay with you!" she pleaded.

"Leave her alone," I screamed.

There was a wall of soldiers between us now, and Ahm was being moved out the door. Ahm turned to face me – she was in the hall now, straining to see me through the confusion.

"I love you, Mac!" she said just before the door was slammed shut.

I could hear her crying as she was led down the hallway. Then there was silence – a crushing silence and a feeling of extreme despair. I stood up. My body was drained from the emotional separation.

Why did they do it like that? I wondered. I had to lie down. I was a mess. *Why the big fucking tortuous scene?* These Cambodian soldiers just couldn't seem to get this malevolence off their minds, this punishing thing that makes them act this way – this fucked up wickedness.

I cried a tremulous wail of mournful despair as I lay on the blue blanket. *Now she's gone*, I thought, and a hollow yearning – a futile desire – filled the pit of my stomach.

~ ~ ~

Hours later, Tarot entered the outer office.

I got up and did my best to control my anger. "What happened, Tarot?" I asked. "What was that whole fucked-up scene?"

"I'm sorry, Joe," Tarot said. "My chief didn't want any problems. He instructed his men to stand by in case there was a problem with your wife leaving you."

"Problem? *They* created the fucking problem!"

"I'm sorry, Joe. These soldiers sometimes do not understand foreigners."

"Foreigners? They just don't understand! Did Ahm make it to the plane all right?"

"Yes, Joe. I take her there myself in the police car. I see her go. She cry all the way to airport and on way to plane."

"Christ, Tarot!"

I sat down next to the desk and held my head, thinking that if Ahm had been there, she would have told me to sit up and be strong.

"Come on, Superman! You can do it!"

~ ~ ~

November 29, 1998.

In between my sweaty, delirious catnaps, I spent most days and nights writing letters to my family and to Ahm.

Half in an attempt to keep in touch and half in the attempt to take my mind off of my biting hunger, I bided my time and kept the pen moving.

"I don't know how much longer I'll be here," I wrote, "but one way or another, the end is near."

~ ~ ~

DECEMBER 1, 1998

I was now resigned to the fact that no one from the U.S. Embassy was coming to bring me food and medicine. I also felt that my effort to bring my message to Hun Sen through the press or my U.S. colonel contact was dead.

I would have heard something by now, I thought. *If Virginia was able to find Daniel, I would have received money by now, so that must have died on the vine as well. It's over, Art – it's finally over.*

For decades, I had been trying to find peace and create a security blanket for my family. And at that moment, I could see that it was beyond my reach. I could see that I had cut myself off from all of those who loved me, and then set myself adrift on a vast sea in a long and dreamless attrition.

I always knew that one is crushed harder when one climbs high. Given the way I felt, I must have climbed very close to the top.

My body was too weak at that point to make an escape. Having no money would have increased the physical demands on me as well. I would have had to travel on foot for many miles and live in the jungle. Without funds, without energy, I would have surely been recaptured.

I told myself that if I didn't hear any positive news the next day, I would activate my final plan. I would take control of my destiny.

It was late in the evening and my watch showed 11:30, so I was surprised when Tarot and his aide entered the outer office. I was lightheaded as I slowly walked from my cell to the chair next to the desk.

Tarot and his aide sat at opposite sides of the desk. It was quiet. Only the faint sound of a Khmer radio playing in the soldiers' barracks outside in the compound could be heard.

"Do you come with news?" I asked in a hoarse, weak voice.

"I do not have any new information to give you, Joe," Tarot said. "I just come to talk to you."

Looking down, I nodded. It felt good to have company. I asked if there was any food around.

"No," he said, "but I will tell the Embassy again to send you some."

"Thanks," I said, knowing that it didn't matter anymore.

"Joe, do you know a man – an American man – named Bob?"

I laughed a little and said, "Yeah, I know him."

Tarot's eyes closed halfway. I could see his anger. "You his friend?" he asked.

"I've known that piece of shit for twenty years. He's part of the reason I'm here!"

"Tell me . . . what he look like?"

"He's a little shorter than I am. He has short blonde hair, beady blue eyes, a big nose, and small mouth."

"Yes, that is him. If he comes back to Cambodia again, we kill him."

Well, I thought, *I'm not the only one in Cambodia he burned.*

"He cause problem here – he no good!" Tarot was visibly angry.

I guessed my assumption that Bob Übel was the beginning of the Hun Sen blackmail scheme was right on.

"Was Bob brought to this building when he was arrested last June the fifth?"

"Yes, we had him here. He work for DEA. He make problem for us!"

I let out a little chuckle. "I bet he did."

"When we first meet you, we think you also work for the DEA or CIA. Now we can see you do not."

I shook my head and said, "And now it is too late to do business with me because U.S. agents and half the U.S. Embassy are all over you and your people. And now, you're forced to hold me and give me up. I also became showcase material for your chief, Hing Peo, and a dozen other ministers and politicians who now stand to gain from foreign aid. I was tortured and exploited for political gain by both countries. My degradation and suffering exists so that a few sanctimonious hypocrites can benefit."

I finished my speech and walked to my cell.

"I have to lie down. I'm leaving soon, you know," I said.

"How do you know that?" Tarot asked with a confused look.

"I just know."

Chapter 35

DECEMBER 2, 1998

I sat at the desk and wrote my farewell letters to my loved ones so that they would all know what was in my heart.

I had read one of the books that Ahm had brought me from the FCC – *Into Thin Air*. In this book, there is a passage written by Joseph Conrad, the author of *Lord Jim*. I copied the passage and sent it to Virginia, feeling that it closely projected my thoughts. It read:

> *Truth is not so often made apparent as people might think. There are many shades in the danger of adventures and gales, and it is only now and then that there appears on the face of facts a sinister violence of intention – that indefinable something which forces it upon the mind and the heart of a man, that this complication of accidents or these elemental furies are coming at him with a purpose of malice, with a strength beyond control, with an unbridled cruelty that means to tear out of him his hope and his fear, the pain of his fatigue and his longing for rest: which means to smash, to destroy, to annihilate all he has seen, known, loved, enjoyed or hated; all that is priceless and necessary – the sunshine, the memories, the futures, – which means to sweep the whole precious world utterly away from his sight by the simple and appalling act of taking his life.*

I also completed writing my will. I spelled out how much each of my daughters, Virginia, and Ahm would receive out of the $600,000 life insurance proceeds and the $250,000 worth of assets. I sealed the letters in their envelopes and addressed them.

The Cambodian guard would soon return. I had given him my emergency ten dollar bill and my replica Rolex watch. I showed him a small box of sedatives that I had brought from the apartment.

I remember Ahm saying, "You cannot use so much. No good for you, Mac."

I had explained to her how I couldn't sleep at T.3, so I had begun to use them there. A Nigerian prisoner had said to me, "Take one and it will put you to sleep. Take two and they will knock you out."

"Suppose you take ten or twenty?" I had asked him.

"Then you die."

I would be taking two hundred of these tablets, plus a bottle of Mekong whisky.

When the guard returned, I would give him the envelopes to deliver to the U.S. Embassy. They would post them and send them out.

The guard returned with the whisky and two more boxes of the French La Roche sedatives. He seemed happy to do this because of the watch – though it was so big on him that it would slide up on his elbow. The money that I had given him had been more than enough.

I handed him the envelopes and said, "Embassy."

He nodded and left.

I retreated to my cell to lie down. As I faced the cobwebbed ceiling, I thought, *Tonight, I embark on a journey; I will go to my father and give my loved ones a life of dignity.*

I thought about my crazy childhood. As young as ten years old, I had to endure what now seems to be incomprehensible. Nightmares, hallucinations – my young life was wracked with pain and confusion.

I remembered my first suicide attempt. I was only fourteen and had a job working for a beast of a man at his bakery business. I had worked there after school and on weekends ever since my father's death. At the bakery, I dealt with my boss' insults and abuse so I could help support my family.

One Sunday, he slapped me in the face in front of a crowd of customers because I didn't count change fast enough. I knelt down to retrieve the fallen coins, not wanting to get up. I was too embarrassed. He later fired me.

I returned home that winter night and gave my mother my paycheck.

"Why are you getting paid today?" she asked.

I told her what had happened and she exploded into a tirade.

"How could you do this to me? They are my friends! You've humiliated me! No dinner for you! Get out of my sight!"

That night was my first attempt to reunite with my father. My bouts with depression saw to it that it wouldn't be my last.

If only I could reach back in time and help that young boy – tell him that he was alright and that he wasn't damaged goods while the adults around him were.

I cried – not for me now, but for the young boy back then.

But I couldn't spend the rest of my last night reminiscing. There were too many painful memories from my childhood to replay. I had to prepare myself for my final journey.

Like the previous night, Tarot returned with his assistant. I couldn't let on what my plans were, so I decided to talk to him as though nothing was going on.

We all sat in the same chairs as the night before. Tarot sat back and asked me why I wanted to stay in Cambodia to do business. I explained how I originally wanted to help Cambodia, how I knew about Pol Pot and what he did to Cambodia, and how I wanted to try to help rebuild the country. Maybe, I told him, I would try to encourage foreign investment, contribute to the infrastructure, and promote tourism.

I watched the anger well up in Tarot's dark eyes.

He focused on me as he spoke. "I don't want to hear about foreign investment!" he said. "Where were America, England, and Australia? Where were all the nations when we were dying by the millions . . . when I lost over forty of my family members? I saw my own uncle knocked unconscious and buried alive after he had dug his own grave. I hid in the bush and watched. I saw my friends forced to build a dome from mud and sticks. They made a small door with a hole on top so the Khmer Rouge could pack twenty-five to thirty people inside. I knew many of them. Once they had it filled with people, they closed the door and poured gasoline in from the top hole and burned them alive. My job was to clean out the dead!

"So I don't want to hear about foreign countries coming here now to build up our economy after everybody turned their backs on us for so many years, Joe. I had to live on one kilo of rice per month . . . for three years, ten months, and twenty-six days! I ate bugs and bark from trees! I don't care about foreign investment! Just because the world saw *The Killing Fields*, everybody thinks they know the truth! Know what it was like? The children were swung against trees, the women were nailed alive to the walls of their homes, and the men were hung up and burned. Foreigners want to come to Cambodia and help us? It's too late! We don't want them now.

"Where were you, Joe Harding, when we needed you? We don't need you now!"

He then left the room. His aide, after shooting a glance of disdain at me, followed him out. I heard the padlock being fastened and locked.

I sat in my solitude in the dim light with my head lowered in pensive dejection.

It was time to go. I was weak and felt so small. I could feel my ribs like never before. The veins in my arms protruded. T.3, and now this, had taken their toll.

Slowly, I moved into my small cell. I cleaned and organized the space. Everything was neatly arranged – the blue blanket folded, my Patagonia jacket made into a pillow. I changed my clothes. I wore my black, pressed pants, black socks and shoes, the dark gray, pinstriped, long-sleeved shirt that Ahm had bought me, and my black Barone leather belt with gold buckle. My uncle John G, the greatest mortician of all time, would have been proud of me. I would go out in style – my body would be properly dressed and my hands folded just as I had seen so many times at Uncle John's funeral home. All of my belongings would be packed neatly so there would be no confusion.

I placed the bottle of Mekong whisky and the three boxes of La Roche sleeping pills on the desk and sat under the slow-moving ceiling fan.

Time has run out for me, I thought. *Forces far more powerful than I have controlled me . . . until now. Now it's my turn to take control of my life. Tonight I'll break away from their sadistic grip.*

In my solitude, I made peace with my God. I asked him for strength so that I could carry out my last mission. Using a small-stemmed glass that the guard had handed me with the whisky, I downed the fiery liquid. More than half the bottle was gone by the time that I emptied out one of the boxes of tablets and piled them on the desk in front of me.

I spoke out loud to my daughters, reasoning with their resonant images that seemed to stand before me. I argued the point of how this would ultimately be best for them – and in the heat of my speech to them, I pounded my fist on the desk.

The bottle of whisky spun under the force of the blows and fell directly toward the pile of white tablets. Immediately, the tablets turned to mush. I quickly scooped it up and tried to separate it from the puddle of brown whisky.

Fuck, I thought. *Of all the directions the bottle could've fallen, it had to fall directly on the pills.*

Now I was left with only two-and-a-half boxes. Instead of 200 tablets, I would only be taking about 140.

That will be enough, I thought.

I swallowed the pile of white pills that I had emptied from both boxes using what was left in the glass of whisky that I had poured just before the bottle fell. The gift of endless dreams appeared.

It's done, I thought. *My life is finally over – peace at last.*

I threw the shards from the bottle, the glass, and the empty boxes of pills out of the barred opening in my cell so the guard wouldn't get in trouble. Then I staggered to my final resting place and lay down. I wiped the tears from my face and folded my hands over my chest and closed my eyes.

I could feel my life evaporating. In my mind's eye, I could see a silent movie playing on an old projector. I could see my three daughters. They were little and dressed in ballerina costumes. They were laughing as they danced in our living room in Milford.

The movie flickered and the scene changed to a recent time in Cambodia. Ahm and I were running in the rain. It was our third night in Phnom Penh and we had gone out to have a drink. It was dark and the rain began to fall harder. Because Ahm was wearing heels, she couldn't run fast enough to keep up with me. She and I were laughing. I could see her beautiful face as I picked her up and carried her through the downpour. We laughed so hard – so freely.

As the silent movie slowed, the flickers intermittently clicked, and then ceased. The film had ended.

Chapter 36

December 5, 1998

"CAN you hear me? Can you speak?" The woman's voice was loud and close to my left ear.

I couldn't respond.

"When did you last eat? Can you hear me? Can you open your eyes?"

I could hear the urgency in her voice, so I tried to move. I couldn't speak. Slowly, I began to focus. Her unfamiliar face was right next to me. In a blur, I could make out her worried, frustrated expression. A man that I also had never seen before sat at my bedside next to the woman. There was an IV in my arm.

I fell asleep again, only to be jolted awake by her voice. "When did you eat last?" she barked.

I couldn't form the words to respond.

The woman and man looked American. An Asian doctor checked my eyes. Then I experienced an excruciating pain as he removed the catheter from my penis. The first sound that I made was a wail of pain from the abruptness of the removal. The woman and man disappeared as the doctor checked my IV. I realized now what had happened.

I failed again, I thought. *Now my family will suffer.*

In a haze, I made out the images of two Khmer soldiers sitting at the foot of my bed. I tried to force words out, but they wouldn't come.

My eyes kept shutting. Again, I tried to speak and to stay focused. Slowly, my words came. I looked at the soldiers, and said, "Do . . . you . . . you . . . have . . . gun?"

One of the soldiers nodded affirmatively.

I fitfully, almost painfully, pointed to my chest. "Shoot . . . me . . . shoot . . . me."

The Khmer doctor quickly stepped between the soldiers and me. "Calm down," he said in a Khmer accent. "You leave us. Now you come back."

He checked my pulse. My skin was raw, my body was emaciated, and my depression complete.

Two men then entered the room and introduced themselves as DEA agents Al Grecko and Joe Marist. They dismissed the soldiers.

A moment of silence hung in the air as the doctor checked me. Finally, almost impatiently, Joe Marist stepped forward, saying, "We ordered some food. And here's a cell phone. You want to speak to your family?"

I gazed straight ahead.

"Don't you want to get back to America and see your family?"

I nodded.

"Here," Marist said. "Your daughter's on the line."

I didn't know it at the time, but the U.S. Embassy had contacted Virginia and told her that I was probably not going to make it. I was discovered at Hing Peo's the morning of December 3, and I'd been in a coma for two days.

Virginia and my daughters got on the phone and told me that they loved me – they wanted me to come home.

"We have no home," I said. "We're losing our home . . . "

"Dad, please! We love you. Just come home!"

"We can build a new house, Dad. Just come home!"

There was too much emotion suppressing me inside. So, instead of talking, I listened and silently cried.

After the call, I tried to sit up. That was when I learned what vertigo was. The room spun so quickly that I literally held onto the bed as if I was going to spin off of it. Slowly, I forced myself to sit up.

Al Grecko returned with a burger and fries. I was still so uncoordinated that I dropped my food as I tried to eat. My body was so small. I couldn't remember ever being that size – not even in high school.

"Art," Joe said, "we're going to try and get you out of here today. I've been tracking you since you arrived in Thailand last January. You've been through a lot. You're lucky to be alive. It's over, Art."

Later, once I had a little of my strength back, we slowly walked to the car in the hospital parking lot. The sun in my eyes made everything seem surreal.

As we drove toward Phnom Penh, Al said, "We'll go back to Hing Peo's where we'll pick up your clothes and you can take a shower and change. We're going to Bangkok. Your buddies Captain Chin and the Bird have already left Cambodia."

I later found out that on December 3, the Bird and Chin had been brought to Hing Peo's to identify my body. Later that day, they were airlifted out of Cambodia by the DEA and the State Department.

I remained silent, still weak and dizzy. All I could think about was that I had failed to save my family from everything that I had tried to prevent, including the foreclosure on our home and the depleted college fund – everything that my death was supposed to have overcome was now vulnerable.

I have to do something, I thought. *I can't give up.*

When we pulled into Hing Peo's base, there were several soldiers and police in the front courtyard. They all turned to see who was arriving. I stepped out of the car and they all started running toward me, yelling and smiling.

"What the fuck is this?" I said.

"They thought you were dead when they carried you out of here," Joe said in a low voice.

The men looked at me as if I was a celebrity. I waved as I walked inside the old structure, laughing to myself, thinking that they had thought I had come back from the dead.

I was led back to the room that was in front of my small cell – the room where I had cried, starved, experienced divine intervention in my blissful marriage to Ahm, and had tried to right all the wrongs by taking my own life.

Joe handed me my clothes and a towel. "Here, Art," he said. "We'll go outside. There's a shower room in the back."

I felt as if I were in a dream, outside the room, seeing things from this perspective, seeing the faces of the people I used to hear but couldn't see. I walked with Joe to the rear of the building. It had once possessed the final curtain in my unendurable odyssey.

The shower cleaned off the sweat and the scent of the hospital – the past.

An image of Tarot and the guard flashed through my mind. They had come to the hospital and had sat next to my bed. I remembered that I couldn't speak. It was in a dream – like a blur – but I remembered their smiling faces.

I stepped out of the shower, feeling rather stoned and separated from reality.

When I'd finished, Joe led me back into the building. The hallway was crowded. Joe and Al, along with several soldiers, stood next to me. There seemed to be some sort of confusion.

Suddenly, Lieutenant Hour, General Wa Nat's aide, appeared before me. He stood close to me and said in a calm voice, "You no have to go. We make arrangements."

I looked at him in silence, trying to detect any deceit or malice, but only saw the caring but frustrated face of an old ally.

"Lieutenant," I slowly said, "if you're going to do something, it better be fast. I'm about to leave any minute."

Al saw us speaking and ran past me. He commented as he blew by, "Where's Hing Peo?" He dodged into an office.

"Come on," Joe said. "There's a car waiting for us out front."

We walked side by side down the stairs to the courtyard. Suddenly, a mass of photographers with video and photo cameras swarmed us. We pushed our way to the car. I could hardly move. I got in the back seat and could see many reporters looking through the front windshield, trying to get more photos. We were surrounded. They tried to ask questions, but the windows were closed.

We slowly moved out of the courtyard and into the Phnom Penh traffic.

Eventually, we arrived at Pochentong, Phnom Penh's international airport. We stopped at the front entrance. Cars in front and behind us also stopped. A half-dozen or so Westerners and Asians stood around our car as I got out. The four Khmer military policemen in my car shook my hand and saluted me.

I was then escorted to another waiting car filled with Western men that I had never met. We drove the rest of the short distance to the departure terminal. The small terminal was empty except for the people connected to my airlift to Bangkok.

This was the same airport where, twenty-three days before, Ahm and I had met after almost six months of separation. How happy Ahm and I had been on that day. Only thirty minutes after I had left T.3 prison, we had been reunited. Now, just twenty-three days later, I was delirious and returning to America.

We walked into the moldy-smelling lobby. I sat in a comfortable chair with a glass table in front of me. In a chair opposite me sat Colonel Hing Peo. He and I faced one another.

I also noticed that all the people from the U.S. Embassy looked haggard and upset. I saw weasel-face, the political analyst. He looked dejected and troubled. Of course, Algers wasn't there. I saw at least fifteen individuals who were connected to my airlift to Bangkok. There were no outsiders.

I could feel, sense, and see the tension. Something had happened. These people were worried and visually upset.

I counted at least four DEA agents. The rest were from the U.S. Embassy, the U.S. State Department, and other agencies that I wasn't sure of. I returned my attention to Hing Peo. He sat in silent contemplation.

As I looked into his slits of eyes, Al approached me and said, "Colonel Hing Peo has been kind enough to give this to you."

It was a blue and gray nylon backpack.

"Your clothes and belongings from the base are inside for you," Al continued.

I looked at this cheap hikers' backpack and exploded with laughter. I laughed so loudly and deeply that I actually slapped my leg.

Everyone in the lobby stopped and looked at me.

As I laughed, I told it like it was. "Hing Peo is giving me this cheap backpack!" I said. I was laughing so hard that I had a hard time speaking, even just at the thought of it! After he stole my money, my expensive watch and leather bag, all of my personal belongings, and my freedom, he's now giving me this backpack! Oh, thank you, Colonel. You are so generous!"

His expression went from confused to angry. He stood up and walked away as my hardy laughter trailed off. I had tears in my eyes from laughing so hard. I held the backpack next to me.

All the agents and government personnel seemed stunned by my unexpected outburst. An Embassy staffer walked over to me, saying, "We're ready to go to Bangkok now."

I slowly got up and walked toward the exit door to the tarmac. I carried my gift from Hing Peo and stepped outside.

The rush of humid air hit me. I could see the heat waves radiating from the blacktop. I was later informed that, on the day that my comatose body was discovered at Hing Peo's, U.S. agents had tried to airlift me out of Phnom Penh at this same airport, but were turned down when they had tried to carry my body on board a commercial airliner. The captain of the jet refused to allow me on board.

"We don't take dead bodies on board this jet," he had said.

That was when I had been brought to the hospital.

I now stood waiting for the shuttle to arrive, and although there were at least fifteen people standing next to me and behind me, everyone remained silent. I could hear the warm breeze blowing against my ears and the Royal Air Cambodge 737 jet warming up in the distance.

I noticed the American agents looking in a concerned manner at a line of Khmer soldiers standing about one hundred feet away from us. The armed soldiers were facing us, at attention, in a straight line on the tarmac. Lieutenant Hour stood at the end of this line of about ten men. His eyes were fixed on mine, while his face carried a stern, readied expression.

I could read his body language and was anticipating his next move. I looked into his eyes and slowly moved my head from side to side, signaling, "No." I knew what he was about to do and I wasn't for it. I'd had enough. It was time for me to leave Southeast Asia – to leave my dreams and leave the place that possessed my heart and soul. I needed to see my family.

His eyes squinted and he nodded affirmatively. His men remained still and at attention.

There were no private passengers on our Cambodian flight to Bangkok on that stifling hot morning, and only our pathetic group of bureaucratic puppets.

As we flew over the green, lush mountains below, my heart felt heavy.

It's over, I thought. *I'm finally leaving Cambodia.*

After all that had happened – the mission, T.3, Hing Peo's – it was over. I would leave Cambodia, but Cambodia would never leave me.

When we disembarked from the plane in Bangkok, no one made eye contact with me. Everyone in our entourage looked guilty – as if they had done something they were ashamed of.

In the coming months, information would be brought forward showing the neglect, the gross misconduct, and total disregard for my life on the part of the government while I was in Southeast Asia.

I couldn't believe that I was in Bangkok. I felt as if I was home – though I felt pretty ill over the fact that the government would never let me break away and see Ahm.

"Listen," Agent Joe said, "you can stay in the immigration office here at the airport. It's better for you than the Thai jail. You'll be here about a week. I can push two desks together and place a mattress on top for you. We'll bring you food three times a day."

"Promise?" I said. It was strange how I feared not being able to eat.

"Yes, I promise. There's burgers, pizza, fish – we have everything here at this airport. I'll personally see to it that food is brought to you."

"Listen, Joe, can Ahm come see me here?"

"I'm sorry, Art. This is a restricted area. No one is allowed in here. I know how close you are to her. I can let you use my cell phone to call her if you like. Just knock on the door when you're done. Someone will be around in the office."

"Thanks, Joe."

The white walls and tan tiled floor accounted for the aesthetics of this room. Off to one side was the bathroom. I could hear the background sounds of a busy airport outside my door. At least here I didn't feel so alone.

I was anxious to hear Ahm's voice.

I dialed Ahm's mother's number. It was early in the day and I thought Ahm would be there, but her mother answered the phone.

"Hello, mom," I said in my best Thai. "This is Mac. I hope you are well. Is Ahm home?"

Her mother sounded shocked that I'd called. She began crying and speaking in Thai so quickly that I couldn't understand her. She lost her ability to speak, and so Ahm's sister Eng got on the phone.

"Eng," I said, "this is Mac. I'm in the Bangkok Airport. Is Ahm there?"

"Mac! Oh my god! Mac!"

Eng was at a loss for English words. She was also crying. I had never heard Eng sound so devastated.

"Eng, what's wrong. Where is Ahm?"

"Mac! Oh, Mac, they say you die in Cambodia!"

"No, Eng! I'm all right. I was in the hospital. I'm out now. Ahm must have received the wrong message. Where is she?"

Eng was hysterical. In her broken English, she spoke. Her words were hampered by her crying.

"Today, Mac . . . Ahm think you die . . . she leave letter on mom's table. She say she go to heaven to take care you! Ahm . . . gone . . . Ahm gone, Mac. Ahm gone forever! Mac . . . Mac . . . "

I couldn't speak. Eng's words crashed into my chest. I began to hyperventilate. A pitiful, almost primordial sound – part wail, part prayer – erupted from deep within me as I called out to God to please not take my Ahm. The blood drained from my brain. I blacked out before I hit the floor.

I don't know how long my body lay there on the floor of the Bangkok immigration holding room. I only remember that in my mind's eye, I could see Ahm. She was in a field of tall green grass near a Buddhist temple in Pattaya. It was the place where Ahm had taken me to show me "lover's leap," where I had told her that she didn't have to worry and that she'd never have to come here because I would never leave her.

I then heard Minh's voice. It was clear as she spoke to me. "Mac, if you ever need me, just call me."

I knew Minh's number by heart, so I punched it in with my thumb while I was lying on the floor on my back. I was too dizzy to stand.

"Sawasdee, Minh's Travel Service. Can I help you?"

"Minh, this is Max!"

"Max! Where are you? I not heard from you in long time."

"I'm in Bangkok. Listen, I tried to call Ahm. Her sister Eng said that Ahm left a letter on her mother's kitchen table. Ahm was told that I had died in Cambodia. It wasn't long ago that she wrote it. She might be at 'lover's leap' behind the temple that is near you. Can you go there now and see if she's there?"

"Oh yes, Mac. I leave right now! Call me back in hour."

Minh left immediately. She would later tell me that she ran out of her office and started her Toyota parked in front. She raced up the hill to the temple, which was only a couple of miles away.

Minh knew Thai girls. Pattaya had thousands of them working as dancers, hotel and restaurant workers, and bar girls. Minh worked closely with these angels from the countryside every day. She knew their vulnerabilities. It seemed that, every week, a Thai girl was found hanging in her bathroom or dead from drinking poison because her man had left her. It didn't matter if they were single, married, or had children.

Minh ran up the wide stone steps into the serene, incense-filled sanctuary, past the golden Buddha statue, and exited through the open-air archway to the field of wild flowers and tall green grass.

Minh searched desperately for Ahm. She ran through the tall grass toward the cliff, calling out to her, and hearing nothing but the sound of the wind and sea.

The sight of long, dark hair blowing in the wind appeared amongst the waves of swaying grass. Minh ran close. It was a girl kneeling in wai position, praying next to the edge of the cliff.

Minh called out, "Ahm!"

Ahm turned around, her face wet with tears and her eyes swollen.

Minh ran to her. "Ahm!" she wailed. "Mac is alive! Mac is alive!"

Minh was out of breath when she reached her. She knelt down next to Ahm and their small bodies embraced.

"It's all right, Ahm. Mac is in Bangkok."

Ahm, Minh told me later, was crying too hard to speak.

As the wind blew their hair toward the sea, Minh told me that the sound of rolling thunder could be heard from the north. It was in this emotional moment, I think, that the completion of something extraordinary had occurred between us.

As was later acknowledged in a packed courtroom in America, I had in fact rescued Minh from the Khmers. Now she had returned the favor.

Not only had Ahm risked her life for me in Cambodia, but her unyielding love and powerful desire to care for me had repaired my heart from my dead marriage to a life filled with love.

Minh had found Ahm at "lover's leap" and prevented her from partaking in an ancient custom that has possessed Thai woman for thousands of years in this land of love and tears.

Chapter 37

7:00 AM: December 10, 1998

THE DEA chief based in Bangkok sat at the head of a glass table in an open café in the Bangkok Airport terminal. He was about 48 years old, 20 pounds overweight, and had a thin face and long hair. He looked and sounded too sophisticated to be a cop.

Seated with him were agents Al and Joe, and myself. The transport agents looked like bikers.

We were having coffee and Danishes as we killed time before my departure to Singapore.

I was still physically unstable, having been diagnosed with vertigo, and mentally disoriented. I was still lucid enough to be sure that no one cared that I had been used as a pawn to leverage and manipulate the Cambodian strongman Hun Sen.

The DEA chief spoke in his distinctive voice. "Arthur," he said, "you're leaving soon for Singapore. We'll have you in the States as soon as possible. I know you've been through a lot, so we'll forego the handcuffs and leg irons during transport."

I nodded. I was still feeling separated from reality.

That morning, the two new DEA transport agents, a Thai police major, and I flew on to Singapore. From there, it was on to Bali.

In Bali, I killed some time in a holding room by talking with the Bali Police Chief, who had joined us upon our arrival.

"So, you here because of marijuana?" he asked.

"Yes," I responded.

I glanced up and saw that Spat, a U.S. DEA agent who had joined up with us in Singapore, and who had had a long and colorful history in both Vietnam and with Sam Übel, was engrossed in a phone conversation. He was too far from the chief and me to overhear our conversation. Joe and Al were also apparently trying to figure out what to do next.

I found out later that because my abduction and airlift out of Southeast Asia were considered illegal in many countries, the State Department and the DEA were now having a hard time trying to fly me back to America without a political incident.

The Bali Chief smiled and whispered, "Large load?"

I nodded.

"Too bad you didn't come here first. We have good weed here, too. And you wouldn't have gotten in trouble with the DEA."

I leaned forward and whispered, "Thanks. Next time, I'll remember to come see you."

He maintained his smile and nodded.

Spat hung up the phone and quickly walked over to us and sat down. I could see the concerned look on his face. He suggested that the chief accompany him while I remained at the station.

"Do you have some place to keep Arthur while we're gone?" Spat asked.

"Yes, I'll show you," the chief said.

The three agents inspected the small outdoor structure in the rear of the office to see if I could escape from it. After they were satisfied that I would be there when they returned, Spat told the police chief to order me some food.

I hung tight for about four hours and ate fried yellowtail as a steady tropical rain soothed my shattered nerves.

After my captors returned, the two transport agents and I flew to the historic island of Guam. The return to this South Pacific island brought back memories of the *Oktedy* rescue mission.

Nothing much had changed – except for me, of course. I was weak and 90 pounds lighter since my last visit to Guam over a year before. At the Guam FDC, I found the Bird and Captain Chin.

Captain Chin had spotted me sitting alone at a table in the detention center. He brought me a cup of tea and sat down across the table from me.

With a big grin, he said, "I see you in Cambodia at Hing Peo's. I say, 'Oh no, he die!' You have eyes open, but no life!" Captain Chin had a broad smile as he laughed. "You have good luck. Very good luck!"

The agents kept the Bird and I separated, but on my first day there I had been able to speak to him through a wire fence. I spotted him outside and yelled to him. He ran over. He also looked like he was just skin and bones.

"Mike," I said, bordering on delusion, "you gotta listen to me. This place . . . this place is a mind-killing farm! Can't you see? They're feeding us so much food and giving us beds to sleep on. We must resist! They're brainwashing us!"

The Bird, wide-eyed, cried back, "Just leave me alone!"

"We must . . . we must call our lawyers immediately."

"Calm down . . . calm down," the Bird wailed in panic as he backed away. "Wait till we return to the States."

The Bird must have thought I was off my rocker. In reality, I was.

~~~

DECEMBER 21, 1998

I was flown from Guam to Seattle via Hawaii, accompanied by two U.S. Marshals.

A year earlier at the Plaza Hotel in New York City, Sam Übel had instructed me to tell my partners to take guilty pleas and be debriefed by the U.S. Attorney's office so that everyone charged in my case would receive a lesser sentence. Everyone would repeat the same truthful information and have their time reduced.

In one way, this plan made sense. However, I wasn't supposed to have returned so soon – I was supposed to have lived in Asia until the case had cooled off. Then I was to have returned and hired the best lawyers to deal with my charge. Instead, I was now in Seattle. Everyone had been debriefed, and most had plead guilty.

There was no way that I could go to trial and win, even if I managed to expose the government's illegal actions and the entrapment case. Without specialist lawyers, whom I now could not afford, I would have a hard time making a jury understand the complexities of my defense.

Needless to say, I was not happy with my plea agreement. My attorney had said that I would receive a five-year sentence if I signed a plea agreement and avoided trial. Others in my case had received less time than that. When the day came to sign the plea agreement, I found that the agreement stated that I would have to serve ten years or more.

I was livid. My attorney was also angry. Either I signed and received ten or more years, or I would have to go to trial.

Still, if I had gone to trial, I would have probably lost and received a lot more than ten years. Thus, I reluctantly signed. My attorney then instructed me to write a letter of responsibility to the judge.

"Write a letter to the judge," he said. "Say that you're sorry. Say that you'll never do it again. Say that you were wrong. Just keep it short and simple."

After our depressing meeting in the attorney-client meeting room, I returned to my cell at the FDC. The attorneys had lied to me. With a knot in my stomach, I prepared my letter of responsibility. When I reread the standardized version that my lawyer had recommended I write, I felt ill.

My desire to expose the truth was overpowering. I rewrote the letter. This time, I wrote what my attorney had advised me to write and, in addition, I wrote the truth about what had happened.

I wrote about how the informants – the Übel brothers – had been friends of mine for over twenty years.

I wrote about the six-dimension plan that informant Sam Übel had developed and contacted me about. I wrote about the new identification I had been given from the DEA via informant Bob Ratner. I wrote about how the Übel brothers, rather than the government, had run the reverse sting operation. I wrote about the questionable relationship between the U.S. Attorney who oversaw my case and Bob Übel, and also about the money the informants stole from the operation. Further, I explained how the informants, with the knowledge of the U.S. agents, took an unwavering position to send our Thai fishing boat through Malaysian and Singaporean waters while knowing that, if captured, there was a death penalty awaiting us. In my letter, I explained to the judge how I was used as a pawn to weaken Hun Sen's stronghold over his country. I exposed the government's self-serving crimes while maintaining the position that I was also responsible for my actions.

I am not above the law as they are, I wrote.

Soon after the judge had received my letter of responsibility, a copy was also reviewed by the U.S. Attorney's office. After reading my letter to the judge, the response that the prosecutor's office presented was an example of their "we are above the law and must win at all costs" attitude.

The prosecutor contacted my lawyer and demanded that I retract my letter. My lawyer told me that the Assistant U.S. Attorney wanted to question me about the validity of my letter. At this private questioning, if she or her staff decided that my letter was false, she would tear up my plea agreement and recommend that the judge give me a longer sentence.

"I think that you should go in there and tell her that you had a bad day when you wrote the letter," my attorney said. "Tell her that you were in a bad mood, and then apologize."

I was shocked over what he wanted me to do. "But Steve," I said, "everything in that letter is true!"

"It doesn't matter. If what's in the letter is true, then the government has big problems and the Übel brothers could also be in trouble. However, they are not going to let that happen. The U.S. Attorney's office will protect themselves by claiming that the letter is false!"

I was pissed. "This is a conflict of interest. The U.S. Attorney's office stands to have a major problem by admitting that my letter, which contains important information about the U.S. government's violation of the law, is truthful. The U.S. Attorney's office is running the investigation to determine whether the letter is true or false, so they have a vested interest in the outcome going in their favor!"

I then wrote a second letter to the judge. I had no one else to turn to. I told him about the outrageous attempts by my lawyer and the U.S. Attorney's office to pressure me into lying about the contents of my letter to him.

On December 3, 1999, a meeting to question me was held. As I suspected, it was a kangaroo court. The AUSA and the DEA agents attacked me and threatened to throw away the key.

The AUSA was beside herself. She repeatedly fired questions at me, never waiting for my answers. "What's this, the Übels owned a sex club?" she asked.

"You don't know about the Superstar Club?" I said.

The DEA agent sitting next to her gave me a look as if to say, "Shut up, man! She doesn't know about that!"

"And what's this about Bob Übel having a relationship with the U.S. Attorney?"

"If you don't know anything about it," I responded, "you soon will!"

"What do you mean that Sam Übel knew about the offload site over a year before the *Oktedy* was seized?"

The DEA agents' faces turned beet red. The AUSA was apparently shocked when she found out that Sam Übel had known about the 1997 operation and that he had been part of it until Ratner entered the picture. She never touched on the issues about the stolen money or the six-dimension meetings in New York City. That would have exposed entrapment, and I later discovered that I indeed had an entrapment case.

She argued over the facts surrounding Bob Übel having a gun. Even she knew that convicted felons were not supposed to carry guns in sting operations. It had been reported in the *Bangkok Post* that Übel had a gun when he was arrested in Cambodian waters. The AUSA and the agents definitely steered clear of the attempted murder situation that I had exposed.

"Why are you doing this?" one DEA agent asked in a pleading voice. "Do you think that you'll get a reduced sentence?"

"No," I said. "I don't think I'll get one second off my sentence. Not one second."

"Then why're you doing this?"

"I'm just trying to create a level playing field. I want the judge to know the truth. What's the matter? Are you afraid of the truth, Mr. Madona?

He turned red and clammed up.

As the three interrogators stood up to leave, the AUSA said, "You should listen to your lawyer. I cannot say what's going to happen now."

Then the three holier than holies left the questioning room.

"Art," my lawyer said, "you have to retract this letter or you'll be doing more time!"

"I'm not changing a thing," I said. "I'd rather do twenty years and expose their corruption, lies, larceny, and attempted murder than say that it never happened."

~~~

I wrote a third letter to the judge, describing my meeting with the government. I took that opportunity to expose more misconduct that had taken place in my case.

I was awakened by surprise early on the morning of December 9, 1999, when an FDC guard said, "Get dressed. You're going to court."

"Why?" I asked.

"Don't know," he said. "Just get dressed. You're leaving in ten minutes!"

I sat quietly in the Seattle Federal Courtroom. Suddenly, my lawyer ran through the large oak doors in a huff, apparently unaware of why he had been summoned. Then he saw me sitting alone at the defense table.

The AUSA and the two DEA agents also arrived.

We all took our places just before the judge entered the courtroom. He announced that he had received my letters and wanted to clear up the situation before my date of sentencing, only a few days away.

I was shocked. I couldn't believe that I had been able to bring this situation to the surface. The judge had been courageous enough to take this highly-improper event by the horns and deal with it.

He asked the AUSA point-blank, "After you questioned Mr. Torsone regarding this letter, did you make a determination as to its validity?"

The AUSA stood and said, "Yes, your honor, I did. Although the letter was colorfully-written, we did not find anything false in its contents."

"Thank you. You may be seated."

The letter in question, my two follow-up letters to the judge, and this hearing had become part of the court records and could be used in my future appeals.

The judge then asked the government employees to step outside the courtroom while he spoke with me in private. When they had left, the judge made eye contact with me and spoke with purpose in his voice.

"Mr. Torsone, I feel as though I know you from reading your letters. First, do you want to replace your lawyer?"

I said that, while I liked my lawyer as a person, I felt that he was unable to handle my case the way I wanted him to.

It was decided that because my sentencing was so close, I would keep my lawyer until afterward. Then he would be relieved and a new lawyer would take his place for my appeals.

I had had my day in court and succeeded in exposing the truth. At least the judge now knew what had happened. If nothing else, I was satisfied that I had been able to get this far single-handedly.

On December 17, 1999, I was sentenced to ten years in federal prison with five-years of probation to follow. It was the minimum mandatory sentence for a category-one defendant.

At my sentencing, the judge said, "I see the government gave you a hard time here. However, I cannot go below the mandatory minimum guideline of ten years."

The U.S. government had allowed the Übel brothers to entice and entrap me as far back as 1993 when I had been involved in a legitimate business. This had occurred after they were released from prison, of course. It was wrong for the U.S. government to allow the Übel brothers to contact me to pull me back into another conspiracy for their own self-serving purposes.

It was wrong for the U.S. government to create severer crimes in order to arrest people for lesser crimes.

They were wrong to allow untrained felons and informants – Sam and Bob Übel, Andrew Pill, and Bob Ratner – to possess the power to promote crimes, develop conspiracies, and make extremely important decisions that were far out of the scope or responsibility for civilians to make.

The Übels often developed the operational scenarios that the Feds used in their attacks on me. It was wrong to allow them to up-load (increasing the accountable marijuana amount in the conspiracy).

It was wrong that the U.S. government had turned a blind eye to the Übel brothers stealing and pocketing tens of thousands of dollars in cash. They then let them lie about it on the witness stand, committing perjury.

It was wrong of the U.S. government to allow the Übel brothers to manipulate the operation so we would be placed in Malaysian and Singaporean waters – where the penalty for marijuana possession is death.

It was wrong of the U.S. government to use me as a pawn to discredit a foreign leader during an important national election. And it was wrong to influence the Cambodian government to prolong our incarceration in T.3 prison.

It was wrong for them to deprive me of my human rights by having me abducted in Cambodia and to neglect bringing me basic care while I was held both in T.3 and Hing Peo's base under U.S. authorization and direction.

The treachery that the Übel brothers had displayed was far more diabolical than anyone could imagine. I later learned that Sam Übel's six-dimension plan had been a well-planned scheme to use us to erase several personal problems that the Übels were facing in Singapore.

One frustrating obstacle that Sam Übel had had in Singapore was his residency status. Because of his drug arrest on the *Encounter Bay* and subsequent felony conviction, he had been unable to obtain residency status. His wife Sukbe and his son Koon Lait wanted to live there as it was near their family. As such, Sam had needed to be pardoned by the Singapore government. His primal need for praise and acceptance was an obsession of his that would be fulfilled by working closely with the Singaporean authorities during the sting operation.

Sam also needed to do business in Singapore. His wife's wealthy family had already helped to improve his image over the years – the image that he desperately needed to groom; the image that his old friend, Mike Forell, had helped to create. Sam and his twin brother had subsequently been instrumental in putting Mike in prison for fifteen years, and his wife May for three years. In short, the Übels ratted out Mike and May so that they could shave four years off of their own prison sentences. The worst part about the whole thing was that every word that the twins spouted out against the two of them on the witness stand was an outright lie.

Sam subsequently made up the story about May leaving Mike and turning him in. The Übel brothers had only served 54 months of a ten-year sentence for being responsible for one of the largest drug crimes in U.S. history.

Sam's pseudo-refined image served him well in Singapore when he conned a wealthy Singaporean family into financially backing him and his brother in a deal to open the largest nightclub in Thailand. Without the forgiveness of the Singapore government, he would not have been able to have done business there and to have pulled off that deal. By obtaining residency, he would be granted an expensive apartment at no cost by the government – a perk that certain valued residents of Singapore enjoy.

In the end, it only took a good word from the U.S. State Department for Sam's banned status to be removed in Singapore. With the help of his new financial backers, who remained unaware of his disloyal, backstabbing personality, he had invested millions into this nightclub in Bangkok, The Ministry of Sound.

It was criminal to allow Sam and Bob to use their newfound power to place me in known danger when they manipulated me into returning to Southeast Asia as part of Sam's six-dimension plan. It had also been wrong to allow Minh and me to become involved with the Khmer intimidators through the instigation of the informant Bob Ratner.

The U.S. government denied any involvement in Cambodia. This was a lie. It had been important that the covert scheme to leverage Hun Sen be kept a secret.

EPILOGUE

I T was at the Federal Detention Center in Seattle that I began to write *Herb Trader* in earnest, soon after my return to the States. I had kept my diary since my departure from America in December of 1997. This diary contained the words that I had written while lying in a puddle of sweat on a concrete floor at T.3 prison in Cambodia during the summer of 1998.

I was obsessed – once I began writing, I couldn't stop. I wrote over a million words before my story was ready to be typed, edited, re-edited, and re-typed.

It took years to pry data from the U.S. government files via the Freedom of Information Act. (Please go to www.herbtraderbook.com) to review photos, and documents.)

There are stacks of documents, transcripts, and photos, and these are only a small percentage of the evidence that exists. Much of the information is being kept secret. The remaining data would likely cause an international scandal and prove that the USG acted illegally, both internationally and domestically.

I cannot think of a single reason why I should have been held to a higher standard of the law than the U.S. government officials who work for the DEA, the U.S. State Department, the American Embassy in Phnom Penh, Cambodia, or even the informants involved in my case. I may have been wrong to do what I did, but I was not quite as wrong as they were. What the agents and informants did was immoral, illegal, and corrupt.

The government could have obtained their convictions without the Übels' six-dimension plan. My partners and I could have been videotaped with the Übels in a New York City hotel, conspiring to import herb from Southeast Asia.

It was not necessary for me to have gone to Cambodia to risk my life and the lives of others – or to have wasted the taxpayers' money.

When Bob Übel and his crew of undercover agents were arrested by the Cambodian Military in Cambodian waters on June 5, 1998, the U.S. Navy had been there assisting the Übel team. When the Navy was alerted that the planned rendezvous between the Übel vessel and the Cambodian Navy gunboat had been aborted because the Übel vessel had been seized by the Cambodian Military, the Navy turned and ran for Singapore before an international incident took place – their mere presence could have sparked an incident that had the potential to explode into a full blown act of war, not unlike a North Korean destroyer entering U.S. waters without permission. The U.S. government has refused our request to show us satellite photos of this incident – probably in an attempt to avoid an international backlash regarding a long history of charting the waters of other sovereign nations, completely uninvited.

As previously mentioned, Bob Übel had a close relationship with the U.S. Attorney who oversaw my case. In the beginning, she even advised Bob to not get involved in the scheme that he and his brother had presented to the government. However, the Übel brothers had ulterior motives. Through their pseudo-charm and charisma, they influenced the U.S. Attorney, Katrina Pflaumer, into conspiring in their bidding.

During our court proceedings, the judge discovered this highly improper relationship and demanded that Ms. Pflaumer make a declaration (see on line) to the court explaining her relationship with Bob Übel. She sugarcoated her explanation to the judge by saying, "We went kayaking together, took long drives together, and had dinner together. When he slept over at my house, he slept in the guest room. We never talked about the case." Yet at one point, she even went to Bangkok to visit him.

I often wonder if she visited his old nightclub, the Superstar, where he sold young girls for sex. I'm sure that U.S. Attorney Katrina Pflaumer had no idea that the man who manipulated her was a dangerous, deceptive megalomaniac.

I later discovered that Captain Damian's arrest was a result of the Übel brothers' cooperation with U.S. authorities after their 1998 *Encounter Bay* seizure.

～～～

In Cambodia, it is business as usual. Hun Sen played his cards well. He won the election and reversed his party's involvement in our operation. This bolstered his image so that he could receive foreign aid for the war on drugs.

Hun Sen's son, whom I tried to contact while I was being illegally held in Hing Peo's base, graduated from West Point Military Academy and is being groomed by his father for his future roll in governing Cambodia.

Hing Peo, the one-legged military police colonel, did not walk away unscathed for his treachery. An article about him was published on November 1, 1998, on this website: http://www.cannabisculture.com/cgi/article.cgi? Num = 1403.

This article exposes how, after his double-dealing against his Cambodian associates in the herb trade, Colonel Hing Peo fared in that infamous year of 1998.

Here is an excerpt from this article:

MILITARY RAID ON TOP POT-COP

A final example of Cambodian pro-pot corruption came to a head when 100 soldiers from the military police launched a full-scale assault on the home of Hing Peo, head of Cambodia's anti-drug squad.

The attack was made because Hing Peo had been successful in charging marijuana traffickers associated with the head of military police, 'Kieng Savuth,' who also sits on the central committee of Cambodia's ruling political party. The attack was a clear message to local anti-drug police that marijuana protected by MP officials is off limits to them.

In 2006, Colonel Hing Peo was arrested for ordering the murder of a judge and several high-ranking ministers. He went on the run and was captured by Interpol in Malaysia. Colonel Hing Peo was convicted and is now serving a 20-year sentence in T.4 prison, which is the replacement for T.3 prison. Poetic justice!

~~~

After my return to America, I discovered that the river in Cambodia that I referred to as "South of the Thunder" had been mistranslated by Captain Chin. What he had meant to say was "Sound of the Thunder" river, but I liked the original interpretation and left it at that.

I will always work to reform U.S. marijuana laws. Take away the black market and you'll take away the crime. It's as simple as that. There are over two million marijuana offenders sitting behind bars in America – more here than anywhere else in the world. Many are in prison for non-violent crimes. They are just like you and I.

Our nation has become a land of snitches and informants, reminiscent of the Cultural Revolution in China, the Pol Pot regime, or the dark days under Joseph Stalin in Russia – when it was neighbor against neighbor and a witch hunt against the meek.

"Those who cannot remember the past are condemned to repeat it."
—Twentieth-century philosopher, G. Santayana

After twenty-five years of marriage, Virginia and I finally were divorced while I was incarcerated. It was the end of a painful era.
As it turned out, my three daughters went to excellent colleges of their choice while I was incarcerated. They are now happy and live productive lives. Our love for each other has never wavered.

My mother, who never turned her back on me, died while I was in prison. My heart and my life will never be the same.

My sweet Ahm wrote me the most beautiful letters from Thailand. She sent photos of herself and promised to love and wait for me.

After I found out that my prison sentence was ten years, plus five years of probation, I wrote to Ahm and reasoned with her. I urged her to move on with her life and not wait for me. In an emotional passage of a letter I wrote to her, I reminded her of the time that we had gone to the Buddhist temple and bought two small wooden birdcages – each containing a small bird. We had held the cages up to the sun, opened their little doors, and let the birds fly away. This was a Buddhist custom, and symbolized the freeing of our spirits to live unencumbered lives. I could not ask her to wait ten to fifteen years for me.

I wrote, "You must go on now like the little birds we released into the sky. You must live your life. If you find a good man with a kind heart, I will under-stand. When I return, I will look for you. If you're not married, I will try to build a life with you again."

I will not be remembered for the landscapes and homes I designed and built, or the love filled family I raised my daughters in. What I will be remembered for is being one of the biggest marijuana merchants on the planet.

With all that behind me, I can now live in peace.

TO CONTACT AUTHOR GO TO.

a.r.torsone@gmail.com

Lightning Source UK Ltd.
Milton Keynes UK
09 March 2010

151135UK00002B/26/P